TWO IN A BOX

MIKE WOOD

OPPERBIRD
Press

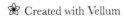 Created with Vellum

Thank You

Thanks to Sarah, Kevin and Amanda, my travelling companions.

Thanks to Janie at Lector's Books for her editorial input and for keeping it all sane.

Thanks to Madeleine K for the lovely cover design.

Thank you to all the campsite owners, managers and stewards for always making us welcome.

To Sarah

More good times

Two in a Box

Mike Wood

PROLOGUE: The year 2006

The car felt empty. The background chatter was missing. Our little boy, Kevin, had flown to the Dominican Republic with his girlfriend. His baby sister, Amanda, was on a plane, with friends, flying out to Majorca. Overnight, it seemed, they'd turned into grown-ups.

So we headed for Brittany. Just the two of us.

We'd all four talked about trying Europe again, many times. Milan was always there, a magnet that sometimes attracted and sometimes repelled. Sarah and I talked about going to the Alps again. But we'd become wary about touring in Europe, at least since that incident in Belgium, and the other one in France when I'd fallen out with the gendarmes. Yeah, I'll get to that.

The children were flying the world. Spreading like dandelion seeds. Me and Sarah were becoming provincial. We needed a caravanning success. We needed to rebuild our confidence for adventure, now that we were two again.

"What about a longer sea crossing?" I said. "Cut out all the driving in Northern France. Let the ship do the work."

"Okay," said Sarah, with a deer-caught-in-the-head-lamps expression.

For a couple who always checked the location of life jackets on the Mersey Ferry, the idea of a nine-hour sea crossing to rebuild confidence had flaws.

First we had to drive to Plymouth. We had a late start after taking Amanda and her friends to the airport.

"Remember that first time we went to France?" I said, elbow out of the window, metaphorical hat tipped way onto the back of my head, more relaxed than a Sunday morning lie-in. "Thirteen hours to get to Dover. Crazy."

Sarah laughed. "We won't have that, at least."

No we wouldn't. We'd made sure of it. Built in double redundancy. Two nights in Plymouth before we sailed seemed a good cushion. Had to be, with only one sailing per day. So even if the gods of road congestion all ganged up on us at once, we'd still win. We'd laugh in their faces. So what if we ended up looking for a remote campsite with just a few directions scribbled on a scrappy piece of paper? I'd added a warning note on the paper beside the last junction, in red felt-tip with exclamation marks and underlines: DO NOT MISS THIS TURN!!! *THIS ROAD GOES NOWHERE!!* YOU CAN'T TURN A CARAVAN DOWN HERE!!

I'd stuck a copy to the dashboard with Blu Tack, too. Precautions. Double redundancy. Avoidance of stress was a priority. This trip was an exercise in confidence building.

We got lost in Shrewsbury.

Shrewsbury is only fifty miles from our home on the Wirral. We know Shrewsbury. We consider it to be almost local. We could never go wrong in Shrewsbury. Except when there are roadworks. And when you're so relaxed, you miss the diversion signs. And when, because you're towing a caravan, it becomes impossible to U-turn, so you continue on along ever-narrowing lanes. And you follow someone else who seems to know where he's going, and that someone else turns into a residential estate then into a cul-de-sac and parks in the driveway of his home.

It took us a whole hour to drive through Shrewsbury.

We hit roadworks in Kidderminster. Then more, just after Kidderminster. What were we doing in Kidderminster? We could have used the motorway, the M6, but...

"No, not the M6. We're *not* getting caught that way again. No way." I was referring to that first journey to Europe. The thirteen-hours-to-Dover journey.

When you're towing a caravan it often makes sense to avoid motorways in favour of good A roads that are shorter in distance. You can't do more than sixty anyway, and on motorways when there's a queue you're trapped. You can't just pull off and divert. I knew what I was doing. I couldn't face getting stuck on the M6 again.

So we got stuck on the A442 instead. Three times. But on A roads I could find another route, couldn't I? Well, no, not with a caravan, along lanes with grass growing down the middle, with no passing places and with oncoming traffic, from the farms nestling at the end. Where the road runs out.

I knew this. I'd tried it before. So we queued. By the time we'd crawled within sight of the M5 – yes, another motorway, but one not so easy to avoid – we were two hours behind plan. I looked at my watch. Amanda would be in Majorca by now, sitting poolside sipping a drink with lots of fruit and umbrellas in it. We were still in the Midlands, not even halfway to Plymouth, and I was fuming, and for once relieved to see a nice bit of motorway ahead.

Except it *was* just a bit of motorway, because two of the

three lanes were closed. *Closed! Roadworks! In June! Holiday season!*

I took a breath. Sarah held up a hand.

"You're going to start moaning again."

Her intuition was sound.

"You're going to do one of your moanicle things," she said.

She knows me.

"Can't you be… positive?"

"You mean, like what? A *posicle*?"

"That would be nice."

I thought about it.

"I am positive—"

"Yes?"

"—that if I ever see the Highways Authority bureaucrat who thought June might be a good month for digging a hole in the M5, I'd—"

She held up a hand again. "Not the positive I was thinking of."

I let it go.

We had expected to arrive in Plymouth mid-afternoon. Park the 'van. Make a brew. Warm some pies for tea. Take a walk. Get to know the countryside.

Didn't happen.

We reached the outskirts of Plymouth an hour shy of midnight. The roads were narrow. There were no street lights. The sky was overcast and the last glimmer of daylight had long gone. Perfect for missing junctions warned against in red felt-tip – and underlined – then heading down those narrow lanes that fizzled out by the sea, with nowhere to turn.

A good thing I had my secret weapon. Home-made satnav.

Satnav devices for cars did not appear until the late nineties, and were not commonplace until some years later. I had something like it, though, a handheld GPS device for walking in the great outdoors. I'd become a bit of a gadget freak. Wherever I was, on whatever remote mountaintop, I could find the exact map co-ordinates for my position. Then I could unfold my map in the wind, misread the numbers because they would be over the fold, and place myself with total confidence somewhere in the wrong county. I love technology.

For navigating the car I discovered I could buy a special wire that allowed me to connect my handheld GPS to a laptop, and I became giddy with excitement at all the possibilities. Here was the future. Tech straight out of Mission Impossible, tracking myself on a map. Of course in those days a laptop battery was only good for about an hour, so I bought an inverter to run the laptop off the car cigarette lighter socket. Still good, but more wires, and the engine had to be running or the car battery went flat.

I stopped the car and fished out my tangled bag of wires. The handheld GPS soon lay on the dashboard, attached by gaffer tape, and with a long, inflexible wire leading to the laptop. The laptop was in turn connected by long, inflexible wires, through the heavy inverter box, to the cigarette lighter socket, which needed a bit of cardboard jammed into the side of the plug to stop it coming loose from the relentless tensile forces of all the wires. It was very fifties sci-fi, but it worked.

I fired up Microsoft Autoroute, waited long minutes, then fist-bumped the air at the sight of the little triangle pulsing on the map somewhere near Wembury.

"It says we're in the middle of a meadow," said Sarah.

"We need to be moving," I said. "It doesn't work properly until we're moving."

I began to drive.

"We're moving across the meadow," said Sarah.

Modern satnav takes into account the fact that you are probably on a road when driving the car, so it puts you on the nearest road and almost never in a field. The GPS used by hikers has no such inhibitions. If it thinks you're in a field, it shows you where. Computer maps of the time were not infallible, either. The one on Autoroute was very fallible, with ruler-straight roads that, in real life, did a lot of looping and swooping. The GPS signal in 2006 also had issues. They're much better now, although I've just checked the GPS on my current laptop and it tells me I'm writing this at the bottom of next door's garden. Hey ho.

"You have to interpret the signal," I said, with techno-geek conviction. "Look for the closest road on the map."

"Okay. My interpretation is that we are in a field," said Sarah.

"Oh, come on!"

Sarah's voice took on an edge. "There are no roads nearby on this map, and none of the distant roads point in anything like the direction we're heading. So watch out for cows."

I stopped the car and looked at the screen.

Without a doubt it said we were in a field.

"It's the trees overhanging the road," I said. "They're disrupting the signal."

"So, what now?"

"We press on. Once we get a good fix we'll be okay."

I drove on.

"Wait, okay. We're on a road," she shouted, excitement in her voice. "I can see where… Oh. The laptop's just switched off."

It did this a lot. If you didn't press any keys for a while the laptop assumed you'd become bored and gone away, so it went into hibernation. I knew there was a way of disabling this irksome feature but could never remember the sequence of key presses to do it. I looked for another place to stop. On a dark, narrow road, with a caravan, safe places to pull over are few.

"Can't you just tell me how to switch it on again?"

I couldn't. When the laptop switched off, the handheld GPS disconnected. I'd never fathomed why, nor how to make all the components work together in harmony, so I had always just switched off the GPS unit and the laptop first then started the whole launch sequence all over again. And I wasn't sure how to even explain; it was just something I did. I knew which buttons to press but I couldn't describe the process.

I found a farm entrance and parked.

It took me a few minutes to fire it all up again.

"Cool," said Sarah. "We're right in the middle of

Plymouth Sound. Better keep the windows closed to keep the sea out."

"We just need to get moving again."

"I don't think we should."

"We have to. That's the only way it can work," I said, exasperation creeping into my voice.

"I think we should go up this farm lane," she said, pointing out of the window.

"What? What the hell for? That's not going to help. You don't just go up farm lanes on a whim. God knows where we'd end up."

"I just think that's the right way."

"And what makes you think that?"

"The sign. There." She pointed. It was a graphic of a little black caravan. And below: the name of our site.

WE SPENT two full days in Plymouth. We needed them, to wash away all the stress. We liked Plymouth. We promised to come back to the area some future time and explore with more leisure.

Just then, though, we had a new chapter to begin. After twenty years we were two again and heading for a big adventure alone. We parked in a line on Plymouth Docks. Ahead of us, one row at a time, the cars and caravans and lorries rolled up the ramp onto the massive *Pont L'Abbè*, our Brittany Ferries ship.

On the tannoy, they were calling for us to board. It was time to go back to France. It was time to see Brittany.

2000 – SIX YEARS EARLIER:
A LAKE IN A FOREST IN FRANCE

Lift your head. Put your shoulders back. Breathe. Now, do you feel all those positive vibes flooding your body? Good. I will bookmark the page in my handy guide to mindfulness before placing it on the coffee table beside the brandy and the cigar. Actually, I've never smoked and I don't much like brandy. They are metaphors. Props for instilling a sense of tranquillity and contentment into the scene. Hold onto that mood while I tell you something good about the British road network. Something positive.

I was thinking about how thoughtful the highways people were in painting buttercup-yellow rings around all the potholes. They brighten up our roads so much. You can see the holes coming from at least six feet away. Plenty of time to swerve. Okay, your swerve might take out the odd cyclist, but hey, they have the same visual aids as you, don't they? Yellow paint could be a progressive system, too. There's room for future upgrades, like yellow paint 2.0, which might be fluorescent so we can see it in the dark. Or can I suggest a 3.0 upgrade? In 3.0, instead of giving the minimum-wage-zero-hours-contract-borderline-suicidal employee a bucket of yellow paint each morning, we give them a bucket of tar and chippings and get them to fill the hole.

MW – Posicle Number 1

Okay, so I've given you a foretaste of things to come: 2006, Brittany, just the two of us. Bear with me on that, we'll get to it all in good time.

For now though, let's return to the year 2000. I ended book one, *Travelling in a Box*, just as we were departing Switzerland after our turn-of-the-millennium adventure. Why would I end the story there when there was more? I had stopovers planned in France, more adventures, and one particular destination that was… well, a bit special.

And what about that junction in the road? Milan. Remember?

There were good reasons not to turn south to Milan. Life reasons. Let's face it, Milan was still far, far away. The sign had said *Milan, turn left*, not *Milan, just ten minutes down the road past the corner shop*. There was the day job – and the certainty of unemployment/bankruptcy which awaited the rebellious non-returnee. But above all we had that special destination in mind, L'Etang du Merlc, a campsite with an evocative name that, to me, suggested access to the full-on, total-immersion, European experience I so craved.

L'Etang du Merle awaited our arrival.

Milan could wait.

When we planned the holiday, our focus had been all about getting to Switzerland, our first-ever caravan trip abroad. We'd built up to it in stages, rather like NASA's nine-year program to get to the moon, taking baby steps: the Mercury missions, Gemini, then Apollo. For us, the preparations for Europe had taken a little longer. We'd been at it for more than twenty years. Camping in Wales was low Earth orbit. Switzerland was our moon, our Apollo 11, and our goal was to reach the Alps, not in a three-day sprint like Neil and Buzz, but to spend a leisurely week doing it.

And it had worked. We'd seen France. We'd been to Paris. Okay, I'd nearly lost all our money at the railway station, then almost stranded us overnight in a town outside Paris, and I'd towed us around pharmaceutical company car parks in Geneva. But I had spoken in tongues, French and German, and I had proved to us all that I could resolve any problem that Europe chose to throw our way.

The return leg, after Switzerland, seemed, no matter how I looked at it, to be anticlimactic. We'd have a thousand miles to eat with our focus being on just getting home, along roads we'd seen before.

I'd been left to do the planning by myself. The family, Sarah, Kevin and Amanda, trusted me.

In hindsight, trusting me with this task had been a little foolish. I was fired up. I had discovered, deep in my soul, a craving for adventure. We choose to go to the moon and do the other things because they are hard, is how Kennedy had put it. Well, I figured maybe nine hundred miles through Britain, France and Switzerland in an antique caravan just wasn't hard enough.

"Leave it to me," I said. "I'll come up with something good on the way back. I'll find us a nice site." This was at home, the four of us, sitting around the dining table during the planning phase of Europe 2000, maps and guide books scattered an inch deep on the table.

"Why aren't you using the Carefree book?" said Sarah,

pulling it from the heap. "Or the one from the Caravan Club?"

This was a good question. These books had sites that were chosen by experts, tested and reviewed. Sites with customer feedback. Sites with lots of stars after their names. But where was the adventure in that? I wanted something a little raw. The kind of campsite that involved discovering the *real* France. By the time we returned from Switzerland we'd have seen enough of sanitised, Brit-friendly sites. Besides, I'd been to Stanfords map shop. I'd bought the Michelin site guide.

"Look at this," I said. "L'Etang du Merle. It's by a lake. In an unspoilt part of France. In a forest."

"Where's the nearest town?" said Sarah.

I smiled and folded my arms.

"There isn't one," I said.

"Hmm."

"Don't worry. I wrote to Monsieur Monet."

"The water lily artist?"

"The site owner. I wrote to him in French. We're all booked."

"In French?" Her tone was loaded with doubt.

So on that summer day in 2000, when we reached the road sign that offered a choice, Milan or home, I already knew where we were going. I turned north… ish. Or a bit westward, maybe.

∾

SARAH HAD the map opened fully so that it filled the car. It was a blue IGN map, 1:25,000 scale, crisp and new, another treasure from Stanfords. Interlaken and Switzerland lay far behind us. Inside the car the temperature increased, as much from the frayed tempers as from the ninety-five-degree sunshine radiating through the windows. We'd already gone wrong many times. Chateau-Chinôn was the only town of any size on the map, and we'd come to know it well after several trips through. The car park of the Super-U had become a favourite place to stop and review the map and fight.

"I don't understand why you didn't just book a proper site," said Sarah. "The sort that gives you directions."

"It *is* a proper site," I said. "Maybe they did give directions. But… my written French might not be so good."

This was quite an admission. I'd felt proud of my written French up until now. I'd booked the site by writing to them, one hundred percent in French. I'd been to the library and looked up the proper format for writing a letter in French. I'd researched each word to make sure my meaning was clear. When I'd received a reply, thanking me for my deposit and expressing excitement about meeting me and my family, I had been elated. Monsieur Monet had written back to me in French. I felt sure that, had he harboured any misgivings about my abilities in his language, he'd have taken the safe option and written in English, because it was a campsite used to holidaymakers from all over Europe, and his English was probably better than mine. But writing to me in French… surely this was a testament to my language skills.

Maybe I should have read it.

Okay, so of course I *read* the letter. I read the letter several times. I read it to Sarah. I read it to Kevin and Amanda, who were both in senior school now and studying French with proper teachers. Kevin, in fact, was to take a GCSE in the language that following summer. Each of them listened to me reading the letter and appreciated my excellent rolling *r*'s and nasal accent. But perhaps I should have taken the same care over the actual translation as I had in writing the letter in the first place. By then, though, I'd been too excited about the prospect of visiting Switzerland to have time to do such mundane tasks. I'd read the letter. I had the gist of the thing. "We have your booking. Looking forward to seeing you."

And some other stuff.

We left Chateau-Chinôn once again, and this time we tried taking the longer route. We took the D978 then followed signs to a place called Saint-Saulge, and, lost in a forest so dark and deep it would have challenged Gandalf and all the elves of Middle Earth, we tried each and every road until, by accident, we pulled up outside a hut with a gate and geraniums in hanging baskets and lake water glittering though the trees, and a sign that said L'Etang du Merle.

I pulled the car through the gate, switched off the engine, and did my best to conceal the need to cry tears of joy and relief.

"There we are," I said. "Easy in the end."

The site looked lovely. Here was everything I had hoped for. The sun shone. The water glittered between the swaying slender trunks of the tall birch and pine trees. A beautiful place. Sarah was won over too. The smile said it all. I was forgiven. My thirst for adventure had thrown up a gem of a site.

I dug around in my rucksack buried deep in the car boot, and pulled out the letter from M. Monet. That wasn't his real name, of course. It's a few years ago, now, and I can't remember his real name but it was like Monet, or like another French artist. Or a non-painting, other well-known French person. I should also point out that the site has changed now. I called up the website for L'Etang today to jog my memory, and I noticed it has changed a lot. There's a pool and a games room and in the section headed "languages spoken" they offer English as one of the options, and the website, or my version of it, was in English.

But our visit was some years ago.

We trooped into the wooden office building. Nobody was inside so I rang a bell and we waited, looking around in wonder at all the postcards and bottles of wine in racks, and jars of... stuff, with French labels. I realised my brain was still wired to German after our week in Switzerland, and I would need a nimble bit of work with a neural soldering iron to tune back into French. I had time, though, to feel rather smug at my multi-lingual mastery, as I rehearsed my opening speech in French. *Bonjour. Je suis Monsieur Wood. J'ai une réservation.*

The door opened and a tall, lean man of about forty years came in and stepped behind the desk.

"Bonjour," I said. I went quiet. I'd been too relaxed. I'd forgotten the rest. I felt annoyed with myself so I thrust the dog-eared bit of paper, the letter, forward and placed it on the counter. The man glanced at it and then began to speak. In French. He spoke very fast. I didn't pick up any of it. He spoke for a long time, pointing to things out of the window, indicating notices stuck to the wall, laughing at things he'd said. He then showed me the produce in his shop with evident pride, saying things about each item. I hoped to pick out key words, like *vin,* and *pomme de terre,* and *chocolat,* but if he used any of these words he disguised them well.

I felt my ears beginning to glow red. I noticed how my GCSE studier and his sister were shrinking into the back of the shop and becoming invisible and how Sarah watched me with pride, waiting for me to respond in fluent, sexy French. I, of course, responded with silence, letting my mouth hang open and allowing my shrugging shoulders and flapping hands to do all the talking.

The silence hung between us for long seconds. I watched monsieur's eyes flick from me to Sarah and back, and occasionally to the children hiding in the back of the shop amongst the postcards.

Then he looked down again at the letter on the counter. He picked it up. He read a few lines and a smile broke out on his face. He pointed to something on the letter: the signature of the proprietor, and he laughed a booming laugh that belied his slender frame. He struck the letter several times with his other hand, each time roughly where the signature was written, and each time he laughed and said something else in French. Then he pointed at his chest. He struck his chest. He boomed out something like, but not quite, *Je suis Marcel Monet. C'est moi!*

This I understood. He was M. Monet, our proprietor, but why he then exploded into howls of laughter completely baffled me.

"Je suis désolé," he said. This also was something I understood. This was getting better. Perhaps I was just taking a little longer to retune than I thought.

The third thing he said, pointing to a line in the letter, was, *"Vous et allemand."*

I nodded with enthusiasm. Yes, I am English. I smiled and gave my most apologetic Gallic shrug.

"Je parle allemand," he said.

I smiled and nodded again.

"Ich spreche Französisch, und Deutsch," he said, beating his chest in pride.

Oh. He spoke German. I'd written *allemand* instead of *anglais.* He roared with laughter again, said something in rapid incomprehensible German, and led us outside.

WE SET up the caravan between two trees for shade, and with a fine view of the lake.

"Why did he speak to you in German?" said Sarah.

"I don't know," I said. "Crossed wires perhaps. He was the one who'd written the letter back to me. He must know he'd sent it to England."

"You kept on saying *ja,* and nodding," she said.

"Didn't want to disappoint him," I said. "It got to that point where it would have been embarrassing to correct him."

"Wasn't it embarrassing enough? You know, not having a clue about what he was saying?"

"I got some of it."

"Really?"

"My German's not that bad, you know."

"Better than your French?"

"No."

"So what did you understand?"

"Well… he said he doesn't speak any English."

"Yeah, I got that bit. And…?"

"That's about all, really." I gave her my enigmatic Gallic shrug but found that it didn't work so well on English wives.

WE DID THE ORIENTATION OURSELVES. We found the shower/toilet block. Sarah took one look at the toilets, the kind with the foot-shaped steps either side of a porcelain hole, and declared she would be using the facilities in our caravan, despite the attendant difficulties. Our toilet cubicle was a small cupboard that expanded out across the caravan doorway, and if you were using it you had to make certain the caravan door was locked, or anyone trying to get into the 'van would swing open one wall and put you on pedestal-like display, mid-ablutions, for the whole campsite to appreciate.

The on-site showers were good though. Clean and well maintained. There was also a row of outdoor sinks for communal dishwashing, covered by a roof for protection from the sun. The site had access to one side of the lake. It seemed very pleasant if you were the sort of person who liked to sit beside a lake and doze all afternoon. None of us were that person, though. We favoured activity.

I BECAME ATTACHED to using the communal facilities as head dishwasher. I enjoyed working away at the plates and pans, listening to all the languages bouncing back and forth between the multinational dishwashers. There was French – we were in France – a lot of German, some Italian, and of course Dutch. It doesn't matter where you are in the world, you will always find at least one NL number plate in the car park. I am in awe of the Dutch. They have turned travel into an art form. For such a tiny nation they have succeeded in sending out emissaries, in their cars and motorhomes, to the four corners of the world. They speak every language as though it is their own. They are knowledgeable. If you are in a town or village new to you and need to find an obscure attraction, ask a Dutch tourist, not a local.

The one language I didn't hear was English. I'm sure the Dutch tourists spoke English, but to approach them with requests for help would have been an admission of failure. I had succeeded in my quest to find a place remote and genuinely European, and without any annoying Brits to spoil it.

On the second day at L'Etang du Merle I was enjoying the conversation, or at least the sounds of the conversation, when several of the dishwashing campers fell silent in mid sentence. They lifted their heads and listened, or sniffed, or otherwise sensed… something. They shouted a few quick words in multiple languages to each other, possibly to me too, then scattered, running with their half-washed pots, as fast as they could, back to their tents and caravans and motorhomes. I found myself alone, staring. The whole communal area was deserted. What had they sensed? I half expected a T. rex to come pounding out of the undergrowth; it was that kind of moment.

I continued washing my dishes in silence, one eye glancing around the forest for stray giant reptiles or cousins of King Kong. Then a strange thing happened. The air changed. A little whirlpool of a breeze stirred the fallen leaves and whipped them into a gentle spiral. Nothing dangerous. Nothing too alarming. But different. Enough to give me a prickling, sixth-sense warning sensation at the back of my neck. I finished the dishes with haste, not rinsing off the soap bubbles or drying. I bundled them into my plastic bucket and headed back to the security of the caravan.

Passing though the campsite I noticed increased levels of industry. Serious trench-digging was taking place. Especially around tents. Kevin waited by our caravan, looking at the activity and looking back at his pup tent.

"What's happening? Why's everyone digging?" he said.

"Don't know," I said. "Maybe they know there's some weather coming."

I looked up at the sky. It looked okay. A bit cloudy, but we Brits are used to cloud. Perhaps if you were used to perpetual sunshine a bit of cloud might be seen as an omen. Or perhaps it really was an omen.

"Tell you what, Kev, get your sleeping bag and put it in the 'van. And any other bits, you know?"

"Shouldn't I dig a hole?"

I looked at the concrete-hard dry clay and shook my head.

"We haven't got a shovel. I don't fancy digging that stuff with a spoon, do you?"

He went into his tent and came out with all his worldly possessions. The first drops of rain hit the ground, kicking up dust like someone had begun practicing shot-put. We both bolted into the awning, stuffing everything we could salvage from the tent through the door of the caravan. Raindrops the size of beach balls began falling on the awning roof. We grabbed everything from inside the awning and stuffed all of that inside the caravan, too. Chairs, tables, bags of laundry, the rack of drying towels. We dived into the caravan to join the girls and the four of us sat by the window, huddled amongst the bedding and laundry, and watched.

We couldn't speak. The roar on the caravan roof drowned out every gasp and squeal. We closed the roof skylight because the rain was coming in. Some still came in with the skylight closed. Water poured from the sky in a continuous flow. Outside, the forest floor had gone, lost beneath water with no surface, just a violent, frothing, swirling mass. We couldn't see the edge of the lake. Not just because of the cascade down the caravan windows, but because there no longer *was* an edge to the lake. The caravan now sat in a homogenous exploding body of water.

And always the noise. The sound of anger. The destruction of the world.

Then it stopped.

The storm lasted no more than ten minutes. The sun came out. The sky turned blue. The rivers and torrents ran across the forest floor, then stopped, then dried, then became hard soil once again. When we stepped out into the open, glad to be alive, we stepped into normality. Our fellow campers were already out on sun loungers. Some played badminton. Washing fluttered on lines between the trees. Over at the communal dishwashing post, all my former comrades were back, scrubbing away at pans and plates as if nothing had happened. They had lived through the end of the world and come out at the other end and their collective memories had been erased. It was the stuff of The Twilight Zone.

We could not feel this way. The inside of our awning was a quagmire. The inside of Kevin's tent, despite a four-inch lip around the sewn-in ground sheet, was full of water. We tipped it out, turned it inside out and it was dry within fifteen minutes.

THAT WAS the only drama at L'Etang. Oh, apart from the waste water. And that was not so much a drama as a soap opera. Something not unique to L'Etang du Merle, either. It was an issue that perplexed us all around Europe, and truth be told, still has the power to confound us to this day.

On UK sites there is a grid for disposing of waste water,

or grey water as it is sometimes called so as not to confuse it with its nasty cousin, black water or chemical toilet waste. We have a device called a Wastemaster – a long tank with wheels at one end and a towing handle at the other, and the Wastemaster is used to haul the outflow from washing and hand laundry – and showers, for those lucky caravanners who have one – over to the waste grid. Sometimes in Britain we stay on small sites or temporary sites, where it is acceptable to tip the waste water into the bushes around the edge of the field. Often, on these temporary sites, it is equally acceptable to loosen the cap of the Wastemaster so that it can slowly drain onto the grass, one drip at a time, to percolate into the soil while all the bits of pasta and sweetcorn and rice stay in the tank to be disposed of with care at the end of a stay.

In Europe we didn't know the drill. What was the acceptable Euro standard?

The first thing we noticed: there were no drains. The fresh water taps sometimes have a small plastic grid beneath them, but it is usually just a soak-away to deal with the odd drip from the tap, and in no way up to the task of dealing with a couple of gallons of soapy, greasy water.

On our tour through Europe we'd gone with the loose-cap soak-away followed by the tip-it-in-the-bushes option. This was not ideal. We hadn't seen anyone else doing it. We tipped it when nobody was watching. But at each site the problem was managed. We made it go away. Kind of.

Here at L'Etang, though, we were stumped. The rainstorm had been a good demonstration of what happens when water hits the ground. It runs along the top. It doesn't soak in. *At all.* I implored us all to be sparing with water. Kevin and I were up for it. We were happy enough to limit our washing routines. The girls less so. The Wastemaster filled. Then it flowed, in a telltale river that snaked out across the site. Fellow campers of all nationalities would walk past, notice the River Wood, follow it with their eyes, trace it back to our caravan, and make tutting sounds and other European expressions of distaste. *Okay, tut all you like,* we thought, *but what are we supposed to do about the stuff?* We walked around the site looking at caravans to see what our fellow campers did to resolve the problem. It got us no further along. None had Wastemasters or even buckets. We could see where the waste outlets exited each caravan but there were no telltale rivers snaking away. They just didn't seem to create any grey water.

I decided to consult Marcel. I rehearsed the French. I didn't know how to say "pour away". I didn't know how to say "waste water". And as to "grey water", was there a French colloquialism, in common use but unknown to the English? I improvised with *l'eau gris.* Straight away I knew I had a problem, because I had never mastered the French word for water. *L'eau.* I knew this because on my many trips to the shop for bottles of mineral water I always came back with something else. It's a pronunciation thing. I know what the word looks like but no matter how much I twist my mouth and strain, it always comes out as some kind of Neanderthal expression of constipation that French people take for an inherited speech impediment.

I found Marcel near the site entrance, strimming weeds.

"Bonjour monsieur."

"Ah, bonjour."

So far so good.

"Ou est le dispose pour the leeoo gris, s'il vous plaît?"

Marcel said some French words and looked confused.

"The leeoo gris," I said again. "Leeoo. Luuow. Er." I searched my fifty-word vocabulary for something else to try. "I know. Old water, er vieux luuow des vieux luuow."

"Ah oui. Un moment." Marcel nodded with enthusiasm. He dropped his strimmer in the bushes and ran to the shop. A moment later he returned with two bottles of mineral water. I paid him and returned to the caravan where my family awaited news. I gave them the water, then slumped into a chair, defeated.

The solution came with darkness. Dressed in black and alone – the family wanted no part in my lawlessness – I hauled the Wastemaster far from our caravan. I couldn't take it off site because we were segregated from the forest by a chain-link fence. I selected a random scrawny bush and I poured. A Wastemaster makes a lot of glugging sounds when emptied. In the silence of the benighted campsite it sounded as though I had set up an illicit glue factory. The pouring took forever. I counted the seconds, expecting to be found out at any moment. I waited for alarms and shouts. *Attention! Attention! Un terroriste!*

My skulduggery went undetected. I returned to the caravan and stripped off my burglar attire. The problem was deferred but not resolved. For the rest of the week I adopted a less furtive approach. At regular intervals I loaded the Wastemaster into the boot of the car and drove deep into the forest for some illegal waste dumping. I still feel dissatisfied with the outcome. The predicament remains. Some European sites have emptying facilities but there are still many that do not. One day I will find the answer. That day has not yet arrived.

I LEFT L'Etang du Merle feeling chastened and a little less triumphant at my European-ness. In language I had failed. In waste emptying and general camp craft I had failed. I vowed to do better. I would study hard to improve my French. I had a dream: to have a conversation with a French person. A real conversation, not just, "A tea and a coffee please." I wanted to discuss the weather and politics and current affairs and exchange views on national stereotypes. I'm not sure why, because I don't have this kind of conversation with other English people. With other English people, strangers, my conversations are usually limited to, "Nice day" or "I think it will brighten up later" or… "A tea and a coffee please." But that is not the issue. I wanted to be cosmopolitan and appear learned and wise, and what better way to do that than to have a philosophical conversation with a French intellectual. Or at least comment on the weather. Or ask him where I could empty my waste bucket.

We drove home from France.

It is 340 miles from L'Etang to Calais. We had to make a ferry connection. We could have done this better, with a break nearer to Calais, but time was at a premium and I had a day job to go to. We thought it would be okay and yes, it was okay. The roads in France are a delight: No traffic queues and no hold-ups.

Arriving in England, in Dover, after our first time out of the country was strange. There was traffic. We had to drive on the left. There were roundabouts that had to be circulated anticlockwise. There were so many cars. Cars everywhere and *rush rush rush* and people who shout at you and make rude hand signals. In Dover we encountered an unexpected thing in our home country. We encountered culture shock.

We had a single night of rest at a campsite in Kent. I was so grateful to find that site and to stop. I needed downtime; my brain had to readapt to the horror of driving in the UK. I needed a night of restful sleep.

The next day we continued home. 300 miles. I felt as though we'd been away for years. Europe had been amazing and terrifying and wonderful. When could we go back for more?

2001: NORTH

A word of thanks to our local authority for the diligent way they maintain our roads. Only this week my mother-in-law's road was resurfaced, and it's only a cul-de-sac with zero traffic flow. Well done them. I think it's marvellous how they have prioritised her road over all the nation's major trunk roads. Those people who complain about the state of Britain's roads, about potholes that rip the suspension off their cars, should try driving up and down my mother-in-law's cul-de-sac; it's lovely.

MW – Posicle No. 2

The aftermath of Europe brought us credit card bills and reality, which eliminated all thoughts of a return to the Alps the following summer. Common sense dictated a UK holiday. But it had to be exciting. We'd had the ultimate thrill. We'd seen the Alps. Would anything in the British Isles ever look the same again? Had we been spoilt? Perhaps we'd return to the Lakes or to Snowdonia and to our eyes we'd see nothing but expansive prairies with little bumps on them that we used to call mountains. We had pigged out on topography, and now perhaps nothing less than the Himalayas would do to set our pulses racing again.

We decided to go to Scotland. At least Scotland had Munros, Corbetts, and Grahams: mountains over three thousand feet, two and a half thousand feet, and two thousand feet respectively. These might sustain us until we could afford to return to *real* mountains. I'm not sure where this warped form of reasoning came from. When in the Alps, we'd done most of our climbing in cable cars suspended from wires. In terms of actual boots on rock, well, the reality was we'd more than likely ascended less than a thousand feet.

We made a firm decision: Scotland. I hadn't been since my schooldays. Sarah and the kids had never been further north than Penrith. We decided to do a tour: up the east coast then down the Great Glen to the Western Highlands. If nothing else we'd be free from the traffic mayhem of the English south coast.

Our first destination was Crail, in Fife, where we decided to stay on a temporary site run by Angus and Perth DA, one of the many District Associations, groups run by volunteers from within the Camping and Caravanning Club. We got as far as the approach to the Forth Road Bridge, on the outskirts of Edinburgh, before hitting the traffic jam, and we parked there for an hour.

"This is bloody Scotland!" I said. "There's not supposed to be traffic in Scotland. It's wild country. They've only just learned about cars." I was exaggerating. I knew they'd had cars for at least a decade or so. I was just annoyed. You make an exchange, a kind of deal when going to Scotland for the summer. You trade in the sunshine and blue sky for crap weather and midges, but then you get empty roads and lots of parking spaces. Hour-long traffic jams didn't seem fair to me.

But I got over it. Our first site was in a good spot. The locals were friendly, even inviting us to their Christmas Party, which I thought was very nice of them if not a bit premature, until we realised they were holding it that night, in July! Now, I know the Scots need more of a lead-in than us, when building up to all that serious Hogmanay drinking, but *July!*

Anyway, we didn't go. We didn't have presents to take, and Christmas wrapping paper and cards are hard to find in July, or at least they were back then. Not so big a problem now, in 2019, when you can pick up most of the Christmas essentials at Asda, Sainsbury's and Tesco from early summer.

Instead, we walked along the coast to Crail, which is your quintessential picturesque Scottish fishing village, with heavy harbour walls, pantile roofs, and where all the houses are huddled into a cosy tight space with barely a gap, to ward against the Scottish winter gales and storms that'll rip the bollocks off you once September arrives. We loved it.

Back at the site the Christmas Party was in full swing. We were the only ones who hadn't gone, so we felt a bit guilty about being party poopers and hid in our caravan so nobody could glare at us. We spent the evening listening to the bizarre strains of Frosty the Snowman and White Christmas as the July sun dropped low, inland, over the Firth of Forth. That in itself felt odd as we are west coast dwellers and used to seeing the sun setting over the horizon out to sea.

We spent our first full day in the area driving, doing a whistle-stop tour of Fife. We did Cambo Secret Garden, which was lovely and unexpected. We did the Scottish National Trust's Kellie Castle, which was heavy and square and would have been a good location for the grimmer parts of Macbeth, and this got us further into the spirit of our Scottish adventure. Then we went to St Andrews.

They play golf in St Andrews and you are not allowed to forget it. They've been doing it for nine hundred years so I suppose they're entitled to be proud of their golf. There are golf shops everywhere, with silly knee-length trousers and tartan socks and golf clubs you could own if you took out a second mortgage on your home, then sold your yacht. We walked around the golf course and crossed the little stone bridge that goes over a little stream because we'd seen it on the telly and we couldn't do anything else with it because the craze for taking selfies was still ten or fifteen years away. Then we walked into the city and found that there was more to St Andrews than knocking a ball around and spoiling a walk. St Andrews is a lovely town. It is home to a university and has lots of history. It is quite a small town so it's easy to explore: the old ruined church, the harbour, the shops. We were very taken with it, but alas, only had an afternoon to spare because the next day we hitched up again. Our tour continued north.

We hit the A9 and threaded our way amongst gorgeous mountain scenery through the Cairngorms. Yes, mountains. Here's where we realised our love for mountains had not been spoiled by the Alps. We also came to understand that Scotland was much bigger than we'd always thought. To reach even Glasgow or Edinburgh was a serious enterprise from our home on the Wirral. But here was the thing: Glasgow and Edinburgh were not even at the midpoint of Scotland. Heading north from Crail we drove for five hours. We passed a heavy iron gate that could be swung across the road, with accompanying signs that warned of road closures in winter. It was the A9, the main route north. And sometimes they closed it. Yeah, at last we were in wild country. This was the Scotland we had come to find.

Some time after passing Pitlochry and Blair Atholl we stopped in a lay-by to eat sandwiches, stretch our legs and use the facilities in the caravan. Each of us took our turn in the 'van. Amanda went last.

"Dad, I can't close the caravan door," she said, getting back in the car. We were anxious to continue on our way.

"What do you mean, you can't close the door? You mean the catch is broken?"

"Not the catch. The door. Won't close."

"'Course it will. Push it."

"I pushed."

"Did you check if anything was stuck in it?"

She gave that teenaged sigh thing that goes along with the rolling eyes.

I gave that adult sigh thing that goes along with climbing out of the car and grumbling a lot. I went round the front of the car to make my route longer so that I could appear more put-upon.

I didn't even need to try closing the caravan door; I could tell it wouldn't close just from looking. The door frame wasn't a square opening. The ninety-degree angles that used to grace each corner were no more. I remembered my schoolboy geometry so I was able to name it. A parallelogram. That didn't help me explain it or fix it, though. By now the family had come to join me.

"The door isn't square," said Sarah. "How did that happen?"

I scratched my head. "How can the door not be square?" I said. "It was square this morning. It was square ten minutes ago. What's changed?"

"We've been in the caravan," said Kevin. "Without putting the legs down. It's bent."

"It can't be bent," I said. But he was right. Two adults and two nearly adults had clambered into the caravan one at a time and we'd twisted the frame. I'd never heard of such a thing. But then, our caravan had more than thirty years behind her. She'd been to the Alps. Perhaps she was getting tired.

"What can we do?" said Sarah.

I pushed the door against the non-door-shaped hole and leaned on it. But it wasn't just catching around the edges, it was miles out. Closing it would be like trying to deliver a widescreen telly through a letterbox.

"We have to do something," said Sarah. "We can't just leave it open."

This was true. I had visions of our journey through the Highlands with a breadcrumb trail of all our worldly possessions marking the route behind us.

"Maybe if I go inside the 'van and stand at the other end," I said. I tried it and it worked. A bit. Not enough to close the door and as the children pointed out, unless I used the window I'd still have to open it again to get out and drive the car.

"Aha!" I said. I wound the corner steady down, below the corner where all the weight had been, to twist the chassis. As we watched, the door frame eased back into a square position. I closed the door. Perfect. I wound the steady back up and all kinds of groaning and straining noises came from the caravan. I felt sure we'd have more issues along the way but for now I didn't want to go there. We had a campsite to reach. It would be a better place to worry about the caravan's new-found interest in topology than out here in the wilderness.

We drove in silence for a while. Sarah was first to voice a thought we all shared but didn't want to put out there.

"She's getting old, isn't she? Do you think…?"

"Talk about it when we get home," I said. But I was worried. Our caravan had served us well. She had been a bargain for five hundred pounds. Bargains like that don't come along every day. We'd been a caravan family for a long time. We could never go back to camping in a tent. I gave a little shudder and dismissed the thought. Perhaps she'd be okay. For a little while longer.

We continued. Our destination lay north of Inverness.

THE CAMPSITE at Rosemarkie is on a spit of land that juts out into the Moray Firth. There's a straight, narrow road, unused by cars, that follows the edge of the coast, and on the inland side is scrubby grass and the odd stunted and salt-blasted tree. On the seaward side there is a line of eighteen-inch white posts with white rope strung between them, which segregates the road from a thirty-foot-wide strip of lawned and manicured grass. The grass strip is the Rosemarkie Camping and Caravanning Club site. Beyond the grass is a short drop to a shingle beach and a few yards further are the lapping waves of Rosemarkie Bay.

We parked the caravan. The view out of the window was of the sea. This was the kind of site that made you stop in your pitching activities every now and again and wonder. What were you wondering? You were wondering, *why did we only book two nights here?* I wanted to stay forever.

It wasn't raining and the sun was shining. We'd been in Scotland for three nights and it hadn't rained yet. I understood this to be unusual. There's a possibility we could have set a new consecutive-dry-day record for the region.

I lowered the steadies and tried the door. It didn't open. I tried varying amounts of pressure on the nearside front steady to no avail. Then I worked on the opposite corner, the offside rear steady, adding half a turn of pressure at a time before trying the door again. On the third go it worked. The door opened freely. I closed it and opened it again a couple of times before feeling happy enough with my work to give myself a satisfied nod of approval.

I noticed the people in the next caravan were watching me. It might have crossed their minds to come out and offer some friendly advice that the way to open a door was with the door handle rather than with the corner steady winder. But then they might have thought better of it, and to stay away in case I turned out to be dangerous.

Both children used their pup tents in Rosemarkie. I shouldn't call them pup tents, it calls up images of tiny tots. The children were now both well into their teens. Kevin, in fact, was driving, so I shouldn't even call them children. But what else can I call them? English is a language which does not have a word for adult children. I've looked around on the internet and it appears we are not alone; I couldn't find a single example from any other language of a word for adult children. It is a curious thing. If I say to you, yes, I have two children, then it leads you to think of toddlers and toys and faces all smeared with chocolate ice cream. (Actually, the chocolate ice cream thing is still valid, and they're both now in their thirties – ha! They'll love me for saying that.) So what *do* I call them? Is it that natural selection decreed we're not supposed to have children of ages beyond early teens? Should they have perished in the mines or up chimneys by now? Did the ancient word makers save themselves the trouble of inventing a word for adult children because, for the negligible few who came up out of the mines or back down from the chimneys, it wasn't worth all the fuss? Or maybe I have it the wrong way round. It is we adults, who, by Darwinian rules, were meant to have been crushed by debt and anxiety and forced into early graves by the time our children reached adulthood?

I've strayed from the point, and I'll stick with the term "pup tents". The camping fraternity probably wouldn't like it, either, if I started calling my adult children's private spaces "dog tents" or "bitch tents".

So the *children* put their *pup* tents up at Rosemarkie because they wanted a view of the sea. Kevin was using his tent most of the time because, at seventeen, he had started to find our two-plus-one-and-a-bit-berth Sprite Alpine somewhat confining. Amanda was more of a fair-weather pup camper. She wouldn't use her tent at Crail because of Patrick, a pushy nine-year-old who had a crush on her and followed her around asking endless questions. She chose to hide in the caravan for most of the time we were on-site.

We'd taken our time getting to Rosemarkie – the non-closing door hadn't helped – and by the time we'd made camp it was late evening and the sun had started to set. We had our evening meal, which took a while to cook because we were still using raw ingredients; convenience meals, like fish fingers, wouldn't keep for more than a few hours in our tiny, not-so-cool refrigerator. It takes a while to wash all the dishes, too. That was my job, over at the communal dish-washing facility, and I missed listening to all the foreign multilingual banter I'd grown accustomed to the previous year. Here in Scotland the banter was in my own language, and I understood less of it than I had in France. I began to tune in to the Scottish accent, though, and annoyed my family by adopting my own version, especially in shops, but more of that later.

I finished the dishes, stacked them away in the caravan, and by this time the sun had begun to set. Hadn't it been setting when we started cooking the tea? I shrugged it off. The evening was still warm, so we headed out on a walk along the promenade in the direction of Rosemarkie town. It took us half an hour or so, *and the sun was still setting*. I checked my watch. It was 11:30. At night. It wasn't even dusk. We'd all noticed how we felt tired, but until now, nobody had thought to check a clock. We are not night owls, and it was way past our bedtimes. We walked back to the caravan and retired for the night, after midnight, with still quite a lot of light in the sky. I thought this was marvellous. It was the first time I'd ever witnessed the astronomical implications of heading far north in June. I hadn't realised you could experience it in Scotland. I'd always thought you had to go to Norway.

The next morning dawned bright and sunny again. Four days without rain. Dared we hope? Amanda came into the caravan and chided us for sleeping late, so we tidied away the bed and Sarah set about preparing breakfast. Amanda, meanwhile, was sent to arrange the camping chairs and table outside. It was a perfect morning for *alfresco* dining.

Kevin came into the caravan a few moments later with dark shadows under his eyes and nursing a grumpy teenage attitude.

"What are you doing?" he said.

"Well, breakfast," I said. "What does it look like? I want to see Scotland, not sleep the day away."

"Do you know what time it is?" he said.

I didn't. I looked at my watch.

"Oh," I said.

"What?" said Sarah.

Amanda said nothing. She'd looked at her watch, too. She knew. She knew whose fault this was.

"It's ten minutes past four… AM," I said.

We ate breakfast then went back to bed.

I didn't sleep. I couldn't. I lay in bed watching the sun streaming through the window, doing a pretty good impression of late morning. I looked at the stack of breakfast dishes waiting in the sink. I wondered what the hell kind of parallel universe this Scotland was in.

WE STARTED our first full day in Rosemarkie feeling sleep-deprived and irritable. We didn't feel much like a long walk. Too tired. The site warden told us about the dolphins.

"If you walk to the point you'll see dolphins," he said.

"Dolphins?" I said. "Not *real* dolphins?"

"Real? Och aye. Bottlenose dolphins." He didn't actually say, "Och aye." That's me, adding regional colour. The site warden was from Yorkshire. I added quite a lot of regional colour to my conversations while we were in Scotland. "Ye'll noo be having a sale?" in every shop was one of my favourites, made famous by a Walker's Crisps advert that was popular at the time. I never said it loud enough so anyone could hear me, of course. That would have been bad.

So we walked out along the shingle beach to Chanonry Point to see the dolphins. We weren't alone. Many others had the same idea. There was a car park and it was full, and all along the beach the technology of dolphin watchers had been laid out ready for the incoming tide, when dolphins chase the fish and perform. There were telescopes, monoculars on tripods, and cameras with big cream-coloured lenses the size of bull horns. There were even some people dangling microphones into the water that were hooked up to heavy reel-to-reel tape recorders to record the dolphins' chatter. We were all very patient.

We waited.

Now and again there was a flurry of excitement, a shout and a pointed finger. Once, we all rushed to one part of the beach and began snapping away with cameras at a bobbing milk bottle. I became adept at focussing my camera on humpback waves, just in case, so I'd be ready.

And we waited.

We became hungry. Lunch time arrived. We turned and walked back along the beach. Today had been our one chance. Tomorrow we would hook up the 'van and move on. It would have been nice to see a dolphin.

Here's a handy hint for wildlife watchers everywhere. Put your camera away, right down in the bottom of your rucksack. The animals know. No sooner had the camera gone when a dolphin the size of a Transit van leapt clear of the water no more than five or six yards from where we stood on the beach. Not one of the thousand or so dolphin watchers back on the point saw any of it. The dolphin turned and did another leap, then another. A whole performance just for us. This never happens. Usually we are the ones watching from the point while the action happens in another place. We couldn't believe our luck.

I've seen dolphins looking sad and jumping through hoops in tanks, but this was a whole new level of thrilling. This dolphin was so full of exuberance and life, and there was no doubt – it wasn't just doing the thing it does while out looking for food. This dolphin was performing because it was fun to perform, and it was performing for us because it knew we'd put our cameras away and that the thousand or so wildlife fanatics over on the point, with their big lenses and their microphones, would see from afar, and they would be bloody livid.

THE NEXT MORNING we woke at a sensible hour – actually we woke at another stupid hour then lay in bed watching the four-in-the-morning sunshine through the closed, non-blackout curtains – and after breakfast we waved a reluctant goodbye to Flipper and departed the Moray Firth, heading west.

The journey was stunning. This was a lonely part of Britain. This was not a place you would want to break down. No, that's not foreshadowing, we didn't break down. I don't like breaking down anywhere, but there are some places I'd enjoy far less than others, and we have tried most of them, but the road to Wester Ross was right at the bottom of my good-places-to-break-down list. It was wild and it was rugged and it was beautiful in a wild, rugged and threatening kind of way. We passed the occasional one-cottage village. We had filled up the fuel tank before leaving Inverness and we were happy to have done so, because there was nowhere to buy petrol or anything else in this part of Scotland.

We followed the A385 Ullerpool road until just after Loch Garve, then the A382 where the countryside became wilder. Here's the thing, though, and something we'd noticed heading north to Inverness a few days earlier. The roads were gorgeous. By that I mean smooth. There were no traffic lights or cones. There were no potholes. No bumping along a patchwork of various-grade tarmac that had been slopped down by an assortment of utility companies after taking turns to dig holes everywhere. These were roads that had seen respect. These were roads, dare I say it, *that were worthy of the Swiss*. We passed lochs and inlets and the road twisted and turned. There were few other vehicles. We had it to ourselves.

Our next site was another Camping and Caravanning Club site at Inverewe Gardens. This time we had a road between our campsite and the sea, but it didn't matter; the road had no cars and beyond was a rocky beach at the side of Loch Ewe, a sea loch. When I say the road had no cars, I mean you could have happily set your picnic table in the middle of the road, if you so wished, and enjoyed lunch undisturbed. And the road is the A382, a main trunk road. When we booked the site we had worried a little about being so close to a main road, especially at night. Well, at night it got quieter.

We stayed in the Inverewe site for four nights, a whole season in terms of this tour. We as good as settled there. From the site we could walk to Inverewe Gardens, a sub-tropical botanic garden on a promontory that jutted out into the loch. Yes, sub-tropical. In the north of Scotland. It was something to do with the gulf stream, and yes, we had warm weather and it stayed dry. The gardens were a constant draw, and we ate in the gardens' restaurant a few times because it was lovely.

Another attraction in the area, and one we just stumbled

upon, was the mountain trail at Beinn Eighe. It was billed as Britain's only waymarked mountain trail, and the route takes you up through scrub and pinewoods until you come out onto bare, ice-scraped rocks. The views were fabulous. This was our first return to mountain walking since the Alps. I was blown away. The Alps were long forgotten. These were real mountains, not the Disney mountains they put on the front of chocolate boxes. These were mountains you could climb without having to buy train tickets. Yes, it was a waymarked path, but it was not a Sunday afternoon stroll to be done in flip-flops. The climb took us to nearly two thousand feet. We needed our boots and we needed our waterproofs, because up on the mountain, for a brief spell, we tasted Scottish rain. The real thing. I loved it. Because then it went away and the sun came out again.

There was petrol in Gairloch. It was open nine till five, Monday to Saturday. We filled up. We were ready to move on, retracing our route back east, and we knew we wouldn't be seeing a petrol station again before Inverness.

OUR FOURTH DESTINATION was something I had wanted to do for most of my life. I had been to Scotland as a boy, on a school trip, and later on a walking holiday in my teens, but I had never seen Loch Ness. I wanted to see the monster.

I have long been fascinated by stories of the Loch Ness monster. I've always believed in Nessie's existence, in the same childish, hopeful, romantic way that I have always believed in fairies. I am Manx by birth, you see. I have always and will always say hello to the fairies at Fairy Bridge, having heard many compelling stories about the fate of those who snubbed them. So, since fairies are real, why can't the Loch Ness monster be real? I wanted to see Nessie. It would be nice to photograph her, but after our encounter with Flipper I was less sure I'd manage that one. A sighting would be enough. I wanted to *know*.

We chose a site right on the banks of Loch Ness. A commercial campsite with small pitches and not enough room for both Kevin and Amanda's pup tents, and I grumbled a lot about being charged for four adults rather than by pitch. If we had advance-booked a pitch each, one for the caravan and one for each tent, then we'd have paid exactly the same and had plenty of space around us. This seemed really stingy to me, and I sulked around the site and muttered things of an offensive nature in my and-yee'll-noo-be-havin'-a-sale accent.

The view made up for it, though. Our pitch was on a cliff edge, fifty feet up. We were right on the lip, almost overlapping, so nobody could walk past and obscure the view, even for a second. We looked out onto the grey waters of Loch Ness, and we could leave the curtains open all night if we wished, and I could stare out into the cold dark water and wait for Nessie. I became obsessed. My obsession became Kevin's obsession, and he lay in the doorway of his tent all night on his own Nessie vigil.

The girls thought we were nuts.

The town of Drumnadrochit had an exhibition, the Loch Ness Monster Exhibition. The car park was full of coaches and the coaches were full of foreign tourists. There are plastic effigies of the monster on the top of buildings, beside the road, and in every direction the eye can see. From the outside it looked appalling. I thought Drumnadrochit would be more tacky than old paint found at the back of the garage and applied onto unprimed metal on a bitter and frosty morning. I feared it would spoil the magic for me forever. But, of course, we had to go in and see it. We were here. This was part of the show. I handed over the cash, drew air through gritted teeth and stepped inside.

Here's the surprising thing. The exhibition was excellent. It wasn't tacky at all, well, not very. The information boards were informative and full of proper science. The exhibition did not give an opinion one way or the other about the existence of the monster, it just laid out the evidence in a calm, fair and unbiased way. It catalogued the various research programs that had been undertaken over the years. There was an interesting section on the geology of the loch, and how this might have led to creatures from the Jurassic era being trapped in the deep waters.

I could not have been more surprised. I had expected to come out in a rage of indignation. I expected to have been ranting all afternoon about the spoiling of a myth and how it was bloody typical and indicative of the general decline in civilisation. Instead I came out smiling. It was brilliant. The exit brought us into the shop, where there were plastic dinosaurs, Nessie tee shirts, Nessie handbags, tea towels, fridge magnets, pencils, rubbers, postcards, soft toys of Nessie, bumper stickers, boxes of shortbread, tins of shortbread, plastic Nessie presentation packs of shortbread…

and I thought… it was great. We bought loads. We bought a pottery Nessie: loops of glazed porcelain that you stand in a line and they combine to look like the serpent shape of Nessie arched out of the water. My favourite was a soft toy Nessie wearing a tartan tam-o'-shanter, with magnets on each foot, and she is, to this day, still attached to our fridge. I was won over. I couldn't get enough of the Nessie tat. It was wonderful.

Another "must-see" in the whole Nessie experience tour is Castle Urquhart. We drove straight from the exhibition to the castle. You will have seen Castle Urquhart. It is the iconic image of Scotland and the ubiquitous backdrop to all artist impressions of the Loch Ness monster. It was an expensive visit, but once again the information boards were presented with lots of thought and good taste. There was a dark and brooding atmosphere at Castle Urquhart. Many castles look better from the outside. Paying to get in usually ends in disappointment. This was not like that. The castle was a ruin, so yes, you don't see any more from the inside than from the outside. But the difference was the atmosphere, the spiritual sense of being in this cold and lonely place with just the sounds of the loch. The waves lapping on the beach. The wind and the ghosts.

Again I parted with serious cash and did not moan once. I found the whole day to be thought-provoking and magical.

And before the spell could be broken we packed and set off on our adventure once again. Change was in the air. It rained. We had a wet pack. We drove the length of the Great Glen through intermittent rain and sun – enough sun to see the mountains, now and again. But I could feel it in my bones. Change. Our weather luck was about to run dry.

I CAME to Glencoe in my early teens as a member of my school mountaineering club. This was where my love of mountains was born. It was an adventure where the memories are perhaps more appealing than the reality. We stayed at the youth hostel right in the heart of Glencoe. Part of the week-long holiday was a climb up Ben Nevis. We had an A team and a B team. I was put in the B team – the support team. We went halfway up, then while still feeling strong and able, we were stopped and compelled to return to the minibus so that our teacher could drive round to the next valley, Glen Nevis, and pick up the returning and triumphant A team. I didn't get to climb Ben Nevis that week. I still haven't climbed Ben Nevis. I still get grumpy about it.

In subsequent mountain hikes with the school that week, I variously lost my lunch and my drinks flask down a gorge, and got into a fight with a school mate. Twice. Became dangerously soaked to the skin high on a mountain when it was found that the waterproof that a friend had brought along for me as a loan – I didn't have one of my own – was his father's floor-length plastic mac, some heavy-duty item of protective clothing perhaps used in the acid industry by Robert Wadlow, the eight-foot-eleven-inch gentleman of Guinness World Record fame. Even with the hem lifted up and doubled over twice, I couldn't walk in the thing. It would unfurl, wrap around my feet and send me tobog-ganing down mountain slopes. Our group's final claim to fame, that week, was having to be rescued by Hamish McInnes and the famous Glencoe mountain rescue team, when we got ourselves lost on top of Bidean nam Bian. Actually they didn't save us, they just spent a cold night on the mountain on our behalf, looking for us, after we stum-bled down, late, via a different route.

Some years later, in my late teens, I returned to Glencoe with two pals from my musical circle of friends. We travelled up to Scotland during one of the longest droughts that Britain had ever known. We wasted the first two days in a pub overlooking Fort William Railway Station, waiting for a pair of old walking boots to arrive by train, after one of our party forgot to pack them. The boots arrived. The drought ended.

It was a funny week. We argued a lot. In something of a *déjà vu* moment – for me – we got lost on Bidean nam Bian, but nobody knew we'd gone up there, so this time the mountain rescue people didn't have to come out looking for us. We didn't die on the mountain though. We came home.

But none of these life-defining wilderness events ever dampened my enthusiasm because ever since that first school trip I have seen myself as a mountain man. Glencoe was the place where it all started. All these years later I wondered if the magic would be the same. Glencoe held a place in my heart as having the most wondrous mountain scenery anywhere. But since those heady and foolhardy teenaged days I had changed. I had seen the Alps. Would the allure of Glencoe hold true?

We pitched our caravan.

Mountains towered all around, stark and forbidding. Glencoe was a place of history, massacre and ghosts. The ghosts were all around in the stirring breeze, the clouds and the rain.

Yes, it was raining.

There was a new visitor centre. They did lunches. After setting up the caravan and two tents, we were wet and cold so we went to the visitor centre for lunch, and to get dry and warm. Then we walked to Ballahulish where we found a cash machine and a small grocery shop. We got wet and cold again. We walked back.

On our second day we climbed a mountain, the Pap of Glencoe. Not quite a Munro, just a Graham, but still, at over two thousand feet it was a proper mountain, with scrabbly bits at the top. The rain held off, mostly. There was a path to a rocky summit, then some exciting hands-and-knees stuff to make you feel like a real climber, and brilliant views from the top. But the clouds were coming back.

I mention the path because when you walk in Wales or in the Lakes, the provision of a path is kind of a given. In many parts of Scotland, though, the mountains are still as wild as nature intended, and apart from the odd cairn there are few marked paths so you need to be good with a map and a compass. I like to think that I am good with map and compass but history has frequently argued against this opinion. On top of a Graham, with heavy clouds moving in, I didn't want to give history the chance to prove me wrong yet again. It had taken us most of the day to get up there and it would have been nice to stick around and enjoy the view, but I didn't fancy a descent through cloud. We made a speedy departure. The rain came, but just late enough to let us get down beneath the cloud line, and so we are still alive. Once more, though, we got very wet.

Our stay in Glencoe had been intended to be one of mountain exploration. The Pap of Glencoe proved to be the last mountain we saw in Scotland. The next morning the rain had become relentless and the visibility was down to yards and feet. We couldn't even see the fence bordering the campsite. We drove into Oban. A holiday tradition required our attention. We needed to find a Kwik Fit. The car exhaust had come loose and was hanging off.

Oban was a very attractive town. There was a harbour, and on the hill, a Roman amphitheatre, built by that famous Roman Emperor, John Stuart McCaig, in 1900. His intention had been to build museums and other buildings inside the amphitheatre, but McCaig passed away before completing his monument, so only the outer circular walls were built.

The buildings in Oban are fine, elegant structures of grey granite that were very much in keeping with the rain. We found our Kwik Fit down a narrow road of grey, slick buildings, and spent the day splashing around the shops waiting for the work to be done.

Then we drove back to the campsite via an hour-long traffic jam at Connel Bridge. This felt more like our kind of holiday. The reason for the delay, apparently, was a herd of wild traffic cones that had escaped onto the road.

We spent a final day in Glencoe locked inside our misted-up caravan playing a game we'd bought in Oban called Pass the Bomb, a timed word game that the children hated from the outset, and which Sarah and I came to hate by the third or fourth playing. We walked to the visitor centre and drank tea, just for a change of scene.

"Och, fine weather," said the man in the gift shop. He wasn't being sarcastic, he bloody meant it. "So long as the rain keeps up it'll delay the midgie season," he added, in answer to my raised eyebrow.

"Midgies? Are they a problem?"

"Och aye, nasty buggers. You don't want to be around when the midgies come."

There was an information board in the visitor centre all about the Highland Midge. *Culicoides impunctatus.* They appear from late spring to late summer. It was now late June, so yes, we *were* lucky. The rain was our friend. I found it hard to decide which flavour of bad news I wanted less: Voracious blood-sucking insects against which there is neither protection nor hiding place, or torrential rain for the rest of our holiday.

Our spirits were low next morning as we packed away a soaking-wet awning and two soggy tents. We were tak'ing the low road to the final stop on our Scottish tour, Loch Lomond.

LOCH LOMOND IS REPUTED to be one of the most beautiful lochs in Scotland. In 2005 a *Radio Times* reader poll placed Loch Lomond as the sixth greatest natural wonder in Britain. I'll take the *Radio Times* readers' word for it. We didn't see it. Apart from the foot or so of water lapping at the shore that is. Our adventure took place in 2003, so I'll assume the mist and rain cleared some time during the ensuing two years to enable *Radio Times* readers to drive up there and offer an opinion. During our stay it certainly didn't seem there'd be a view of the loch any time in the next decade or so.

We unpacked the wet tents and the wet awning and erected them, in the rain.

A wet pack is hard. It is a miserable process that is always followed by a cheerless drive with all the windows steamed and the heater blowing and roaring in vain. But a wet *pitch*: one where the tents are already soaked through, and the ground is squishy and your wellingtons are cold and wet, or your walking boots are stiff with peat-bog water, and your glasses are misted over so that you can't find the tent poles or the tent pegs, and the guy ropes are stiff and rough and cold in your chapped fingers, and if you've knotted them to be tidy and avoid tangling the knots are swollen with water and are *never* going to come untied, no matter how bloody and broken-nailed your fingertips become. This is a special kind of purgatory. It is only improved by having a warm dry caravan in which to change into dry clothes, cosy up and sip tea afterwards. The days when we had a cold wet tent as our only shelter were thankfully gone. Except the caravan's plug-in fan heater was at home. We had taken it out of the caravan to save weight. After all, who needs heating on a holiday in June? Then the gas expired. Okay, I could have gone back outside, into the rain, in my dry clothes, and switched the bottles over. Instead, we climbed back into the car and drove to Balloch.

Our site was on Millarochy Bay, on the west side of Loch Lomond, so the drive to Balloch was farther than we'd thought. Our craving for tea and warmth grew exponentially with every mile. We reached Balloch. We found a tea shop.

If you've ever watched the UK TV program, The Apprentice, you may recall there's a tea shop where they send the losing team each week. It has Formica table tops and styrofoam cups and steam and even on the TV you can smell the grease. The tea shop we found wasn't as nice as that one. We took our cups of tea, stirring them with the communal spoon that had stood erect in a mug of brown water since Nessie swam the open sea, and we considered our options. We had three days left. It could rain every day and we'd have nothing to do. I'd wanted to climb Ben Lomond but had no intention of doing it in the rain and mist. I'd have settled for a *view* of Ben Lomond, or even of Ben Williams, the guy in the caravan pitched next to ours. Then again if it stopped raining the dreaded midge would come and feast on our blood.

I was for staying, then I was for going home, then I was for staying. We all felt the same. We couldn't decide. If the rain ever stopped, we'd find our caravan in what appeared to be a beautiful position, looking out over the *Radio Times* reader poll's sixth wonder of the world. In the end we decided that we'd paid for it so we'd just have to hunker down and make the most of the few remaining days. We came up with a wet-weather action plan. Part one involved a walk around Balloch. We were already there, so we walked around Balloch. It looked okay. The drains and gutters worked well under the extreme conditions, so that was a tick on the hypothetical list; we approved of the civil engineering at least.

In the caravan, we spent a wet night listening to rain hammering down on the roof. Amanda decided to forgo her cold pup tent and join us in the cold caravan. Kevin braved it outside in his tent, figuring he was warmer out there.

Day two: We went to Hill House, the home of Charles Rene Mackintosh, full of interesting art déco stuff. Everyone else in Scotland came, too, because where else could they go in the rain? We enjoyed Hill House though we did our absolute best not to let it show. We'd reached that point; the place in a holiday where we all knew it was never going to be salvaged. Sarah and I snapped at each other over every little thing, and the children worked on their teenaged sulking personas. In the evening we made paper boats and raced them in the awning. And we came to a decision. We decided that, next morning, we'd pack and go home.

I half hoped that the decision to leave would tempt the weather gods into offering a slap in the face and show us some sunshine just to spoil the decision we'd made. But it rained all night and in the morning we faced another wet pack, worse than any before, because the tents and the awning were just as wet on the inside as they were on the outside, as were our clothes. It was a sad end to the holiday because overall it had been a success. We'd had far more fine days than wet. We'd seen fabulous countryside and mountain scenery. We should not complain.

We had one other piece of good fortune, for our journey home was easy, and yet mere hours after leaving the outskirts of Glasgow we heard on the radio that the M74 had suffered a landslide and had closed and there were twenty-mile tailbacks on all roads. They were behind us. Scotland was behind us. We crossed the border at Gretna Green and the sun came out. Should we stop for a night in the Lakes?

No. We just wanted to go home.

THE REST of the year we had uneventful weekends. I re-packed the fan heater. It wasn't needed. We had a good bank holiday, walking on the Long Mynd near Church Stretton. The door-fitting problem continued but we perfected the levelling trick so we could straighten the caravan chassis each time without too much effort.

And we looked forward to our first Feast of Lanterns.

The Feast of Lanterns is a huge end-of-season rally organised by the Camping and Caravanning Club, and it has live entertainment and trade stands and a big torch-lit parade. We'd never been to one and we were looking forward to our first, which was reasonably local, at Vaynol Park near Bangor.

There would be plenty to do even if it rained.

It rained.

I finished work on Friday afternoon and we headed out to Wales. The roads were well signposted and we expected to find more caravans heading out there, but we seemed to be the only ones on the road. At the entrance we were met by a volunteer in a yellow oilskin with water pouring off his sou'wester. He looked like an advertisement for Fisherman's Friends.

"Sorry, closed," he said.

"What?" I said.

"Too muddy. Can't let any more units onto the site."

"We're okay with mud," I said. "We're used to mud. And rain. We've been to Scotland." I added that last bit as a kind of qualification. A certificate might have helped:

This is to certify
The Wood Family
Have camped in Scotland
They know about rain.

BUT THE FISHERMAN'S Friend was having none of it. He looked at our Mondeo with the gaffer-taped front bumper.

"We're not even letting 4x4s on, now," he said. "Been towing caravans on with tractors, but the tractors are getting stuck."

He told us about a couple of nearby temporary sites that might take us. One was in the Conwy Valley. We went there. It wasn't much of a site. It rained. It was cold. The weather was starting to take a toll on the caravan because we found a leak in the corner where rain was getting in. We hung up our tea-light lanterns and felt sad about the whole thing. Our payment for the Feast of Lanterns would be refunded, we knew that. But still, it was sad. I had a feeling. The caravan was getting older and beginning to fail. I knew that our family was getting older. The children were no longer children. They would have lives of their own, soon. Our holidays were becoming endurances rather than holidays again. How long before the four of us stopped sharing these moments together?

2001: CHANGE

My goodness, aren't these LED information signs useful on the motorway? They tell me, for instance, how long it will take to get to junction 21a. Or that there's a delay of 30 minutes between junctions 35 and 38. Marvellous. Although I confess, I sometimes struggle to make full use of this valuable resource. I should try harder and learn the location of every junction number for every exit on the 2,173 miles of motorway in the UK. Can't be too hard, can it? Someone must do it, because why else have all these electronic motorway signs? Or perhaps I'm just being silly, because I could look at the junction numbers in a road atlas instead. Except I have a feeling there might be some risk involved in unfolding a map while driving along the motorway at 70 mph. And isn't it illegal to stop on the motorway for anything other than mechanical catastrophe? No worries. I'm sure the traffic will come to a halt soon enough. It usually does.

MW – Posicle No. 3

Our caravanning year had been one of dissatisfaction. Scotland had been a good holiday, but our memories of it had been saturated by the rain. We'd been looking forward to the National Feast of Lanterns and then seen our weekend sucked into a mud pit. We knew, deep down, that being stopped at the gate of Vaynol Park had been a good thing. We saw the evidence. Our journey home at the end of our substitute Light Lunch of Lanterns in Conwy was the same route that others who had gained access to the festival site were taking, and as each sad-looking unit passed us on the road we saw the mud: caravan windows opaqued by mud, tyres brown with mud, cars − nearly all of them 4x4s − looking like shell-shocked survivors of the RAC rally (the old one, not the sanitised public spectacle they have now). Were the 4x4s the only ones that could get out? The two-wheel-drive cars are probably still there today, trapped deep in the mud, awaiting tractors… or palaeontologists. Perhaps we'd been lucky. We didn't feel lucky. Who knows, it might have been fun. It would have made a grand tale to take back to the office on Monday morning. Much better than, "We couldn't get in."

It was only the first week of September and yet we felt compelled to begin our traditional season-end close-down; we drained the tanks, ready for the first frost; we removed the bags of pasta from the food cupboard. (We always end the season with more bags of dried pasta than when we started − why?) Then we dragged out the heavy canvas cover and sealed her up, bracing ourselves for the long winter.

We have neighbours who also like to caravan. Their season always stretches on into December. We had considered delaying, trying another weekend, maybe in the Lakes, but cold nights in September or October were too much for our 500-watt fan heater to cope with. Caravanning was meant to be fun, not an ordeal, and we didn't have the kit for October fun. We wondered how long it might be before we didn't have the kit for July or August fun. Our little Sprite was bending. The chassis was rusty, and no amount of crawling underneath with pots of Hammerite paint was going to fix this. She needed welding. Or something. The bendy thing was also having an impact on the topside of the 'van. I was sure the flexing and movement had a lot to do with the water coming in at various places when it rained. Our Sprite had been a sturdy and reliable home from home, but we had punished her. We had dragged her thousands of miles through all weathers, through mud, along rutted farm roads, down continent-spanning fast autoroutes. We'd spent over three hundred nights in her and she'd visited five countries. Perhaps we had reached the point where she had to be replaced. She was only a two-plus-two-at-a-stretch berth, and we were a family of four adults, and although two of our adults slept in pup tents much of the time, size still had to be a factor.

But our Sprite was part of our family. I liked how she was quirky and historic. I liked how she attracted attention wherever she went. Very few original Sprite Alpines were still in active service, and she was distinctive. But her age and quirkiness were not the reasons we had bought a caravan all those years ago. We didn't want her for historic rallies, we bought a caravan because we wanted to go caravanning. But could we afford to replace her?

We began looking around caravan dealers in the area. Since the last time we looked, the price of caravans had risen. There would be no five-hundred-pound bargains this time. We had to spend serious money. There didn't seem many caravans out there that would give us much change from ten grand. We didn't have ten grand. Nothing like it. We had some savings. Our finances were considerably better than they had been. But we were not in the market for anything new or nearly new or even not long past nearly new.

We saw the Avondale in a dealership in Port Sunlight. They were a new company; they were local and we were customers, buying gas canisters and toilet chemicals since they opened. We always looked inside the new caravans whenever we went because it is nice to fantasise. Yes, they had lots of new 'vans, way beyond our reach, but also they had a good range of used, part-ex caravans. The Avondale was a model that appeared in the 1970s and was often associated with luxury, not a thing we had ever associated with caravanning. This one was an Avondale Leda Cheviot, and was about twelve years old, so not ancient. She had features. She was a four berth, and that was significant. She was only two and a half thousand pounds, and that was very significant, for it was right on the edge of our budget. Not an amazing bargain this time. No free awnings or anything like that. But she was a good, solid, non-quirky caravan, and we were already calling her "she".

Before we took delivery we had the most painful part of the transaction to undertake. Our Sprite had to go and she was too old for Port Sunlight Caravans to take any interest in doing part-ex. I have had the painful task of taking many cars to the scrap yards around Wallasey Docks. The day I took our Sprite on her last trip still brings a lump to my throat and a tear to my eye. I still feel bad about that day.

She deserved better. I don't know what "better" could have been. A chicken coop? A construction site office? But leaving her alone in that scrap yard on that cold wet morning, standing lost amongst the broken cars and mountains of scrap, in a puddle of stinking gearbox oil instead of in a daisy-spotted meadow surrounded by snow-capped peaks felt wrong. I felt like a bad person. I felt I had let her down. *We've finished with you. We've got something better.* Even now, writing this thirteen years later, I still feel the old emotions welling up inside.

SO OUR AVONDALE moved in on the patch of ground outside the house. We cleaned her and replaced the odd bits that were broken and itched to take her away on a holiday. It was October. We had to try her out.

We found a temporary site near Blackpool for the illuminations. This seemed a good idea, so on a Saturday morning we packed for just one night and headed north.

The site was a cinder car park, straight off the main road. No grass. No view. Kevin objected. He had his tent, and despite our now having a caravan with four good bunks he still wanted to use his tent. He had become a camper; he had no truck with the soft world of caravanning. Amanda objected. She wanted a grass field. Sarah objected. She didn't want to spend the night in a car park. She wanted beauty around her. I gave way. In part I was glad of their objections; the car park was horrible and it was on the main road and easy for anyone to pull in, hitch up our fine new caravan and take her away. We did a U-turn in the car park and drove. We didn't have a clue where we were going. It was lunch time. I had a sinking feeling we would drive until we arrived home again. I didn't want to. I wanted to try our new 'van.

"There's a site in Clitheroe. Not far," said Sarah, reading from the sites book as we travelled. She rang and they had room, so we drove to Clitheroe.

Setting up the caravan was a joy. I watched the door as I wound down the corner steadies, and beamed once I realised the door opening wasn't changing shape. Normal caravans don't do that, and our Avondale was a normal caravan.

There's something special about that first cup of tea on a new site. This time that first cup was extra special. It marked the transition of our Avondale going from being just a caravan to becoming our new, second home. She became part of the family. Here's what she had:

She had a *fridge*. We'd never had a fridge in a caravan before. All our holidays had involved long-life milk on our breakfast cereals, and long-life milk is horrible and often a good reason to go home. Now we could have fresh milk and cheese and margarine and even, at least for short periods of a day or two, we could have frozen food, because there was a small freezer compartment and it kind of worked.

She had a heater. Not a 500-watt fan heater but a proper plumbed-in gas heater that brought the inside temperature up to toasty warm in a few short minutes. She also had *double glazing*, so the heat we made inside stayed inside.

She had a cassette toilet, so I could do the emptying operation from the outside without having to dismantle an obstructive plastic beast of a toilet all over the awning floor, and not only that but the toilet compartment was a proper closet-sized room that could be used without having to partition a space across the caravan entrance, and more, the toilet compartment had a fold-away wash basin *and a shower!* Remember the paddling pool and the hand-pumped shower bottle we used to use in the awning? A thing of the past. Our own shower. With hot water. The whole caravan had hot water, in the hand basin, in the sink. We could wash our hands *in hot water!* We could not comprehend such luxury.

We sat on the spacious bunks, in our tee shirts, drinking tea and smiling. We had never known such decadence in a caravan. The features were so numerous, there were things we hadn't even found yet.

There's not much point coming to a place and not having a look around. So we went for a walk into Clitheroe to see what was there. But we didn't care what was there. Clitheroe was lovely but irrelevant. We wanted to enjoy our new caravan, so we hurried back.

Sarah cooked our tea. She had *three* gas rings to work with, not two. And an oven that worked. *And* there was a grill, so now we could have toast in the morning. In the evening it got better because there was plenty of light. The caravan was cosy and comfortable. We set up the beds. Kevin went out to his tent.

"Goodnight, John-boy," we said.

"Goodnight, Jim-Bob. Goodnight, Elizabeth," he said.

Amanda climbed into her bed and oohed and aahed.

We climbed into our bed and stretched and purred like contented cats. The bed was bigger than our bed at home. The bed was more comfortable than our bed at home by a factor of ten. We slept soundly, dreaming of toast in the morning and warm showers.

In the morning it was cold. I skipped out of bed to turn the heater on, watching my breath cloud around my head. The heater would not light. The process involved some dexterity but I'd done it the previous evening without problem. Hold down the gas knob and press a button to fire a piezo electric spark. I could see the spark but no flame.

I decided to boil a kettle. We had an electric kettle because we were on an electric hook-up, but I thought using the gas ring might take the chill out of the caravan. The gas ring wouldn't light. The hot water heater, for the shower, would not light. None of the gas worked.

The door opened and Kevin came in.

"Freezing out there. I'm glad we've… Yow, it's freezing in here. Haven't you got the heating on?"

I gave him a look.

Through the open door I saw the frost, white and glittering on the grass. I knew what had happened. Our gas tanks were butane. We always used butane because we only ever went away in the summer. When butane tanks get cold, they stay liquid. They don't work. In the winter you use propane. Why hadn't I thought of that?

I remembered I still had the old 500-watt fan heater from the Sprite – we'd transferred everything, even the things we didn't need. I dug it out of a cupboard. Switched it on. An hour later the temperature became bearable.

When the caravan got warm the butane bottles got warm and the next time I tried the gas it worked. We cheered.

The caravan was soon warm and cosy with steaming hot water. We had our showers. We ate toast. We looked at the frost outside and it felt good.

We'd always known there'd be things to learn. Now we knew we'd be needing propane and a propane regulator before we ventured out again, but this was only a glitch. Our Avondale had won our hearts. She was part of the family.

2003: BACK TO THE ALPS

I live on the Wirral. It has a wide swathe of countryside down the middle – a green belt at the time of writing but probably not by the time you read this if the local authority get their way – but I'm getting off the point; this segment is meant to be upbeat, so let's get back to the positives. There's a roundabout between Clatterbridge and Thornton Hough. It's rural. It's miles from anywhere, and the authorities have just completed a massive amount of work on it. They've added kerbs and lots of red paint on the road, and pavements all the way around the outside with those nifty ramps that improve access for wheelchairs and mobility scooters. I think it's so thoughtful of them. Also very forward thinking because there's no pedestrian access for at least a mile in any direction. So whenever a wheelchair user is beamed down from space he can travel around that pavement forever, and in comfort and safety.

MW – Posicle No. 4

A new season and a new caravan. We couldn't wait to try her out for real. It's funny though, we'd bought a 'van that was capable of winter caravanning and yet apart from our brief one-nighter in the frozen tundra of Clitheroe we then waited until March for our first outing. Somehow, throughout the long, cold winter, we didn't feel any spark of enthusiasm to even leave the house, let alone go on holiday. So we waited for a glimmer of relief from the frost and it came in early March.

We went to Keswick. The journey was terrible. Heavy traffic. Heavy rain.

We pitched on hard standing. All the grass pitches were closed or submerged. We were warned not to stray far from the 'van; the site was under flood alert and could become part of Derwent Water at any moment, and we were advised that if that happened we should be ready to move, fast. Kevin put up his tent of course. He wasn't going to let a bit of rain spoil his camping. I wondered where he'd got that from. Anyway, it rained of course, continuously, for every moment we were there. We tramped around Keswick looking in shop windows. We didn't see the mountains or much of the lake. Then the gales came. We went home. We couldn't do more than forty/forty-five mph on the motorway into the head wind. A miserable season opener.

We tried Church Stretton at Easter, in the back half of April. The winter still refused to quit. It was lovely being in the caravan but we didn't want to go outside. I insisted. We stomped up the Long Mynd where I knackered my knee and then couldn't walk for the rest of the weekend. This was not going well.

Our third outing of the year was a trip to Lyme View Marina, in Cheshire. At last we had a successful few days, but the weekend was significant because it marked the first time that only three of us went away. Kevin stayed at home. He was twenty years old and holidays with parents were becoming less cool. Here was the beginning. That word, child, was losing its meaning. More than ever before we needed a better word because adult child was just too cold.

We had a few weekends that followed and sometimes there were four of us, sometimes just three. Our main holiday beckoned though, and we would certainly be together for that one, because we were challenging our Avondale to mirror a journey that our hardy mountain goat Sprite had pulled off without complaint and with aplomb. We were returning to the Alps.

WE DECIDED NOT to attempt the folly of a three-hundred-mile dash for a pre-booked Dover ferry. Been there, done that, failed. It couldn't be done. Somewhere along the three hundred miles of British roads there would be problems: roadworks, accidents, oil spillage, escaped poultry... the laws of probability demanded it, and traumatic stress is never a good overture to a holiday. So instead we left early in the morning and stayed one night at a small farm site in Kent. A good plan.

We arrived early, before lunch, no traffic problems – we could have made the ferry with ease, wouldn't you know it – but at least, with a mid-afternoon, next-day sailing, we had a whole afternoon and morning to explore the orchards and outlet shopping malls of Kent.

We made sure to arrive in Dover early – stupid early – where the delays to the day's ferry sailings were being announced. Not a problem though, I let it go, because I'm mature and patient and positive and never one to grumble, and because we had miles of empty French autoroutes on the other side along which we'd have plenty of time to catch up to our schedule. I even stayed calm on the boat when they wouldn't let the ferry into Calais harbour to dock until an hour later than our delayed ninety-minute crossing should have been.

We hit the road in Calais at six thirty PM and headed south. Our plan was to put as many miles behind us as we could before spending the night in an *aire de repos*, the pleasant and restful lay-by on a motorway that the French do so well. I hadn't wanted to drive in the dark; now I'd have to. But apart from the odd, sub-vocal *zut alors*, I let it go, because this holiday we would be unfettered and free-spirited. In other words I hadn't booked any campsites; we planned to dawdle along, reaching Chamonix some time during the next day, find a site, stay for about a week. No stress. No preconceived ideas. The truth was, we did have a site in mind, in Chamonix, but for some inexplicable reason they didn't take advanced bookings. *"Pas de problème. Beaucoup d'emplacements."*

Northern France is big and wide and dull. The first time we drove this way it was new and thrilling and everything we saw was worthy of comment. That first time in France was special, I always knew it would be. Only now did I appreciate how special, because the second time it was... just France. And dark. A tasteless entrée to consume as quickly as possible so we could get to the main course. The Alps.

We stopped at an *aire* at Troyes. There was only one

other vehicle in the car park. A motorhome – with Dutch plates, of course.

The Dutch couple came straight up to me. "Are you staying the night?"

"Yes, I think so," I said.

"Good," said the wife. "So long as there's someone else here. We feel… vulnerable, camping alone."

We chatted about the journey down for a few minutes then they bade us goodnight and retired to their motorhome.

"What did they mean, vulnerable?" said Sarah.

"Oh, nothing," I said. "It's just a bit lonely here. There's only the two of them. I imagine they're glad of some company."

Sarah was happy with that. I wasn't. There was something about the way they looked around and over their shoulders as they spoke. Their fears had nothing to do with satisfying a need for sociability. These were Dutch people. Dutch people know how to travel. They have been everywhere. They know the safe places and they know… the other places.

We dropped the legs on the caravan. Another significant thing, tonight, was that it would be the first occasion (and in time we'd realise, the *only* occasion) when the four of us would all sleep in our big four-berth caravan. The layout of the 'van had the door placed just in front of the two bunk beds that went across the back wall. In the centre was the galley kitchen, with the wardrobe on one side and the bathroom on the other. In the front was the dining area that converted into a double bed. So the children slept in the bunks by the door. We slept at the other end.

"I'll tell you what," I said. "Amanda, you sleep up front with your mum. I'll have your bunk."

"Why?"

"I just think it would be better. Me and Kevin by the door."

They looked at me.

"This is a car park, not a caravan site, yeah? Go along with me."

We didn't talk about it again. They could see in my eyes that I had a reason. Our Dutch friends had rattled me. Before we'd left home I'd read about an English couple who'd been gassed while sleeping in their caravan at night, on the autoroute, and then all their possessions had been removed. The perpetrators had run a rubber hose through an air vent.

I went to bed fully dressed. I took a heavy socket wrench with me and kept it under my pillow. Soon I could hear snoring all around. I could hear owls hooting. I could hear every step on the tarmac outside. Several times I heard sounds. Then whispering, a rattling sound. Was someone fiddling with the lock? I leapt from the bunk. Well, not so much a leap as a wild upwards lurch and a crashing head-butt into the heavy timber frame of Kevin's bunk. To any would-be gassers/kidnappers I'm sure it sounded like a seven-foot road-digger-stroke-Tarmac-spreader was rocketing out of bed, blaspheming and itching for a fight. I looked outside. Nobody was around.

The night passed without further incident, and for me, without sleep.

In the morning we lifted the caravan legs and prepared to move on.

The lock on the caravan door was jammed. I couldn't re-lock it. Interesting.

I decided we should skip breakfast. The Dutch motorhome was still there. I debated knocking on the door and telling them we were going, but it was light and the world looks safer in daylight. I didn't knock and later felt bad about not doing so. I hope they were okay about it. I'm sure they were fine.

The night had rattled me. I didn't feel quite so safe any more. Maybe I was just spooked. Jumping to conclusions. Maybe if I hadn't heard about the gassing incident beforehand, I'd have slept and been fine.

But the caravan door lock was jammed. It had been okay the day before. And try as we might, we couldn't lock it.

THE GOOD THING about having a twenty-year-old along for the trip was that we now had three drivers. I let Kevin do the next couple of hours while I snoozed in the back seat. Our route took us past Dijon and along the spectacular A40 towards Geneva.

We skirted Geneva, staying on the French side, and where the A40 turns into the mountains, through Bonneville, we stopped for a break. Only for minutes though. We were soon on the road again heading through Cluses and Sallanches. The road climbed higher and higher, towards the Egratz Viaduct, an amazing feat of engineering that took the road high above the valley floor on dizzying 68-metre piers. It twisted and turned for a kilometre and a half, and for all that time we felt exposed, suspended in mid-air, supported by nothing. Especially in the rain. Because it had begun to rain. Not just rain. We got special rain. Alpine rain. The kind of rain that turns mountains into waterfalls and roads into rivers. The climb towards Chamonix was relentless; even the lower parts of the town are higher than Snowdon. I obsessed over that fact, turning it over and over in my head. We were towing our caravan up Snowdon. Up a river. It felt like it, too. I am not a nervous driver but as we rose up the exposed viaduct, with bottomless drops to left and right, and with a struggling, oxygen-starved engine, and rain like ball bearings bouncing off the bonnet of the car, it is fair to say I was nervous. I had wanted a holiday with adventure. Here it was, by the bucketful.

We drove into Chamonix and the rain continued to deluge. The road surface was slick, the painted direction markings rendered invisible. Ordinary road signs were lost in the curtains of water. We toured Chamonix.

In a car, if you go wrong you can do a U-turn. This is not an option with a caravan; with a caravan you make sure you don't go wrong. We went wrong many times and had to find circuitous routes to get back onto the roads we should have taken, all the time terrified that we'd stumble onto the downward section of the A40 and have to go all the way back to the valley floor before finding a place to turn before having to climb up the skeletal viaduct to Chamonix once more.

We argued a lot.

All four of us.

I drove through the town, around the town, in and out of the town.

It was Amanda who spotted the sign, a little wooden plaque the size of a postcard.

"There!" she shouted. "Les Rosiers!"

We had passed this place three times before.

I turned right over a wooden-railed bridge and we pulled into Camping Les Rosiers. For a while we just sat in the car, panting and trembling, and letting all the adrenaline drain away.

But we couldn't relax. Not yet. As I mentioned, we hadn't booked.

We walked through the campsite looking for the site office.

"It looks very full," said Sarah.

I nodded, my expression grim. I'd written to them to make a booking. *"Pas de problème. Beaucoup d'emplacements."* That's what the reply had said, and then gone on to explain how their policy was not to take any bookings at this time of the year; it wasn't necessary. We saw a campsite layered with dome tents, their guy ropes overlapping so they could fit into tiny spaces.

I looked up. The rain had stopped. *Good*, I thought. *It might make it easier when we go to find another campsite.*

The site office was on the upper floor of a chalet, at the top of some stairs.

"Parlez-vous anglais?" I asked.

"Oui, of course," he said. He was about twenty, long hair, wiry, and was looping a climbing rope on the top of the desk, sweeping all the paperwork and clutter down onto the floor with every motion.

"Do you have room for a caravan?" I asked without conviction. "I tried to book, but…" I showed him the letter.

"Yes, we are always not so full this time of year, *avant l'été*. But…" He shook his head and closed his eyes, giving the problem some thought. "Perhaps… yes. Come."

We took him to the caravan. He looked at its size and sucked air through his teeth, then gave an apologetic and very Gallic shrug.

"Okay. We try. Follow me *avec votre caravane*."

There was a space. Not very big. We had to unhitch the 'van and the five of us manhandled her into a tight corner between a Spanish caravan and an Italian motorhome. Kevin found room for his tent by adopting the overlapping guy line technique that was prevalent around the site. He was determined to camp. This was a real campsite. Outside every tent were ropes and crampons and jingling metal climbing equipment. This wasn't just a campsite, this was an *Alpinists'* campsite.

Amanda decided she didn't want to be an Alpinist; she'd seen Alpine rain. She preferred the idea of being safe from the mountain elements, cosy in our caravan.

"We're a bit cramped, here," said Sarah.

"I know. It's not what I expected. Maybe we won't stay so long. We can always move—"

And the clouds lifted. Ahead of us, in clear line of sight,

the snow-capped summit of Mont Blanc. To the left, a glittering shard of a peak. One that I recognised straight away from the mountain books I'd been reading at home. The Petit Dru. Iconic mountains. Snowy peaks. The Aiguille Du Midi. The sparkling red Aiguilles Rouges. No caravan view had ever come close to this, even in Switzerland. We stood and gaped. Thoughts of moving on evaporated. Yes, we'd be staying in Les Rosiers for as long as they'd have us.

THE SUN SHONE, it was late afternoon but there was time for a walk into Chamonix. The small bridge we crossed entering the site spanned the Arve River. Alongside the river ran a gravel path that led into the town. A few hundred yards downstream, the river merged with another, the Arveyron, where the path led across another footbridge. Two things struck us about these rivers. The colour, a vivid turquoise – and the cold. The afternoon sun felt hot on our backs but crossing the bridge we could feel the intense cold welling up from the water below and chilling the air. This was glacier water, no mistake. The Arve, now merged, was bigger, colder and more ferocious. As the wind gusted, we felt variously the heat from the sun and the deep, bone-penetrating cold of the river. We had no doubts: this was not a river in which to swim.

The path continued through pine trees, past a sports complex and brought us to the town of Chamonix, with which we became enchanted in an instant. The wooden chalets, the red geraniums in window boxes, the ornate roofed bridges over the chilly Arve River. There is a statue in the centre of the town of two figures, one pointing to the summit of a mountain high above the rooftops. The mountain is Mont Blanc. The statue is of Balmat and Paccard, the first to climb it.

But in Chamonix we had business to conduct. A task to perform. Amanda had left her prescription sunglasses at home. Here in the Alps the combination of sun and snow provides abundant potential for snow blindness. Probably an overreaction in July, but we Woods can be chock full of overreaction when we put our minds to it. I suggested we try to buy some clip-ons, perhaps in a pharmacy or a gift shop, or, failing that, maybe even try an optician.

I only said the latter to appease her. I had not the slightest crumb of optimism that an optician would stock clip-ons, or even discuss the matter with us. Back home one traditionally waited three weeks just for an appointment, then spent a long afternoon having various eye-health examinations, culminating in that death-ray air-blast thing they fire into each eye to remind you that this is serious medical stuff, and worthy of the inflated bill. Then you are ushered, after a wait, into another room where the expensive frames are sold, where an attractive young girl tells you which ones suit your face, and of course they're all over a hundred quid, and yes, you *can* get frames for under sixty pounds, and you are shown to where they are displayed on the bottom shelf only, off the rack marked "under £60", and you try a pair, and you realise they'll only work if you're happy to look like Fred Dibnah after a steeplejack accident. So you end up with "designer" frames. You write a cheque and wait for two more weeks before going back to have your new, ill-fitting "designer" spectacles bent into shape around your awkward-shaped head. I always wondered about that word, "designer", tagged onto specs and jeans and stuff. How would they make non-designer frames, anyway? If nobody designs them what process forms them into glasses? I picture maybe a room in which an infinite number of monkeys play around with an infinite number of plastic injection moulding machines.

So yes, after failing on our pharmacy/gift-shop quest for clip-on sunglasses, we came upon an optician in Balmat Square and I led us all inside. I felt certain it would be a short visit but I had to demonstrate a preparedness to eliminate every option. My French remained sketchy, a make-do-but-willing-to-try kind of French. I had no idea how to say "clip-on" in French so I went for the full-on fancy option instead. Even so, ordering a pair of designer prescription sunglasses would likely involve a lot of words I barely knew in English.

"Bonjour." A good start. Baby steps.

"Je voudrais…" *I would like.*

"Pour ma fille." *For my daughter.* Wow, I was motoring here. But now came the hard part.

"Des lunettes de soleil." I knew *lunettes* were glasses but then the word for sun came to me in an epiphany.

"Oui, je comprends," said the optician. *Yes, I understand.* Woo hoo! But what about the prescription part? I knew that English words with "-tion" at the end usually worked if you said them with an accent. So I gave a pained and apologetic half-smile and said:

"Prescription?"

Again he nodded. He indicated to Amanda to pass him her glasses, which he put into a machine, turned a few dials, then announced, "Bon." He showed Amanda to a cabinet of frames. She selected a pair of very stylish designer frames that looked as though they would cost me my home, and the optician said, "D'accord. Très chic." Or something like that. He turned to me and said, "Demain. Après midi."

I looked confused. "Demain? Tomorrow?"

"Oui, tomorrow," he said.

We left the shop. I hadn't paid a thing, not even a deposit. Had we bought something other than sunglasses? What would they cost? I felt nervous. What had I done? But I also felt a little proud. Whatever happened tomorrow, I had conducted the entire transaction in French. Not exactly a conversation, but a big step up from *bonjour*, *merci*, and *au revoir*.

WE DID some shopping in the SuperU, where I felt just a little too cocky about my superlative French language skills and tried to make a comment on the weather to the checkout girl, but instead caused her great confusion. She thought I was asking about the provenance of the milk we were trying to buy. Several of the other staff got involved and I wished I'd stuck to my usual three-word repertoire. We left the SuperU with milk, though, and were happy to do so. We had bought *real* milk that could go into our real fridge, instead of the nightmarish French sterrie that we'd had to endure on our previous visit. We went back later, after the shock waves of my weird conversation had settled down, and bought something frozen to go in our freezer box. We weren't one hundred percent sure what we had bought, or whether it was a main course or a dessert. I'd work on the instructions later, in the caravan, with the dictionary. The surprise might be fun.

Back at the caravan we enjoyed the red-orange alpen-glow setting the mountaintops ablaze, then watched as the stars came out, one at a time, crisper and brighter than we'd ever seen before. It felt good to be back in the Alps. We couldn't wait for the next day.

THE STATION for the Montenvers railway is in Chamonix. We walked there. Most attractions around Chamonix could be reached on foot from Les Rosiers, and this added further to the appeal of the site location. These same attractions then involved clambering onto a train or cable car, and a considerable amount of deep mining into the darker folds of my wallet. We learned quickly that our stay in Chamonix would coincide with a serious depletion of funds. The Alps don't come cheap.

I paid with a smile, though it was a somewhat tight-lipped smile. Four adults. I would hold back the tears until home. I felt in my heart that the Montenvers railway would be worth every penny, and I was right. The railway climbs up the Aiguilles de Chamonix. It is a funicular railway, and it ascends loony gradients, twisting and turning, looping through tunnels as it scrabbles up the impossible mountainside. Whoever thought this would be a good spot to build a railway must have been insane. It would be hard today, to build even a goat trail through this terrain, and they built the railway back in the 1900s.

The destination was Montenvers, where there was a cafe and the main attraction, the view of the Mer de Glace. As it was summer, we were able to walk down waymarked paths to the glacier and enter the ice tunnels that are carved into the moving ice itself. The sun filters from above causing the tunnel walls to glow bright turquoise, the same colour as the rivers in Chamonix, and inside the tunnels there are ice sculptures. The ice sculptures had melted a bit when we were there, but so what. The whole experience was sublime. Explaining it seems like just a bunch of words. I'll never get across how it felt to *walk inside* that immense river of ice. To feel the cold. To hear the creaking and groaning and snapping sounds as billions of tonnes of ice moves, a millimetre at a time, down the valley, and all of it just above your head and around you. It was a fabulous experience.

Like all such experiences, though, it was hard to know when to leave. We exited the tunnels and retraced our steps towards the station where we stood and looked. But what is the required time period for standing and looking, in awe, at one of the world's greatest wonders? After a while you get the sense that, okay, seen it. Is it too early to move on? Will I appear shallow if I suggest we go now? Should I stay and admire it a little longer? But while you feel you have seen enough and should move, you also know that the chances are, this is your one shot. You probably won't be back because there are so many other things to see in the world, so when you turn and go you will never see it again. So, just one more look. Take another photo in case none of the other four hundred turn out. One more look up at the mountains, too, the Drus and the Grandes Jorrasses. And you turn. You take a final glance back over your shoulder, you walk to the train station, clamber aboard the train, and it's over.

ON OUR WAY back through Chamonix we returned to the optician's. I had trepidations. That's probably a French word too. Possibly my only one at that moment. You have to be in the mood for languages, and I felt preoccupied wondering what kind of financial crisis I'd negotiated us into yesterday afternoon.

"Bonjour."

"Ah, monsieur. Mademoiselle." He led Amanda to a chair in front of a mirror and with a gentle touch, placed a pair of sunglasses on her face. He handed her a card full of French words that got smaller as they went down the page.

Amanda smiled. "Do I have to read?" She sounded nervous about it, like it was her GCSE aural all over again. "They're fine. The letters are clear. Perfect. I love these sunglasses."

The optician gave me the bill. I swallowed. It was in both Euros and Francs. The numbers seemed small. I did some mental arithmetic. Again and again. *This couldn't be right.*

"But this is… it's only forty or fifty pounds. Er… is there more?" I realised the shock had thrown me into English. "Er… C'est tout?"

"Oui," he said, and some more that I didn't catch, but I could tell from his tone that it was all just pleasantries.

I gave him my credit card. Done. I thanked him. Again and again. I might have even cried a little. Amanda thanked him. We staggered out of the shop that we had only found at random, the day before. Amanda wearing her *designer* sunglasses and a big white smile. I had lost the ability to speak. I was doing financial sums and deciding that we should come to France for all our family's ophthalmic needs from this moment on.

I WANTED to walk in the Alps. Our campsite was full of Alpinists, with their ropes and hard hats and their jingly karabiners and things, and I wanted to feel like a mountain man rather than a spoilt, fat tourist. The only way to feel like a mountain man is to walk in the mountains, so we took the téléphérique – I use the word téléphérique because I like putting in all the little lines above the letter "e", it's really a cable car – which lifted us high above the Chamonix valley to La Flégère. From there we set out along the ridge, the Grand Balcon Sud, towards Planpraz, another téléphérique station from where we could catch a car back down to the town.

Our walk in the Alps was good but not great. The clouds came down and wrecked our view for the most part.

We never felt in any danger of a misty whiteout, causing us to stumble around lost before striding out over a precipice, because the clouds here were white and fluffy-dry. Not the sort of clouds that lay down a cloak of invisibility and fog your specs, like they do in Scotland, Wales or the Lakes. Somehow, at six thousand feet it felt safer in the Alps than on some of those Munros we never got to climb in the Highlands the year before. Probably something to do with the regular signposts that pointed along the way at every junction and said things like, "Planpraz: 1 hr 20 mins". A very civilised way of doing the Great Outdoors, I have to say. But the clouds, for all they were nice, cotton-wool, benevolent clouds, still obscured the view, and without a view the strenuous walking felt kind of pointless and frustrating. Now and again the fluffy clouds parted for a fleeting second. Just long enough to show us a breathtaking glimpse of what we were missing. The walk took us a couple of hours; it was only about three miles, but we took our time and we stopped for a picnic lunch along the way, at a perfect spot for cloud watching.

We arrived at Planpraz, and the clouds parted, and we were at last given a wicked-cool view of the whole valley right across to the summit of Mont Blanc on the opposite side. But I wasn't happy. Planpraz was a cable car halt. Anyone with cash could ride up here and take in the view. This wasn't a mountain-man view, the sort we should have had for the whole length of our walk along the Grand Balcon Sud. I suggested we turn around and go back but nobody agreed. So then I had another idea.

"Let's walk down," I said.

From up here we could see the whole route winding down below us. It looked easy. We could be real Alpinists without all that unpleasant sweaty toil of an ascent. Gravity would do most of the work for us.

Again I was alone in my enthusiasm, but I worked on the others, and I whined a bit, and I pimped it all up and built their interest, gaining allies one by one, and told them it was only the height of Snowdon, don't be a wuss, and if we could climb *and* descend Snowdon in a day, then strolling down this well-made path would be a doddle. I gained my victory, and we set off walking down an Alp.

Here are some of the differences between an Alpine descent and a Snowdon descent:

1) Snowdon has slope-y bits, then steep rocky bits, then long flat bits, then slope-y bits again. One's body has time to recover during the transitions.

2) None of the Snowdon paths go all the way down to sea level, not even Snowdon Ranger, so they're not actually 3,560-foot descents. And I lied a bit about this descent. This was further. Much further.

3) When we last did Snowdon I was fit. I hadn't knackered my knee a few short weekends earlier, when I had tearfully struggled to descend a mere 800 feet down the gentle tourist path of the Long Mynd.

These inconvenient truths spoiled my argument so I kept them to myself. The first part of the descent was steady, steep, on gravel, and relentless. I noticed my knee beginning to throb. At this stage I could have gone back. I could have climbed, but it was hot and the gravel was loose and my knee hurt even more when I experimentally went up. I said nothing and continued to plod down.

We moved into pinewoods where no two steps were the same, where roots snaked out to turn an ankle and jolt the weakened parts of the body. I began to lag behind.

"What's up?" said Sarah.

"Just enjoying the view. Savouring the walk."

Sarah looked me in the eye. "Your knee?"

I nodded.

"We'd better go back." She said it without conviction. We'd come down a long way. Chamonix was still a toy train layout far below. With good eyes and freshly polished specs you could see the little moving dots that were cars. Planpraz was a toy téléphérique far, far above.

I pooh-poohed the idea and we continued. I limped and stumbled and the descent remained punishing. Yes, gravity helps, but with each step all that body-weight momentum needs to be stopped, and you need good shock absorbers. Good knees. My thigh bone felt as though it was connected to my calf bone via an earthenware pot filled with broken glass.

We each had telescopic walking poles. We'd bought fiendishly expensive models the last time in Switzerland, and I'd left mine on top of an Alp and been heartbroken. They'd since become fashionable in the UK and I'd bought a replacement for a tenth the price of the original, and I had it with me. They are meant to help propel you along as you walk. I used mine as a crutch.

We continued down without options. There are no bus

stops. Nowhere to wait while the others go for the car. I limped on and the pain increased. I tried keeping it bent, I tried keeping it straight. I tried binding my knee with my tee shirt, I tried hopping. I took Kevin's walking pole and used the two to take as much weight off my knee as I could, but it was hard. The slope went on and on. The path twisted and turned with no respite from the gradient. Every now and again we came to a clearing in the trees and looked up as the cable car hummed above our heads. We could have been on that cable car. But I would have been sulking about not getting my way and not being allowed to walk. I would never have known how lucky I'd been. People waved. We waved back. We walked. I hopped. Our stops became more and more frequent. Our progress became slower. I apologised again and again. I could feel my knee filling out the space in my trouser leg, pressing against the fabric in all directions as it ballooned.

The descent took us hours. We passed the lower cable car stop, shuttered and closed. And still we were only in the upper parts of Chamonix with lots of downhill to go.

The light was fading as I hobbled into Chamonix proper. The shops were closed. The street lights were coming on. I reckoned my knee would feel better walking along the level path beside the glacial river, but it didn't. I wanted to put my knee in the river and numb it in the icy water, but I'd have probably slipped and been swept away to Geneva and that wouldn't have been so good.

We reached the caravan. I have never felt so grateful. I lay on the bunk and put frozen peas on my knee and groaned. We discussed going to hospital. I refused. I was in no mood for languages, especially looking up the French for "Yes Doctor, I buggered up my knee three weeks ago on the Long Mynd then walked down an Alp today and it hurts again. No, I can't bend it. Yes, it does hurt. Yes, I do have one of those UK National Insurance cards that probably mean naff all when it comes to settling the medical bill."

Sarah made tea. I drank a lot of cheap SuperU wine to numb the pain. I had a fitful night because it hurt to lie on the knee.

In the morning it felt easier. Less pain. No swelling. Except when I walked.

We had a laundry day.

SOMETIMES THE SIMPLEST things give pleasure. Every morning I enjoyed walking through the site to a gap in the hedge, behind which the mobile boulanger parked his van. This is another thing the French do better than anyone else. They wake up at stupid o'clock and bake fresh bread and croissants and pain au chocolat, and then bring them to the campsites still warm from the oven. I loved the routine of lining up with other Alpinists of all nationalities to buy bread and croissants. From my place in line there was always time to stand and stare at the magical scenery towering high above in every direction.

On our last full day in Chamonix the sky was clear of any clouds, the sun felt warm on my face and, high above the valley, it glistened off the metallic church-steeple-like spire atop the Aiguilles du Midi.

I wanted to go there.

"We should go up the Aiguilles du Midi," I said, dropping the bags of warm bakery products on the caravan table.

"Is that wise?" said Sarah. "With your knee?"

I waved it off. "Two cable cars. No walking."

"How high is it?"

"Hmm. Twelve, twelve and a half thousand feet."

"And how long would it take?"

"Oh, nothing. It's just up and down. An hour. Hour and a half."

"Okay. No thanks. You go with the kids. I think I'd rather do some souvenir shopping. We can go for a walk somewhere after lunch. A *gentle* walk."

Amanda decided she'd rather shop, too, so they walked us down to the cable station and we split up. Kevin and I would do the Aiguilles du Midi. It was then ten thirty. We said we'd meet them back at the 'van at noon.

A large crowd had just gone up and we were lucky to be at the front of the queue for the next ascent. Twenty minutes later we were at the Plan de L'Aiguille, the halfway point. Here we were not so fortunate, because those intrepid Alpinists and tourists who'd gone before us were still waiting for the next cable car, the one that climbs to the top. We waited. Some boarded. Some didn't. We were amongst the "didn't" group.

Cable cars are different to chair lifts and their constant conveyor belt of tourism. Cable cars are more binary. One car goes up and one car comes down. I looked at my watch. Okay, so maybe a noon return had been optimistic. It was already twelve thirty. We'd still be fine for a walk in the afternoon. Late afternoon. Once we were at the top, a quick look around would suffice, then we'd head back. I knew that many of our fellow travellers had bought the full ticket which meant they'd be transferring over to the cable car that crosses the Mont Blanc Massif to Pointe Helbronner in Italy. So demand to go back down would be less and we could bank on our return trip being quicker.

The cable car arrived and we squashed aboard for the next departure. We were used to cable cars by now, but it is still scary to follow the line of the cable with your eye, up and up into the thin air, and to know that we would soon be hanging from that slender thread of wire along with sixty or seventy gourmands, shot-putters and weightlifters all packed into a little metal box.

Out we swung. Everyone gave a "whoa!" followed by nervous chuckles, and we climbed, yawning and swallowing all the way to counteract our popping ears. We'd secured good positions in the sardine pecking order, if you'll excuse me mixing my clichés, and we could stand, faces squashed against the glass, and see climbers dotted far below, heading up the hard way.

At the top, in the Aiguilles du Midi station, we were handed a ticket by a cheery, perky young man. A student, from the look of him.

"What's this? Er... qu'est que c'est?"

"You are English, yes?" he said.

"Yes. Oui."

"These are your boarding passes, sir."

"Oh. No. We don't need boarding passes. We're not

going on the cable car to Italy. Just a look around then back down."

"No, monsieur. A timed boarding pass. So many people. Return trips have to be timed. That is the time of your return trip down to Chamonix."

"So we can't choose?"

"Non, monsieur."

"Even though we're not joining the next cable car. To Italy."

"Non, monsieur."

I shrugged. I led Kevin in a slow shuffle off the car, down a cold corridor and out onto the viewing platform of Aiguilles du Midi. I looked at the boarding pass. No language difficulties. 17:45. Three and a half hours.

I went back to argue but the English-speaking student had gone, and been replaced by a surly Frenchman who did not want to make an effort with my attempts at explaining, in French, how we'd arranged to meet the rest of our family an hour and a half ago. That they might be worried. He dismissed us with a flick of the wrist, sending us back to the viewing platform.

There was a cafe on top. I bought us drinks and sandwiches. I didn't moan about the prices because we were twelve and a half thousand feet up a mountain, and it seemed nuts there'd be a cafe up here at all, so I forgave them on price and even on the maturing condition of the bread, which seemed to let *la belle France* down a little after all my waxing lyrical about the quality of French boulangerie products.

We looked around. We looked down on Chamonix. We

commented on how rapid movements tended to make us gasp and see stars because of the thin air. We went over the bridge between the two peaks and got the lift to the top of the pointy bit, then looked out again at the same view, but 140 feet higher. Kevin mentioned how the extra 140 feet didn't seem to change the view much when you're already twelve and half *thousand* feet above the valley floor. I agreed. But we looked around then went back down the lift and across the bridge, and half an hour had passed. Only another three hours to go.

It wasn't just the waiting. We'd promised the girls a walk. We'd promised lunch in the caravan at noon. How could we let them know? We had a mobile phone and they had a mobile phone. Early millennium technology was rampant in the Wood family. But high in the Alps, British Telecom didn't seem to have a signal, and roaming was a thing I'd read about in some tech magazine and wondered what it meant. I tried texting them but kept getting *text undelivered* messages.

I was worried that the girls would be worried. I was bored, too. Kevin was bored. I'd given this whole, how-long-do-you-look-at-a-spectacle thing some thought a few days earlier, and my answer had been within an envelope of minutes. Three and a half hours was a long time to look at a view. I also wondered, well, since there wasn't much air up here, would we both start to get altitude sickness? What were the symptoms of an embolism? On the plus side, if I passed out or started coughing blood they'd maybe bump us up to an earlier departure time. Then I thought about the surly Frenchman who'd replaced the perky student, and I thought that if I passed out, he'd more likely allocate my slot to a more deserving, able-bodied traveller.

We waited. We sat on the floor, our backs to the parapet wall, bored with the views of snow, and waited, breathing long slow breaths to maximise the oxygenation of our cardiovascular systems.

For three bloody hours. Felt like thirty.

But our time came. We clambered to our feet, relieved to find that our backsides hadn't welded to the tiles from frostbite, and then we shuffled down the long corridor in amongst a press of excited travellers, newly returned from their Italian adventures. We waited. We shuffled. Far below we saw our cable car begin the ascent. We'd been in it before. We knew how long it took. We waited. I tried my best not to faint from all the physical exertion of standing and shuffling.

At last the car arrived. We squashed aboard. When the car was full we waited while some more weightlifters and sumo wrestlers were encouraged to board just to stress-test the cable. Then we dropped. The cable stretched and hummed and made plaintive cello sounds.

We shuffled into the midway station at Plan de L'Aiguille where there awaited another surprise. When we had joined the queue for the summit leg so long ago this morning, we noticed that not everyone wanted to go all the way to the top. Some had gone onto the mountain at Plan de L'Aiguille, to walk, to sunbathe, to dine at the cafe, whatever. These people were now also coming back down. So were many more that had walked all the way from Montenvers, having gone up on the train.

There is no boarding-pass system for the last leg. Everyone takes pot luck. And in the late afternoon the cable cars stop running, French style: *Nous sommes désolés*. We're sorry. *Fermé maintenant*. Closed now.

Our small army of summiteers mingled with the several thousand others from the midway station and its environs, all vying to make one of the last three or four descents. It would appear that those of us remaining would be sleeping rough on the mountain… or we'd have to walk down. Plan de L'Aiguille is 7,600 feet above Chamonix. I thought about how my knee had fared on the 3,000-foot descent from Planpraz a couple of days ago. It had already begun to throb a little from all the shuffling and standing. Yes, the girls would be worried. It occurred to me now that they might have something to worry about. These are serious mountains. I had proved I was as much an Alpinist as Long John Silver.

We shuffled. I even barged a bit. I used my weedy elbows, which are not so effective against high-protein-diet American weightlifters. Kevin was younger, but had grown taller than me. He had stronger elbows. The time for British reserve was over. Kevin made a path.

I'm not sure if our cable car was the last one or not. There couldn't have been many more after ours. I wonder what happened to the hundreds we left behind. Perhaps they do keep the cable car running as a matter of civic duty, to clear the Plan de L'Aiguille station before closing. I didn't know. I no longer cared. We were heading down.

We stepped onto the firm ground of Chamonix a few minutes before seven. We sucked in deep draughts of oxygen-rich air to feed our red corpuscles. Halfway back to the caravan we met Sarah and Amanda. I could see from their colour-drained faces that I had been right about the worry thing. Sarah shouted at us then hugged us, then I shouted at her because it wasn't my fault, then hugged her. We told them our story. They told us theirs, about fruitless shopping then sitting in the caravan awaiting news of a cable car crash or the airlifting to hospital of some asphyxiated tourists or some other mountaintop catastrophe.

We had our noon lunch at eight thirty. Too late for an afternoon walk in the pine-forested foothills. And tomorrow we had to leave.

But we couldn't leave Chamonix just yet, because I had to get arrested first.

2003: LUCERNE

*S*ince I've been praising the disability ramps on Wirral's roundabout to/from nowhere, I should also add my admiration for these knobbly tactile kerbside ramps in general. They do make it easier for those reliant on wheeled access. Of course it would be better if the authorities put ramps on both sides of the road, but perhaps that would be making it too easy. My mother-in-law uses a mobility scooter and we've been helping her find a route to the local shops that doesn't leave her stranded in the middle of a road. We haven't found one yet, but the search satisfies our innate human need for exploration. One access ramp shows, too, that our local government officials do have a sense of humour. It passes either side of a tree with only nine inches of pavement on each side. Perfect for all the disabled unicyclists in the community.

MW – Posicle No. 5

I HAD BECOME friends with the young man who managed the site at Les Rosiers. I gathered he was a student who had taken on the site-management job for the summer. His English was excellent. I saw him each morning on my daily trip to the mobile boulangerie and had progressed from *bonjour* to comments on the weather and had fallen into the habit of trying a new line of French out on him each day. It was he who suggested the Grandes Balcon route from La Flégère to Planpraz as a safe introduction to Alpine hiking.

His name was Jacques. Each morning I would say *bonjour Jacques* and he would say *bonjour Monsieur Wood*. Then I said *mon nom est Mike*, so from then on it was *bonjour Jacques, bonjour Mike*. At one point during our week I dared to use the *tu* form of address, the familiar form only used between friends, and he had been delighted, called me *mon ami*, and we were friends. I worked hard to always use the *tu* form from then on. Stay with me because this is important for what comes later.

On our last morning I met Jacques while on my way to buy bread from the boulangerie. I explained how our week was over and that we had to move on, and how sorry we were to be leaving. We ate our breakfast, then Jacques helped us to manhandle our caravan out of the tiny corner we had occupied for a week. We said our goodbyes then pulled away.

Outside the site I turned right instead of left. This was partly because it is a tight turn and with a caravan it would have been difficult to turn left without scraping the 'van along the bridge parapet, and it was also due in part to my mind being elsewhere, and my being an idiot.

No worries, I was confident I could find my way. There was a series of junctions I knew well, then a roundabout. At the roundabout, I missed the correct exit because I was still in drive-to-the-centre-of-Chamonix mode. I should have taken the previous exit for through traffic instead. Again no worries. I did a full circuit of the roundabout so I could take the correct exit on my second pass.

There was a whoop of a siren. I looked in my mirrors and saw a police car. The gendarmes. Blue lights flashing. I pulled over.

I watched in my mirrors as two of them, with shoulders like Schwarzenegger, swaggered slowly down the length of the caravan, reached the car and tapped on the window. I wound it down. One spoke in rapid French. I shrugged.

"Répétez s'il vous plaît," I said.

He repeated. I processed the words and thought I heard *voiture* and *sortie* amongst them – car and exit. He was telling me to get out of the car.

I got out of the car.

I felt insignificant standing between the utility belts, body armour and muscles.

"Votre permis?"

I looked blank.

"Votre permis de conduire?"

Sarah, Kevin and Amanda had also climbed out of the car, and we all formed a little group at the side of the road.

"He wants a permit," I said to Sarah. "Do we need a permit here? What kind of permit?"

"Je n'ai pas un permis," I said. I meant to say *I don't understand permit*, but it came out as *I don't have a permit*, and that was okay, because I didn't.

The gendarmes' faces darkened and they conferred in rapid French.

"I think he means your driving licence?" said Kevin.

Yes, of course. That would be the first thing the police would ask for.

"Yes, good," I said. "Er… Un moment. Oui. J'ai un

licence." I said licence in my best Peter Sellers, Inspector Clouseau accent.

I dived into the car and fished around inside the glove compartment, then came back with my licence.

I didn't have a modern photo licence. I still don't. I passed my test in 1973 and my licence is a museum-exhibit pink sheet of paper that unfolds from a small plastic wallet. Few English people still alive have seen one like it. I imagine there are even fewer French police that would recognise it.

"Qu'est-ce que c'est?" said the larger of the gendarmes.

"C'est mon licence," I said.

I felt the time had come, as with all police interactions, to do some humble apologising and subservient grovelling for whatever crime I'd perpetrated. I thought it might be a good idea, too, to find out exactly what it was I was supposed to have done.

"Je suis désolé," I said. "Très désolé. Quel est le problème?" I then went on to explain that I only spoke a little French. "Je parle à un petit… um, français."

"Excusez moi, monsieur?" said one of them.

"Er…" How could I say in another way that my French was bad? "Les français sont mauvais."

I have a French pen friend. Her name is Joelle. We've written to each other for years, first by email and more recently as Facebook friends. We met online some time before my first trip to France because I saw it as a good way of improving my French. She in turn wanted to improve her English, so we connected via a website that puts language students in touch with one another. We've never met in person but we have remained friends. I emailed to tell her what had happened some weeks later. I remembered much of the conversation because I wrote down all I could remember in my caravan diary that night. When I shared extracts with Joelle, she told me that instead of saying I only speak a little French, I appear to have said something along the lines of "I am speaking to a little Frenchman." This explains why the shorter of the two gendarmes, who was only about six foot four, straightened his back and stood tall by another two inches, then placed a hand on the holster of his gun. A gun that I only noticed for the first time at that moment.

Also, I should have said *mes*, not *les*. And maybe *est* instead of *sont*. I never could get the hang of pesky French grammar, so I tended to adopt a scattergun technique, salting my sentences with whatever words sounded right according to my recollection of the French tapes I used. So instead of saying *my French is bad*, I said *the French are bad*. Also I started gabbling. Making light conversation. Inspired by conversations with my friend Jacques from Les Rosiers, I realised I was doing a lot of *tu*-ing instead of *vous*-ing, which is how you speak to small children and close friends and is taken as quite insulting when used on policemen who are not your friends.

They were both glaring at me now, with cold eyes. I didn't know what I was saying but I sensed I might be digging an ever-deeper hole for myself. Visions of ten years' eating bugs on Devil's Island came to mind.

The two were now looking more closely at my licence. There's an endorsement on there, and they were pointing to it and making questioning noises. The endorsement was twenty years old, going back to 1984, and would have been expunged years earlier had I updated my licence. But to me the endorsement is a symbol of the social injustice that prevailed then and still to this day.

I was convicted for having a car on the road without valid tax and MOT. The truth was the tax expired because the MOT expired a few days before pay day, at which time I couldn't afford to get the required work done, get the car MOT'd and buy the tax. If I'd been more wealthy, I'd have lived in a house with a driveway, as I do now. The car would not have been parked on the road and I would not have been committing an offence. I always felt I was convicted for poverty. It is a modern Dickensian tale of judicial inequity and I get all het up every time I tell it.

So now I had my chance to tell it in French. I tried not to look angry because I sensed it wouldn't help. But I had to explain because the first column in the endorsement section was headed "Convicting Court Code." And this looked more incriminating than it really was. A mere motoring offence made me sound like some kind of gangster. I explained with increasing desperation about how my home had no drive. "Je n'ai pas un maison, un drive."

I said how it had been an injustice. "Il est une injustice."

I explained how it had come out badly for us. Very bad. "Nous sommes mal. Très mal."

All the time I was trying to explain, they were leading me by the elbow towards their police car. One of the gendarmes kept saying, "*Vous dois arrêter.*"

"What? I'm under arrest?" I pulled my arm free. I still didn't know what I had done. "Pourquoi? Pourquoi?"

Then they had a discussion. Led me back to my car. Opened the driver's door and pointed to the handbrake, shouting "*Vous dois arrêter. Le frein de stationnement.*"

The handbrake. Ahh. I got it. *Arrêter* meant stop, not arrest, and in France you are meant to apply the handbrake at stop signs. You have to stop. I had merely slowed. I nodded and apologised with enthusiasm.

"Je comprends. Je comprends. Je suis désolé. Je suis *très* désolé."

Joelle explained to me later that a spot fine would have been normal in such cases. I'd been very lucky. They should have taken me to a cash machine and made me withdraw money for a fine. That would have been normal. Prison was unlikely.

Joelle said, as far as she could figure, it sounded like I'd told them I had no home and this was an injustice. They probably took us for a family of New Age travellers. Then I apparently told them we were all sick. Very sick. Perhaps the gendarmes didn't want a diseased Englishman in their car with them. Not only diseased but demented, if my French was any evidence. Perhaps they preferred it if this homeless, demented family got the hell out of Chamonix as soon as possible.

This seems to be a good explanation for their actions. They pushed me back in the car and told me to go. *Aller! Aller!*

We all piled into the car. I drove. I was careful to apply the handbrake at every junction, because they followed us out of Chamonix, always there in my wing mirrors, all the way to the town limits.

We travelled in silence. My hands were shaking. My soft spot for Chamonix had hardened a little. Next time I came back, I thought, I might have to do so in disguise.

We returned down the spectacular viaduct to the outskirts of Geneva. We were heading for Lake Lucerne in Switzerland but our route had been subject to much debate. I'd been on internet forums to ask opinions. The route straight through Chamonix and up to Martigny then on through Montreux was shorter. Eighty kilometres shorter. It looked interesting and scenic and avoided repeating the route we had taken to get to Chamonix.

On the other hand, it went over the Alps. On the map it was one of those twisting, turning mountain roads that looked fun in an open-top Ferrari or on a mountain bike, but less so with a ton of caravan dangling off the tow bar, and your rear-view mirrors full of the local constabulary wondering what kind of *merde* these crazy Brits were getting up to now.

So we took the low road. The long way round.

We entered Switzerland in Geneva, and felt the way it should have, years ago. The way we'd pictured it, rather than the way we had blundered, via the back door, through the car park of some pharmaceutical factory. There were Swiss flags and armed guards, and they just waved us through. Obviously their colleagues in the Chamonix police department hadn't phoned ahead to warn them of our arrival.

France became Switzerland and Switzerland became flat. God seemed to have taken a jack plane to Switzerland and shaved off all the pointy bits, then finished the job with grade 000 sandpaper. We found ourselves on featureless motorway indistinguishable from the East Midlands M1. Actually, that's not fair. This was a clean motorway with no cones and little traffic and some low hills, but not much interest because the distant Alps became lost in the heat haze. We went over a lake at Gruyère, and it was pleasant. It could have been Bala only the mountains weren't so high around Gruyère and it wasn't raining. Near Fribourg we crossed another lake, the Schiffenensee, and this too was... pleasant. A break from the motorway monotony. The road was nice. It was clean. It got us from A to B. If I were reviewing for TripAdvisor, though, this would not score as one of the great motoring routes of the world.

The road became smaller, a road rather than a motorway, and we passed through verdant countryside, but not spectacular countryside. We didn't feel an urge to stop and look around because we were getting quite close to our destination and becoming a little worried. This did not appear to be the Switzerland of chocolate-box fame. Good roads, though. Very smooth.

But then the landscape perked up. We began to get glimpses of Lake Lucerne. We saw real Alps in the distance. We passed by the town of Weggis and there, behind and above the lake, were snow-capped peaks. Alongside the shore were dotted picture-postcard white churches with slender orange spires. We felt a wave of relief. This would do.

Our site was at Vitznau, up and away from the road, arranged in terraces so that every pitch had a fine and unimpeded view of the lake. Every pitch except the one behind the wooden barn. That pitch, ours, had a fine and unimpeded view of the back of the wooden barn. The site was full. Every other pitch was taken. There would be no point making a fuss about our lousy position, even though we had booked months in advance. What could we do? Ask for someone else to be kicked off their pitch? No. We just had to suck it up.

We were tired. We'd driven 250 miles through unremarkable countryside, during which I had remained obsessive about handbrake application at every junction, those with stop signs or otherwise. We pitched the caravan. The kids put up their tents; they had plenty of room. Amanda was excited because it was the first time in the holiday that she'd had enough space and felt confident enough to use her own tent. We hadn't eaten lunch because we are veggies, and the motorway services only sold sausages. So Sarah made a pan of something and we put our feet up and admired the view of the brown, Swiss barn wall.

We noticed a lot of people with plastic fly swats coming back from the site shop. In fact, everybody who returned from the site shop carried plastic fly swats. What could this mean?

We ate our veggie stew, made a cup of tea, then watched the wasps move in.

Half an hour later we each had a colourful plastic fly swat we'd bought from the shop. The site owners were taking no chances; they had a stock of hundreds. They worked, too. Better by far than a rolled-up magazine. (In fact, I still have my Vitznau Fly Swat in our current caravan. I used it only last week. It still works a treat.)

We spent a happy hour eradicating all the wasps in Switzerland, which delayed our evening walk down to the lake for just long enough to save us from being caught outdoors in the hell-and-damnation thunder, lightning and rain storm that swept in from the mountains. It lit up the early evening sky and washed the road clear of dust, leaves and vehicles.

WE TOOK the steamer to Weggis.

It was lovely sailing across Lake Lucerne, but it was Sunday and Weggis was closed. We'd forgotten about that. We were in Europe. Not European-Union Europe, but the wider, continental Europe, although that didn't matter, because something we should always try to remember – they close all of continental Europe on Sundays. Everything. Shops, cafes, the lot. Closed. Shuttered.

We walked around and commented on how lovely it would look if it was open. But it wasn't. We sat by the lake, a thing we could have done in Vitznau, but without the intermediate and significant expense of a boat trip. We walked back to the quayside, boarded the steamer again and sailed back to Vitznau.

Vitznau was closed, too. Of course it was. We wandered about a bit, admiring the clean shutters on all the shop windows, then walked back up the hill to the caravan and killed some more wasps.

ON MONDAY we took the steamer to Lucerne. We were more successful. Lucerne was open. It was also a beautiful city. There was a bus station near the steamer dock, and most of the buses were trolley buses, and I proved I am not a transport geek by only taking about fifty photographs. I just wanted to capture the atmosphere of the place. Nothing to do with buses, I swear.

The temperature was pushing a hundred – kind of hot for walking around a city. But there's a covered bridge across the river Reuss called the Kapellbrüke and beneath the pitched roof and above the alpine water was shady and cool, so we crossed it a few times. It has a tower in the middle. Very attractive. We recuperated in a cafe, the kind where you sit in the street and watch people rush past making money. Then I marched everyone up to the Museggmauer, the historic city walls, that are at the back of the city up a long steep hill, and when it's a hundred degrees and you are all carrying heavy rucksacks, as you do when visiting a new city, your family members tend to get a little ratty with you, and we'd all lost interest in scenery by the time we reached the top. Lovely view from the top, I'm sure, but you know, a hundred degrees.

So we came back down. Sat by the river. Consumed liquids. I tried to interest everyone in the Richard Wagner museum but it was a half-hour walk each way so my heart wasn't fully committed to the argument, because, as I say, a hundred degrees.

I liked Lucerne. There were many things we didn't get to see. I'd go back, but I'd want to do it on a cooler day. We were all a little surprised by the heat. We'd come to Switzerland, not Death Valley, California. It was hard to do sight-seeing in those conditions. We needed mountain breezes and some of that snow we could see on the peaks all around. It was time to gain some altitude. So the next day we climbed the Rigi.

THE RIGI IS a mountain area right on the edge of Lake Lucerne. Our campsite was, in fact, perched on the lower slopes. At over five thousand feet the Rigi is a decent height for a mountain, taller than Ben Nevis. Not something to be taken lightly, especially in the heat of summer.

So when I say we climbed the Rigi, what we did was we caught the train.

The train runs from Vitznau. There were round trips one could book, but most of these involved the steamship from Lucerne. We'd done Lucerne. We just wanted the train.

It cost a lot. I wanted to explain to the ticket clerk that we only wanted to make a return trip, not buy the whole railway, but my German wasn't up to the task.

And the fare didn't even take us to the top, just part-way up, to a station called Rigi Kaltbad. We couldn't afford to go to the top. I didn't mind though – about the shorter journey that is; I minded a lot about the train fare. The shorter journey gave me the chance to do some knee-friendly Alpine walking.

We clambered onto the train and it hauled us up through dense pine forests, so dense we couldn't see anything. We sat and we looked at green, passing by the windows on both sides.

At Rigi Kaltbad we alighted, as did many of the other passengers. The station was a surprise. Very modern. Very clean. Lots of sharp concrete lines. And also a view. The first chance we'd had of a proper view down to the lake and over to the bigger Alps on the far side. Spectacular! Stupendous! A great many other superlatives, but the view was almost too much. I found it hard to believe that what we were seeing was real. There's something real about a Scottish mountain when viewed from the inside of cold, wet clothes, with raindrops clinging to your eyelashes, and iced water in your boots. The Alps, all the Alps we'd seen, were more like virtual reality. Perfect and maybe just too comfortable. So I thought about the money I'd spent, and the pain acted a little like pinching myself to prove it wasn't a dream.

Then we walked. A lot of people walked. We followed a wide gravel path beside the railway track. So many people were with us, walking, we felt a little like we were heading to a football match. Me and Sarah and the kids were all togged up in our mountain boots and our hiking gear. We had our Alpine climbing poles. In our rucksacks we carried extra jumpers because we knew from past experience that it *always* gets colder with altitude. Everybody else wore trainers and sandals and vests. They shambled along with hands in pockets, chatting.

What was going on here? We were up above the four-thousand-foot contour line and it felt like a Sunday afternoon outing up Moel Famau, the little hill we often stroll on near Ruthin in North Wales. The scenery on the mountain was similar to Moel Famau, too. The Rigi did not feel like a mountain at all. Here there was grass and trees and paths.

Don't get me wrong, it was lovely. The sun was shining, and thankfully a little cooler than down by the lake. But I do Moel Famau a disservice. People at home take it seriously. They wear boots… sometimes. It's only 1800 feet. It is officially a hill though it *feels* like a mountain. This mountain, this Alp, felt like a hill, a pimple. Perhaps if we'd walked all the way up from Vitznau it might have earned more respect, but then we'd have been just stupid, because there is no reason to walk all the way up, and we'd have had sunstroke before getting halfway to Rigi Kaltbad Station. That's not mountaineering.

On top of the Rigi there was a TV mast, painted red and white. It added to the hilltop as opposed to mountaintop ambience. The view was good but we expected better. Something… more Alpine.

Let's take stock of what was happening here. We'd driven a thousand miles to the Alps. We'd paid a week's food money for a train to save our legs. And we'd found ourselves on a mountain that we were comparing to Moel Famau, for which you don't need a train, or a thousand-mile drive, just a spare forty-five minutes on a Sunday afternoon.

We took out our sandwiches and ate lunch and looked at the view and the TV mast, and felt… well, not a lot, really.

To mix things up, we walked back to the station a different way. We headed along a lesser-used track, through meadows and past farm buildings, with narrow tracks running to them.

It was okay. It was beautiful, even. But…

∾

ON OUR LAST day we did a local walk along the road to the Republic of Gersau, a separate microstate, at least it was until 1817, when it rejoined Switzerland. I didn't know any of this. There is still a sign at the side of the road marking the border. The Republic of Gersau. Fascinating. We had a beer there, on a veranda overlooking Lake Lucerne. The location was a delight. The waiter spoke perfect English but when he saw I was trying hard with my German he let me continue, encouraged my attempts, and prompted me in some minimal-vocabulary conversation, which I thought was very nice of him. Very classy.

All around Gersau there were sculptures, in parks and at the side of the road. The town had a lovely feel to it. Very European. We stayed most of the afternoon then caught the bus back to Vitznau where we killed some wasps and packed. It was time to move on again. Our route would take us north to a new country. We were heading for Luxembourg.

2003: BENELUX

Number six. A sixth good thing to say about UK roads? Okay, this is hard. I'm struggling a bit. Might have to come back to you with number six. Let's call this one a placeholder. And Sarah says the first five sound kind of snarky. Not positive at all. She says I might as well go back to moaning. Huh. Well, I tried.

MW – Posicle No. 6

We packed and headed north. Three hundred miles. In Berne we stayed east of the Rhine, heading through Germany. We'd never been to Germany so this was a way to tick off another country. At lunchtime we stopped, at first one, then two, then three autobahn services, where, like in Switzerland a few days earlier, all we could find to eat were sausages. Europe didn't seem to offer much in the way of good eats for veggies, or even part-time veggies like us, who might eat fish or even chicken now and again if pushed.

"Okay, enough," I said, once noon, then one o'clock, then two o'clock had come and gone. "We're hungry. Let's go to France and eat there." How often do you get the chance to say a thing like that?

We crossed the Rhine and bought cheese sandwiches. It

has to be said, the French know a thing or two when it comes to making a cheese sandwich.

Our route continued north, past the outskirts of Strasbourg. If we hadn't been towing a caravan, we might have been tempted to make a diversion. But you don't do diversions with a caravan. Not on purpose, anyway.

We skirted the Vosges mountains, pointed west towards Metz, bypassed Metz, crossed the Moselle south of Thionville, where we also wanted to stop, explore, eat. But no. Onward to Larochette, in Luxembourg. We arrived just in time for tea.

THE SITE WAS LARGE, spacious and welcoming. We had no language problems even though we were the only English people staying there. Everyone else on the site was Dutch. We were surprised. We expected a mix of nationalities in Luxembourg. We were happy about it; the Dutch speak better English than we do, and they are always friendly. But it was strange to come to a multicultural country like Luxembourg and find ourselves to be the only non-Dutch on the site.

The bar had a terrace on which, in the evening, we relaxed and listened to Frank Sinatra. He was a one-man tribute band and he was amazing. I don't normally like singers who use backing tracks. As a sax player, I always look upon such a performance as one in which a band has been swizzed out of an honest gig. I was willing to forgive this guy though. I'd tell you his name but he just started singing and didn't tell us. He looked like Frank Sinatra though. Not just a superficial resemblance, he *was* Frank Sinatra. His voice was *exactly* Frank's voice. His mannerisms. Everything. I could have sworn we had come to this campsite in the middle of Luxembourg and Frank Sinatra just happened to be staying there, too. But because the Nelson Riddle band had chosen to take their holidays back in the States, Frank had been enticed into doing a spot with some backing tapes, because it was the perfect evening on which to sing, with the setting sun casting red streaks on clouds floating in an azure sky turning to purple. A still evening, and warm. Not even a hint of a chill in the air.

Only two things spoiled the idea that this was Frank: One, Frank Sinatra had died four years earlier. Two, and this was an even bigger giveaway: The chat between songs, the audience repartee, all of it… was in Dutch. And you know what is amazing? It didn't break the illusion. It was fine. A suspension of disbelief was entirely possible. Francis Albert Sinatra had somehow cheated the grave and come here tonight to entertain me and my family, and there was no anomaly whatsoever in him speaking fluent Dutch. So what? He must have learned the language especially for the campers in Larochette. That evening has stayed with me. Perfection. Sipping a glass of wine under a perfect sky with Sarah and my adult children, watching and listening to Ol' Blue Eyes. I'll never forget it.

Luxembourg golden memory number two: Next day we needed petrol. I called in at the nearest garage, filled the tank, and it came to less than twenty pounds. Let's just revisit this. In 2003, a full tank of petrol, at home, would have cost forty-five quid or more. I gave the attendant in the shop an argument.

"Are you sure? Thirty-two euros?" I showed him three fingers on one hand and two on the other to eliminate translation errors, but the numbers were up on the till. "Thirty-two euros. That's…" I did the sums again. "Nineteen pounds and change. Really?"

"You are English, yes?"

"Yes. Do we get some sort of tourist discount?"

He smiled. "Visitors are always surprised. No, that is the price of fuel in Luxembourg."

As I returned to the car, I checked the euro price per litre on the pump just to be absolutely sure. Yes. Fuel was better than half price in Luxembourg. I squeaked the news in the car.

"I just paid twenty quid for a full tank."

"No way," said Sarah.

"Yes way," I said.

But there was a cruel twist. We were only here for two nights. We were heading into Luxembourg City today, and Luxembourg City is only fifteen miles from our campsite. Thirty miles round. If I filled up after that, before we hitched the 'van and drove back into the real world, it would cost, what? Five pence? It would be embarrassing. Luxembourg is only twenty miles across, east to west. I had to accept that this tankful was a one-off. I would never again, in my whole life, ever, fill an empty tank for less than twenty quid. A mean joke. A tragedy.

We drove, cheaply, into Luxembourg city and left the car in an underground car park. They don't often do these in the UK. In the UK we build car parks vertically and keep the cost down by making them as ugly as possible. We like to place these tributes to brutalist concrete architecture right next to our most beautiful and historic buildings, just so that photographers can't get a good shot any more, and we do it so that wherever you are in the city you can never lose your car, because the multi-storey car park is there, visible, towering above all the historic buildings.

In Luxembourg City you have to remember where you left your car park by memorising the street name, otherwise you would never find it again, hidden below all that annoying fine architecture. Also unlike the UK, in Luxembourg they don't bring in teams of homeless people to urinate all over the stairwells for ambience.

Luxembourg City is how you imagine Europe should be. It oozes European-ness. In the centre there is the City Hall. A splendid but understated building. Also the attractive Grand Ducal Palace, right on the street, not miles away from prying eyes or protected by chain-link fencing. The shops are historic and… European. Inside, the shopkeepers' language will morph into English or French or German or Dutch with ease, often mixing several languages into each sentence, depending on what sounds best and who their customers might be.

The city is beautiful. A gorge runs through the centre with a river, though when we visited there hadn't been much rain, a first for the Wood family, and it left the river as little more than a shallow drain at the bottom of a concrete channel. In full flood it would have looked wonderful, with the old town nestling on either side.

It felt like a safe city. There were no hoodies or scruffs. There didn't seem to be a poor part of town at all. Everything was understated and not at all tacky. Okay, there were no particular landmark buildings that made us say, "Oh, *that's* here, I never realised." There was no Eiffel Tower or Colosseum or Parthenon. Luxembourg is a whole package of genteel, fine buildings. Luxembourg is Europe. I loved it.

OUR STAY WAS TOO SHORT. Two days. The holiday was nearly over but not the adventure. Another country awaited our tick list; we were to pass through Belgium on our way to Calais and home. First though, an early and unexpected wake-up call. I awoke from a deep sleep in the early hours. Something had disturbed me. A noise. Several noises. Kind of short, punctuated roaring sounds. Very loud, though.... Familiar. Was it the caravan? Something wrong? Something to add an unpleasant spice to the final leg of our journey home? Again, that sound of… gas combustion! Oh my God, that was a gas burner. *The propane bottle!*

I leapt out of bed. I listened. The sound again, but no, not the caravan, at least not *my* caravan. It came from outside. The kind of sound that maybe the burner on a hot-air balloon might make, but too close. It would have to be right on top…

I flung open the caravan door. The roaring noise, much louder, came from directly overhead. I looked up and all of the sky was hidden by a hot-air balloon, the basket just a few feet above the caravan roof. I yelped, but I needn't have worried, the balloon was going up. A crowd of Dutch holidaymakers stood in the field and watched. Did they notice me standing there in my underpants? Did they care? No. They were fascinated by the balloon. I ducked into the 'van, shouting to Sarah and pulling on trousers.

"Sarah, wake up. You have to come and see this. Quick!"

She joined me outside. The balloon over our 'van had climbed away, but another had appeared, even lower. And another, right behind it. *The sky was full of balloons.* They were coming from the next field, and they passed so low over the campsite that many of the campers were able to have conversations with the balloonists without having to even raise their voices.

I went over to Kevin's and Amanda's tents and kicked the guy ropes.

"Wake up. Come and look."

For an hour or two we watched as one balloon after another rose from the surrounding fields and filled the sky. Some kind of balloon rally? I don't know, but it was a marvellous sight. None of us had seen anything like it before.

It made us late packing. We had 250 miles ahead of us and a ferry to catch. We rushed breakfast. The children took down their tents. I folded the awning away. It was hard to concentrate while the air all around was thick with coloured balloons, but all too soon it was time to go.

≈

I WONDERED how it would be, leaving Luxembourg. Would there be a border? No. Luxembourg was the home of Shengen, the place where the agreement was signed eliminating control of persons crossing borders in Europe – Britain excluded. If any country were to have a minimal border, then that country would be Luxembourg.

The passage into Belgium, as it happened, was obvious, and marked by three things of note:

One. A small rusty signpost, no different to driving from England to Wales.

Two. A dilapidated petrol station, with fuel at normal, rest-of-Europe prices. It begged the thought, who the hell would be soft enough to buy petrol there, when they could get it for half the price just a few yards up the road? And could this explain the prevalence of Dutch spoken on our campsite? Were they in fact Flemish Belgians over for a cheap-fuel holiday, a bit like the famous cross-channel booze-cruises the Brits used to do to spoil Calais? After all, Flemish is indistinguishable from Dutch, certainly to my untrained and confused ear. My magical evening of music could have been courtesy of a Flemish Frank Sinatra. But I'll never know.

And what else? Oh yes, item three. The roads turned to crap.

Item three was by far the most significant, especially after enjoying the roads in Luxembourg, which were just like the roads in Switzerland, magnificent. The thorough-fares of Luxembourg were not just laid, they were crafted. Artisans must have toiled and laboured with passion and spirit-levels to create roads so smooth they could hold a shine deep enough to rival that of antique mahogany.

Belgian roads were the opposite. Belgian roads were a haphazard pile of crap. Tarmac seemed to have been thrown into the fields and left for car and lorry tyres to tamp down into vaguely useful rutted surfaces. Line markings did not exist. Potholes were deep. Some probably had cars and dead people in them.

And I'm not talking about back streets or country lanes, though they were bad enough. I'm talking about the motorway, the N4, the main thoroughfare from Luxembourg and the southeast of Belgium into Brussels. This was the saddest strip of highway I have ever seen. Line markings were gone, or had never been painted. Central crash barriers were broken, or missing, or had never been constructed. The most scary parts were the viaducts that passed high over river valleys. They had no fences, no crash barriers, no lines and no cats' eyes. At night it would not have been improbable for drivers to become disorientated while avoiding the many holes in the road and to have headed right out into the void, unimpeded by any safety restraints whatsoever. For the entire length of the motorway, as we bounced and crashed along this concrete proving ground, we saw lines of forlorn cars on the strip of wasteland that passed for a hard shoulder. Most had flat tyres. Many, though, just lay low on the ground, abandoned by their owners after lamenting the final and inevitable destruction of their car's suspension systems.

There were no motorway services. None. The answer to bladder control, from multiple examples we saw, was to pull over onto the hard-shoulder wasteland, climb out of the car, and pee into the road. It seemed a suitable expression of contempt.

Our timings, too, were in jeopardy. We had a ferry to catch. My calculations involved an average motorway speed of fifty miles per hour. On these roads? Not a chance. At fifty our car and caravan would have been trashed. Here was serious off-roading. The N4 was the Paris-Dakar Rally. A car breaker. We were lucky to find any strips of road surface that were level enough to maintain thirty-five mph.

I need to protect myself a little here. I'm talking about the year 2003. We've never been back to Belgium. I'm sure the Belgians have brought in some road-building expertise since that time. Maybe the roads are better now. Maybe the N4 is a thoroughfare to rival the best the Swiss roads craftsmen have ever created. If so, then hats off, they've worked bloody hard over the last fifteen years.

Also, I'm comparing Belgian roads of 2003 to UK roads of 2003. Looking back from the vantage point of 2019 it is fair to say that UK road builders have seen how low the bar can be set and gone a peg lower. Many of our once-adequate UK roads are now worse than the N4 of 2003. The mechanical damage to our cars is not so great in the UK though, because we have a workaround; we cone off our motorway lanes to stop the traffic from going fast enough to cause any damage.

Anyway, back to Belgium, 2003. Disappointing. I thought Belgium might be a country we'd want to visit properly, some time. It has beauty spots like Bruges, and… well, Bruges. One day we may go there. When we've bought a tractor. On this day it was all we could do to get out in one piece. We longed to see the sign on the road ahead that said, "Welcome to France".

And so we got lost.

Soon it wasn't the N4, it was some other road. Something unsignposted and with deeper holes. I'd been so boggle eyed staring at what passed for a road surface, and swerving to avoid the more rustic agricultural patches, that I'd missed the turnoff. We searched for some clue as to where we might be. The only comfort was the sun's position in the sky; at least we still pointed in something like the right direction. The post-apocalyptic road bounced us along, on and on, until we came to a signposted junction and corrected ourselves, but we now realised we faced ten miles more of Belgium than had been necessary on our original route. We gritted our teeth. I gripped the steering wheel with hands that were steadily succumbing to vibration white finger, and we prayed for France.

We nearly made it, too, but just as we dared to become complacent the car screamed and swerved and in the mirrors I saw a plume of orange sparks bouncing off the front of the caravan. I pointed the car onto the wasteland hard shoulder and we skittered to a halt.

"That didn't sound good," said Sarah.

"No," I said.

I didn't move straight away. I still gripped the wheel while my heart pounded and my body flooded with adrenaline. In my mind an image appeared of our cross-channel ferry, sailing off to England with one empty space on its car deck.

None of us were surprised to be here. We'd seen the wreckage of vehicles all along the road since we'd left Luxembourg. That our venerable Ford Mondeo had got this far was a testament to her rugged construction.

I wanted everyone out of the car and away, but we'd picked a part of the motorway that was hemmed in by four-foot concrete walls. Sarah and the kids could have climbed, but the other side was a graveyard of vehicle components and spent bodily fluids, and the drop was farther on that side, too, so once over they might not have got back.

By law, in one of the European countries through which we had passed, I'd been compelled to carry a warning triangle. I'd been annoyed about having to buy the thing, but now I fished it out of the boot in a panic, and ran down the road to position it. Our location was precarious. A fast entry ramp swept around a blind corner and joined the motorway about fifty yards away from the wreckage that used to be our car/caravan. Cars came fast and blind. I wished I'd paid more and bought a bigger triangle. Something around the size and weight of a bus would have been good. The whole area should have been painted red and marked DANGER!

As I trotted back to the car, I still didn't know what had happened. Specifics had been a low priority. Now I let my imagination run amok. Collapsed suspension, sheared tow bracket bolts, broken engine mounts... the list went on. What was certain was that, from the moment I heard the noise, the handling had gone all Torvill and Dean. I had coasted onto the hard shoulder. Coasted is not the right word, we had freewheeled in the way a builder's skip might freewheel. The obvious and most likely cause was broken suspension mounts or springs. Or perhaps the gearbox had rattled loose and fallen onto the road. Whatever, it would not be an easy fix. Today was Sunday. As I may have mentioned before, Europe is closed on Sundays. The level of assistance we might expect from garages would be minimal to zero. What would we do? We couldn't spend the night here, that was for sure.

Kevin was already lying on the hard shoulder, looking underneath the car. I noticed how the back of the car was raised up in the air. Higher than it should be, at least. Not a good sign. I felt there would be scant good news.

"Exhaust's gone," he said, as I joined him on my knees. "At least most of it. Doesn't look so bad as it sounded from inside the car."

Yes, I could see the problem. Yes, it might be repairable. Yes, but, *we'd* have to do all the repairing.

Kevin was right. The exhaust pipe had gone. At least the middle section. Where to? Who knew? Bouncing along somewhere on the road to Brussels I expect. Our bigger problem, and the cause of all the pyrotechnics, was the tail pipe. When the centre section had waved goodbye, the forward-facing end of the tail pipe had dropped, dug in, and pole-vaulted the rear of the car up into the air. And it had stayed that way, acting like a jack, lifting the rear wheels almost clear of the ground, hence the skittery, Ice Capades handling.

Right, all I had to do was shift the tail pipe. I could try reversing to un-pole-vault the car, but I didn't fancy reversing car and caravan, blind, into oncoming traffic zooming onto the entry ramp, traffic that was already performing death-defying circus acts to avoid slithering into the back of us.

I could jack up the car. Best option, but I'd be spending a long time working exposed, out in the road amongst the 120 kph traffic, whose eye-fatigued drivers were already mesmerised from scoping out all those potholes.

So I went with option three. I lay in the road and kicked the exhaust.

"What are you doing?" Sarah screamed. "Get out of the road."

"I'm… just… trying… to kick…" I pulled my body tight-in to the car while an eighteen-wheel juggernaut roared past, inches from my ear. What was a juggernaut doing on the road on a Sunday? I looked back down the road. Car-free for a few more seconds, then pulled back my leg and recommenced the kicking.

"Mike, for God's sake get back…"

Crunch.

The car fell back onto four wheels. The tail pipe lay on the road. I kicked it underneath the car onto the other side and scampered around. I felt the irrational need to be tidy, so I picked it up and tossed it over the wall where it crashed down amongst all the other discarded bits of mechanicals that had rattled free from similarly afflicted vehicles over the years. Then I ran back down the hard shoulder to collect my triangle.

The return run was even more scary, knowing that I no longer had the security of my flimsy, £4.99 plastic triangle to guard my back from the wacky races behind and around me. I tossed it into the back seat for the kids to fold away, then gunned the engine, keen to escape.

Once up to speed I looked over at Sarah. She looked back at me. Her face looked pale. Two weeks' of Alpine tan was gone. She shook her head.

After a while she spoke. "How far?"

"Don't know. An hour and a half. Two hours."

"Sounding like that?"

"Yeah."

With most of the exhaust system missing, the car sounded like a nitromethane top-fuel dragster.

I sniffed the air. "Fumes coming in, too," I said. "Better open all the windows."

A few minutes later. "What were you doing, lying in the road? You could have been killed."

"Yeah." Couldn't argue with her there.

The road was still rough and I worried about what all that bouncing might do to the remaining front section of pipe. If we lost that too, we'd have the potential of fire coming into the footwell to add to our woes.

Just west of Tournai we came to a place with twenty-, then ten-kilometre speed signs. Dozens of lorries were parked at the side of the road.

And then, over a neat and precise boundary line, the road went smooth.

We'd reached France.

An hour and forty minutes later we drew up at the ferry port in Calais. I made a point of switching off the engine when we stopped at passport control so as not to cause a panic. The girl on passport control didn't seem to notice and she processed our boarding passes quickly, saying if we hurried we could take the next sailing.

We thought the car sounded loud outside. We rolled into the big tin echo chamber of the P&O ferry sounding like the opening laps of the Silverstone Grand Prix or the Indy 500. Heads turned, perhaps expecting a thousand-strong Hells Angels chapter. I seemed to be the only occupant of the car. Sarah and the kids had ducked their heads below window level so nobody could see them. I didn't care. I was ecstatic. We'd made it. I had been convinced, back there in the Belgian wastes, that it might be weeks before we saw merry old England once again, if ever. Broken exhausts? Not a problem in England. ATS, Auto-Care, Kwik Fit, National Tyres... Whatever! I could speak the language. I could find them in the phone book. I knew the drill. They'd probably be expecting my call, missing me; I hadn't given them any business for months. And this was a Wood holiday. It's hard to remember the last time we *didn't* visit an exhaust/battery/brakes/clutch specialist on holiday. It's what defines us. What makes us Woods.

We stayed the night at the same site in Kent where we'd stayed on our outward journey abroad. It's hard to say if I was more excited then, to be going away, or more excited now, to be coming home with most of the original car. The next morning I roared into Ashford, just with Kevin, and we returned to the girls, purring, an hour later with a fine new exhaust.

We packed and drove home.

2003: SEASON'S END

≈

Yay, here we go, posicle number six. Told you I'd think of one.

UK roads are better than Belgian roads.
(At least, they were in 2003.)

MW – Posicle No. 6

≈

Our trip to the Alps turned out to be the last major holiday we'd all take together. The season wasn't over. There were weekends to do. The four of us went to a DA in Glossop, where it rained, but we had fun. Then came the National Feast of Lanterns in Ipswich.

We'd almost been to an NFOL before, the previous year, but the mud stopped us. Of the four of us, Kevin had been the most disappointed about the way it turned out, because he'd had big ideas for the lighting-up, a feature of the Feast of Lanterns. This year the weather was good, we were all booked in, but then Kevin found a girl. He stayed at home.

So now we were three.

We loved the Feast of Lanterns. The live entertainment in the tent was brilliant. We toured the trade stands and bought armfuls of caravan stuff we didn't need. We were amazed by the lighting-up, the street scenes, where rows of caravans created an illuminated tableau around the central theme which this year was Toy Town. We were wowed by the cleverness of each idea, but for me and Sarah there was a little empty space. Kevin would have loved it too, but now he had other priorities. Hormones tend to trump families most times, and so it should be.

Kevin was back with us, at least for part of our last outing of the year. We went to Torver, in the Lakes. In mid-September the light was failing, and travelling on a Friday after work meant driving much of the way in the dark. Three of us went ahead and arrived even later than we'd hoped, at ten PM, because of all the cars crashing in the wet conditions and messing up the M6, which they often do, but the light went early anyway so it wouldn't have mattered.

It continued to rain on Saturday, when Kevin joined us in his own car and set up his tent for just one night. It rained all Friday night and all Saturday, and all Saturday night and it was still raining on Sunday morning when we packed and called it quits. We hadn't walked in the mountains; we hadn't *seen* the mountains. We'd slipped and slithered our way down to Lake Coniston in the driving rain, just to stave off the onset of cabin fever, and hadn't seen much beyond the near shore. The far side of the lake had been completely hidden from view. We made two useful scientific discoveries – we found that none of our waterproofs were waterproof, and we noticed how the Lakeland sheep had a genetic instinct to line up two-by-two.

Had we reached the end of our first season with the new

Avondale? In September? Here at last we had a caravan that would withstand the harshest winter, but we didn't feel much in the mood for withstanding winter, not even a mild one. We would have relished the cold. We would have laughed in the face of wind or even snow. But rain? Day after relentless day?

We shut down the 'van – drained the water tanks, brought in the bedding – and called it quits. Spring would be here soon enough.

2004: CORNWALL

And I'm back – in the comfort zone of a good old moan. Ah, that feels good. Like finding a long-lost pair of comfy slippers.

So here we go. Am I the only one who finds that it's getting harder to drive at night? Car headlamps are just too bright. It wasn't always like this. I have a theory that the reason we have red tail lights is because in days of yore someone wisely realised that if we are following another car and have to stare at his tail lights for hours on end, red would be less damaging to our night vision. (Another version is that it evolved from the railways' standard of using red for danger, but I prefer mine because it gives a better basis for a good moan.)

So having adopted a sensible, eye-friendly red, we then invent xenon headlamps for oncoming traffic – lights with a gazillion lumens that scorch the lining off our retinas, leaving us with a constellation of dancing purple blobs to blink away while trying to remember which way the road went. Progress.

—No. 85 from the Moanicles of Michael.

We started our new season by getting the caravan serviced. A fine, new(ish) caravan deserves proper love and care, so we splashed out £140 and were told:

- Serious fault! Running electrics defective.
- Serious Fault! Water heater is defective.
- Serious Fault! Much damp detected in the walls.

This came as a surprise. The dealer who performed the service was the same dealer who sold us the caravan just over a year ago. When we bought it, the caravan had "just been fully serviced" and in the space of a mere thirteen months she seemed to have succumbed to rampant damp and serious failures in most of her inner workings. Okay, so we'd shown her some rain and we'd towed her a few miles, through eight different countries, including the geological roads of Belgium, but isn't that what you are meant to do with caravans? Tow them around? Get them wet? It all sounded a bit dodgy to me. Very suspicious. And we'd bought the caravan with twelve months' warranty, *thirteen months ago*.

I shook my head and I grumbled a lot, but I realised I'd just have to get on with it. I changed a stop bulb, and this solved the "Serious fault! Running electrics defective." problem. The gas water heater was a little harder. It wouldn't light. My father-in-law had just taken the same model of water heater out of his own 'van, so I examined his dismantled version and saw how it all worked, then sent away for a new burner unit from Ebay, and a week later she was back together and burning with a lovely blue flame. The damp warning was something we'd have to live with. Too big a job. And we rationalised, damp isn't as bad as wet. So we were still drier on the inside of the caravan than the outside. I could have entrusted these jobs to my local dealer, but I make it a rule only to get stiffed once. I can say these harsh things with impunity because my local dealer went bust earlier this year. Well, of course he did.

Easter was in early April, so the four of us headed off to a temporary site near Ludlow. It rained. The evening darkened early. The lights in the caravan flickered and died. The battery had expired. One of the service items was for them to check the battery condition. They'd put a tick against it. So much for that one. A hundred and forty quid for a service and we spent our first evening sitting in the dark. Brilliant.

Next day we drove around looking for an accessory shop where we could buy a new leisure battery. We found one in Craven Arms. Holiday saved. Apart from the bit about having to be towed off the field.

As I say, it rained. A lot. The field was clay and soon performed like an ice rink, so all the four-by-fours formed into rescue teams while those of us with closet four-by-four envy waited our turn to be pulled onto the road. This is one of the great things about DAs and temporary sites though. There are always people happy to help. Over the years we've been towed off sites numerous times, and on two occasions we've even had to be towed *onto* the site. Did I mention that we get a lot of rain on our caravan weekends?

I talk as though every weekend we ever had was a wet washout. That's not the case. In this particular year we had many outings in lovely sunshine, and I had even worn shorts and left the wellies at the bottom of the shoe box.

Our visit to Llangollen was sunny, and one of several occasions when I have arrived on-site wearing a dinner jacket and bow tie. I'd been booked to play in a pit orchestra for a production of *Oklahoma*, so rather than travel out to Wales every evening, we took the caravan. You get some odd looks emptying the chemical toilet dressed like a waiter, but I've done it a few times since, people ask about it, I tell them, next thing you know, they're in the audience. It all helps to keep these events sustainable.

By the time we came to August and our main holiday, most of our weekends had seen good weather. Our fortunes had turned. The rain gods had packed their bags and gone off to find someone else to terrorise.

And since the weather was kind, we chose Cornwall. We'd had enough of Europe after our Belgian fiasco. We felt scarred and bruised. Belgium had made us feel vulnerable. The attempted gas attack in France, at Troyes, hadn't helped either. No, this year we felt the need for safety and security, a holiday of relaxation rather than adventure and abject fear. A shorter journey would be nice, too. We didn't want to spend our holiday driving across continents.

Well, I hadn't realised how far you can travel in the UK. We picked a campsite near the Lizard, booked it, then worked out it was 370 miles away. The Wirral, where we live, is quite central; I had no idea we could go *anywhere* on the UK mainland that was 370 miles distant.

We decided to split the journey and stop somewhere en route. Motorway services had worked well for us over in France – apart from us being nearly gassed, and that could never happen in the UK. Our villains don't go around gassing people to steal their stuff; our villains just load brand new caravans onto low loaders and haul the lot away while you're in the cafe enjoying breakfast. And while ours was new to us, it wasn't likely to be so attractive lined up amongst all the twin-axle, fixed-double-bed, panoramic-roof variants still gleaming in their showroom polish.

This year would be our first long holiday without Kevin. Three in a box. We hitched up and headed south on Friday evening. Our plan: drive as far as we could, then stop for the night. "As far as we could" turned out to be Cheshire, where we hit our first traffic jam. We crawled, stop-start, and watched the light fade from the sky.

"So, why not break the journey here?" said Sarah.

"In Cheshire? We've only come twenty miles," I said.

"I know a nice place nearby," said Amanda. "Just turn off at the next junction, then back the way we've come, about twenty miles. Cosy beds. Warm showers. We can even watch *Friends* on the telly."

I scowled at her. Leaving on Friday night had been my idea. The girls had argued hard against spending a night camped in motorway services. I gripped the steering wheel and willed the traffic to clear. And you know what? It cleared.

"No problems now," I said. "The roads are getting quieter because it's late. Just as I said. We'll be fine."

Just north of Birmingham they closed the motorway. We didn't know to begin with; we had to queue for an hour before we got to the road signs telling us about it.

"They can't close the M6! It's the main artery south. They can't just close it!" I slapped the steering wheel a few times. "It's August. People are going on holiday. They're going south to the sun, like they do every year. Whose stupid idea was it to close the motorway?"

We followed the diversion signs which led us to the centre of Birmingham then cast us adrift. In the dark, with no clue where we were, and with a caravan, so no U-turns allowed, I vented my frustration on every set of lights, every other road user, every badly laid out road junction.

"This travelling at night thing," said Sarah. "It's going well."

At about one AM, quite by chance, we stumbled upon the M5 and resumed our journey south. Sarah did another driving stint, then I took over again, but we were getting tired, and bored, because at night there is a limit to the amount of stimulation one can get from staring at two converging dotted lines lit by one's own headlamps.

We pulled into Brent Knoll Services. I dropped the legs. Locked the car, and we fell into the beds we'd already prepared.

UK services proved to be different to those in France. Lorries roared and hissed their air brakes. Cars zoomed and screeched. Coaches disgorged yobs and hooligans sixty at a time, and always the guy at the front of the group had to curse the guy at the back of the group, while the guys in the middle of the group sang and jeered.

But at least nobody tried to gas us.

And I must have slept because I woke up. Sarah and Amanda were still asleep so I shook them awake. Dawn had arrived. We ate breakfast in the one corner of the restaurant they hadn't roped off in pretence of cleaning, then returned to the car to continue our journey south. I felt vindicated.

This was how to do it. We'd put two hundred miles behind us. The rest would be easy because we were ahead of everybody. Nobody would be driving in Cornwall at this time in the morning.

I was only half right. They weren't driving, but this was because they'd got there first and were already queueing along the A30, from Bodmin to Dartmoor.

There's always a delusion when driving to Cornwall. You reach the end of the M5 at Exeter and you think, give or take a few local roads, that you have arrived. There are road signs that say Cornwall. You feel all ready to surf and eat pasties. But this sticky-out bit at the bottom of England, the part called The Southwest, is long. There are still more than a hundred miles to go, and they can be difficult, irritating miles, especially when the queue to get into the town of Bodmin stretches back forty miles to Okehampton. Not just any old queue, either. This is invariably a professional queue. The kind where you can switch off your engine and get out of the car to shake some life back into your legs, because, just like your own circulation, nothing is moving and nothing has moved for a long time.

We crawled over Dartmoor. Moved a bit. Stopped. Came to Bodmin Moor and arrived at Jamaica Inn, as in the Daphne du Maurier novel. We had time to study it. To watch people coming and going, driving into the car park, entering the inn, having breakfast, getting back in their cars, rejoining the queue.

Morning became afternoon. We became hungry. We crawled, slower and slower, stop and start, as we approached the pinch point that is Bodmin, where there appeared no reason whatsoever for any hold-up, because suddenly we were driving along roads with no traffic problems at all and only fifty miles more to go. But fifty twisty, turny slow miles through junctions with stop signs, T-junctions and pointless roundabouts, until at last, at tea time, we arrived at Mullion Cove on the Lizard.

We fell out of the car. We lay on the grass, exhausted. We had taken turns with the driving, but we felt we'd been around the world. Other than a short sleep on the motorway we'd been on the road for twenty-four hours. I felt we could have driven to Nice in that time.

But, on the plus side, the campsite looked good. The sun shone. Clouds scudded across the blue sky. Who needed Europe? We could have a lovely holiday here in Cornwall.

Just so long as we didn't stop to think about the journey home.

We set up the caravan. Amanda delayed pitching her tent until the next day. Sarah cooked a veggie stew for tea.

And the science fiction noises began.

We were in the caravan when they started. *Whoo-oo-oo. Whoo-oo-oo.*

In the fifties a Russian inventor named Leon Theremin invented a musical instrument. It was named after its creator. The theremin appeared in numerous science fiction films and TV programs. Listen for it in the 1951 film, *The Day the Earth Stood Still*. The theramist – I'm guessing that's what you call a theremin player – waves their hands around in the space between two aerials, which generates a spooky, out-of-this-world sound. As we sat in the caravan, staring at each other with wide-open eyes, it sounded as though a theremin band had descended onto the site to serenade and spook our evening. But outside there was no sign of any musical activity at all.

"It's Goonhilly Downs," said Sarah.

Goonhilly was nearby, with its dishes and antennas, and this seemed a good bet. Except…

"Goonhilly is a listening station," I said. "It doesn't make any noise. It listens. And it's closed."

"Closed?"

"It's a visitor centre. Nothing more."

"But—"

"It doesn't make strange noises."

"Something does."

"There it is again," said Amanda. "Listen."

Whoo-oo. Whoo-oo.

"Damn, it's creepy," I said.

But then it stopped. No more. I walked around the site, looking. No little green men. No indication of anything at all that could make that sound. It appeared to be coming out of the air itself. What made it worse, nobody else on the site appeared to notice. They all went about their water-fetching, toilet-emptying, awning-pegging activities without so much as a flinch. If aliens were coming, we were the only ones who knew anything about it.

We ate our stew, on edge, ready to start at any sound. But all was silent. Not even a wind.

Our evening walk took us over the cliffs to gaze down on the village of Mullion Cove below. It was a beautiful location. We decided we'd have to visit Mullion Cove – stroll around and admire it, but not tomorrow. After a night and a day on the road we needed activity. We felt the urge to seek out a place for an adrenaline-burning swim before the fine weather had a chance to quit.

WE ALL THREE awoke the next morning at the same instant. We awoke with wide and staring eyes.

Whoo-oo-ooo!

Today it sounded louder.

"What the hell is that?" I shouted, sitting bolt upright in bed. I heard Amanda, at the other end of the caravan, scrabbling around for her glasses. I was peering through the curtains. I hadn't reached for my own glasses so for me the act of looking outside was all a bit of a waste of time because I wouldn't be able to see anything, even if an army of giant robots had arrived and were stomping around the field.

"There's nothing there," said Amanda.

I retrieved my glasses and looked, as if she might have somehow missed the robot army and flying saucers. But she was right. There were a few early risers on the campsite, pottering around their breakfast barbecues, and oblivious to the sounds of the cosmos that filled the air. I pulled on my trousers and stumbled outside and the sound was louder.

Whoo-oo-oo!

But still no sign of what it could be.

A shadow flicked across the field. I looked up, and there it was. I heard a shriek from Amanda. She had seen it too.

A glider.

It sailed across the field only a hundred feet or so above us, without a sound, except then I saw the wings ripple and vibrate, and… *Whoo-oo-ooo!*

We discovered that the gliders launched from the next field. A winch pulled them along the ground until they leapt into the air, over the hedge and straight across our site. Had they been RAF fighter jets I might have been a little miffed at camping next door, but these were not fighter jets, they were graceful and poetic and wonderful. We loved the sound they made, all of us. For a day or so we watched them fly over the field. They became part of the soundtrack to our holiday. Restful music, like the overpriced relaxation CDs they sell in garden centres.

Mystery solved, we went to the beach.

One of the main reasons we chose this part of Cornwall was its proximity to Kynance Cove. Kynance is owned by the National Trust and we had stumbled upon it a few years earlier. It is the most enchanting of beaches, hemmed in between cliffs, and with a strip of sand leading to a part-time island that is only separated from the rest of Cornwall when the tide comes in. The warm waves break over the sand bar from both sides, and paddling along it at the right tide level was a delight the last time we were here. We were so happy to be back, and only three miles along the cliff path from our site. We could see people swimming and longed to get into the water.

We got a surprise. It was cold. Very cold. There would be no delight in paddling this year, just excruciating pain. Other people swam, and splashed, and didn't seem bothered in the least, but all three of us howled and wailed as soon as we put just a toe in the water. There was no way we were going in past our ankles. Here's the thing. They all had wetsuits, which seemed to have become compulsory for swimming in Cornwall. In fact, we three were the only ones showing any skin at all. Amanda owned a wetsuit because she'd started sailing lessons at home. She'd brought it with her on holiday but left it in the caravan. Wetsuits are heavy and not the sort of kit we wanted to haul three miles along cliff tops. Besides, I felt sure a wetsuit wouldn't help. I'd still have to go in beyond my ankles before the sea got to the rubber part.

So we towelled off our feet, bought tea and biscuits from the cafe on the beach, then, after admiring Kynance for a little longer we headed back to the caravan. We decided we'd return in the car later in the week so that at least Amanda would have the chance of a hermetically sealed, vulcanised swim. On other days we focussed on Praa Sands, where the waves were less threatening and the water was a luxurious half-degree warmer. We could at least paddle up to our knees there. But Praa was a twenty-mile drive, a long way along Cornish lanes, and we also felt it carried the risk of our being arrested for indecent exposure, being the only people on the beach who were revealing flesh. And then it rained, so that was okay. Not too much rain, but enough for an excuse to finish our day of endurance at the beach.

On Tuesday we stumbled into a zone that had a mobile phone signal – none at the site, none at the beach – and our phones went berserk. Frantic calls from each of our parents and even one from Kevin, wondering if we were still alive.

"Of course we are. Why?"

The TV had been full of images of the seaside village Boscastle being washed out into the sea after torrential rain, the worst in memory. Hundreds of homes destroyed, businesses ruined and caravans washed away. The impression given by the media was that Cornwall in its entirety was a disaster area. We'd had a bit of drizzle. What was going on here? If there was any record-breaking bad weather doing the rounds, we were normally magnets for the worst of it during our holidays. Perhaps we were shedding our rain-god misfortune. It put us on edge, though, because if we'd missed this one, then maybe the real weather was still to come.

I called ahead to all the sites we were booked into next, just to make sure we could still come, and to make sure they were still there. All of the sites were on the north coast of Cornwall, and one was only a few miles from Boscastle, but they were fine. Like us, they hadn't seen a lot of rain. Boscastle seemed to have copped it on behalf of everyone.

So on our last day before moving on, we looked to the sky, noted the heavy clouds, and chose a safe option. We went where civilisation gathered in numbers. We had a townie day. We went to Falmouth.

"THERE'S a car park at the National Maritime Museum," I said, pointing to the sign.

"Do we want to go there?" said Sarah.

I shrugged. "Could be good. Boats and stuff. It's a modern building" —I always enjoy a bit of modern archi-

tecture— "so yeah, I suppose it looks okay." You can probably sense my bubbling enthusiasm.

The car park was small and they wanted £2.20 and it
looked almost full. I noticed a sign that suggested visitors use
the Park and Ride/Float.

"What's a Park and Ride/Float?" said Amanda.

"I suppose they use a boat instead of a bus," I said.

"Cool."

"It says on the sign that it's more ecologically friendly to
use the Park and Ride/Float. Better for the environment,"
said Sarah.

"Yeah, I'm all for Park and Ride." I was. This was the
truth. I'm a bus man. A champion of public transport.

"I sense there's a *but*," said Sarah.

"After all these years I'd have thought you'd know me
better—"

"But?"

"But wouldn't the environment have been better served
if there'd been a sign on the way *in*? The other side of
Falmouth? This way we've driven here, we turn around,
then drive back. How's that better for the environment?"

"You're moaning again, Dad."

"I am moaning. And how much will it cost to do this
boat thing?"

"It says there's a reduction to the entrance price for the
museum if you use the Park and Ride/Float," said Sarah.

"Fair enough," I said. "We'll see. Sounds kind of fun,
anyway."

I hadn't wanted to admit this, because I'd been building
up a head of steam for a rant, but yes, I rather liked the idea

of arriving at the National Maritime Museum by sea. That seemed right. Besides, my ears had pricked up at something Sarah had read from the sign. My opportunities for a good old rant were far from exhausted.

"So how come there's money *off* the museum? It's the *National* Maritime Museum. National museums are meant to be free. They're free in London. They're free at home. How come they get to charge people here in Cornwall?"

"I'm sure it isn't a lot," said Sarah.

We drove back the way we'd just come, filling the pure Cornish air with double servings of noxious exhaust fumes in the name of environmental friendliness. Amanda pointed out the large sign for the Park and Ride/Float that we'd driven past on the way in. Okay, so maybe they had told us. I decided to let them off.

Except the car park cost £2.90.

"The museum car park was only £2.20. How is that meant to encourage ecological awareness?"

And there was more to come. The ticket machine was defective and not giving change.

"So now it's cost us three quid. Marvellous. We're racking up the spends here."

The girls gave me a stare that could not be misinterpreted: Shut up with the moaning.

We followed large signs to a warehouse-like building. Inside there were few people but lines and lines of barricades aimed at controlling the flow of vast crowds in zig-zag formation, much as they do in airports. I had no experience of airports but I knew the way it worked.

"They're expecting a lot of people here," I said. "I wonder where they are."

This should have been the first warning, but we commenced to zig-zag, ordered to do so by enforcement notices, walking fifteen miles instead of the mere fifty-yard straight line to the reception desk.

Above the desk was a small notice. The Park and Ride/Float was going to cost us £4.50 each. We stopped a few feet short of the desk for a conference.

"*That's going to cost us £13.50!*" I said, in italics and with at least one exclamation mark.

Sarah and Amanda said nothing. They could sense the embargo on ranting was over.

"I thought I'd paid already. *Three quid, in the car park!*" The last bit was not just italics but delivered in the kind of squeaky voice they haven't invented punctuation for yet.

The worst of it was, they had me. If I turned and walked, they'd have already got my three quid, and for nothing, because it was a long walk to Falmouth from here. We'd have to drive back through the town. Again. Then pay again to park at the museum, if there was still room in the car park. I shook my head in despair. There was no hope for Planet Earth.

I turned my heat-ray eyes on the girl behind the desk.

"I've already paid for the car park," I said. "Now we have to pay for the Park and Ride/Float?"

"Yes," she said.

"Seems unreasonable," I said.

"You think so? Most people enjoy taking the boat over

to the museum." She looked me up and down as if she was seeing a rare specimen of miserable old git for the first time.

I sighed, not for the first time, and handed over fifteen quid. She gave me a paltry handful of silver by way of change, and three tickets.

"There you are, sir. Now, just follow the signs and show your tickets to the bus driver," she said.

"Okay, thanks." Then I stopped. "Er, bus driver? We've paid to go across by boat."

"That's correct, sir. But the boat doesn't run from here at low tide. At low tide the Park and Ride bus will take you into Falmouth Harbour. There's a short boat crossing you'll take from there."

"But I thought we'd paid for—"

"Tide'll be high enough in a couple of hours. You'll get to come back on the boat. Last crossing is five-thirty."

Sarah grabbed my elbow and steered me away.

"Let it go," she said.

"But—"

"Leave it. Chalk it up to experience."

We stood and waited for the bus. The bus came. We went up to the top deck so that we'd at least have a better view. On a hot day, though, with the bus unmoving for fifteen minutes, the greenhouse effect of all the glass on the top deck was significant, and I regretted our seating choice within the first few seconds. And yes, we'd come to Falmouth for a wet-weather day and yet the sun was turning the puddles to steam. Too late to change our seats though. The lower deck was full.

We waited, we sweated, I fumed. I watched several

service buses go past on the main road. We could have caught one of them. I bet they'd have cost less than thirteen quid, too.

At last, though, the bus moved, and in Falmouth we were shown where to queue for the "Float" part of the deal.

We stood in line along the jetty, swaying in the relentless heat of the midday sun for twenty minutes, wondering who'd be first to faint into the harbour.

Our boat arrived. We boarded. We sailed.

It wasn't like a cruise. It wasn't even like the Mersey Ferry. Ten minutes, max. We watched people walking from where we had waited for the boat. They were walking faster than our boat. The walk would take them less than seven or eight minutes. Had we boarded the service bus from the car park we'd have been here twenty minutes ago. We could then have walked and we'd have been inside the museum for the last half an hour. This felt, to me, insane. Beyond insane. I wanted to shout at someone but all the staff who worked here – directing the queues, running the boats, manning the ticket offices – were young kids who seemed to be doing a summer job while school was off. They were not to blame. I wanted to find The Man. The one who thought all this up. It's probably just as well that I didn't because I'd have peaked too early. There was more to come.

Entrance to the *National* Maritime Museum: £6.50 each. So, £19.50 for the three of us.

I felt Sarah's hand on my arm. "Don't forget, we can have a discount for using the Park and Float. Show her the tickets."

"Ah, yes, of course sir, there is a discount for using the Park and Float. Sixty pence."

A silence formed between me and the reception desk. A tangible, thick silence, that masked the rusty-hinge-creaking sound of my jaw swinging open. But as I say, she was young, a schoolgirl. She did not deserve my wrath. Somebody did: the museum curator, the mayor of Falmouth, Prince bloody Charles, Duke of Cornwall. But not the girl. I handed over the cash and stumped into the museum on wooden, angry legs.

It was a good museum. Light, modern, informative. Somehow, though, I knew that today I would not be informed. I would not be entertained. There was nothing, *nothing*, they could do at the National Maritime Museum that would please me today. Besides, there was to be a final turn of the screw.

"See that," I said to my girls, pointing at another sign. "Museum closes at five thirty."

"That's okay," said Sarah. "We've got three hours."

"You think? The first money collector, over in the car park, said the last boat was five thirty. That's our only chance of getting the full Park and Float experience."

"So? That works out okay."

"Except the boat holds, what, seventy people? How many in the museum, now, are planning to catch that last boat? More than seventy?"

"Okay, fair point."

"So if we miss it, then what? We walk to Falmouth. Then we *pay* for the service bus to take us back to the car park, because the Park and Ride bus won't be running because now the tide's in and there's a boat. Yes?"

"Yes. So you think we should leave earlier?"

"I do."

"When? Four thirty? Five?"

I wanted to say, "How about we leave now?" but I sensed eggshells. So I said, "Five should be okay."

It made sense. We went to the boat dock at five and watched two sailings leave before we could board one at a quarter past. Only fifteen minutes until the last boat and there appeared to be at least three hundred anxious Park and Floaters waiting on the dock behind us.

Maybe they extended the service hours for them. We'll never know. We were, at last, getting our Float deal. And it was fun. Best part of the whole museum thing.

Back in the caravan, though, I did some sums.

"Mike, let it go."

"I will, I just want to… if I include… there. It cost us an extra twelve pounds and forty pence to be sensitive to the environment. I hope the environment appreciates it."

And with that, we began to pack. Our Cornish holiday was to be a tour of Cornwall, and tomorrow we'd be heading for Sennan Cove, near Land's End.

IT TOOK us just one hour to reach Sennan Cove. We knew it wasn't far so we didn't hurry. We even found time to walk into Mullion Cove in the morning and have some lunch at the Mullion Meadows visitor centre, and a fine lunch it was too.

We arrived at our new home mid-afternoon, and after setting up the 'van we drove into Sennan Cove, looked at the lifeboat station, strolled around the gift shops, then back to the site. We took a walk down to the beach to try out the sea. Dipping a toe in the sea was scary stuff. *Big* waves. The kind of waves you have to look up in the air to see the tops. The kind that could whip your legs out from under you and carry you out into the North Atlantic on a whim, so a rapid toe-dipping was enough. For the rest of the time we stood back and watched the power of the ocean with a sense of terror and awe.

I couldn't understand the big sea. We didn't have any wind. We had quite a grey day with lots of drizzle, in fact. How come the waves?

The wind arrived in the night. Now I understood the sea. We rocked and swayed on our dry-land hard-standing caravan pitch and I snuggled deep under the duvet and wondered how it would be to be out there in a boat. I thought about the size of the waves we'd been watching on the beach that afternoon. I could hear the boom of the sea crashing on the rocks more than half a mile away. I thought about the lifeboat station we'd seen earlier, which is the base for the Royal National Lifeboat Institution's search and rescue operations for Land''s End, and wondered what kind of person could, voluntarily, for no pay, clamber out of a snug warm bed on a night like this, pull on an oilskin and wellies, leap into a lifeboat and launch into a sea with waves as big as a house. Very special people, that's who. I snuggled deeper under the covers and waited for morning.

The weather stayed blustery and changeable for a few days. No swimming, but there were plenty of iffy-weather options nearby. We visited St Michael's Mount, free to us National Trust members, where we walked out over the causeway, explored the mount and came back in a boat because the tide came in. Loved it. The boat was much cheaper than the Park and Float debacle, and all three of us enjoyed it so much more because I had nothing to grumble about.

We had a day in St Ives. A very pretty town but the day was spoiled for Sarah when a seagull snatched an entire Cornish pasty out of her hand. It had been her lunch. I bought her another and we sat on the beach and watched in fascination to see the coordinated strategy the seagulls used to take food. They worked the beach in teams, two screeching and performing in front of each picnicking group, while others worked around behind, then swooped in while the victim was distracted. Edgar Allan Poe should have written about seagulls. Bloody sight more scary than ravens.

Land's End Airport. Yeah, it doesn't seem to be a promising destination for a day trip, does it? I had a hankering, though, so we decided to go to the cafe there for lunch.

It turned out to be fascinating. It wasn't Heathrow or LAX, that's for sure. The runway was grass. The airport buildings were a row of huts, but there were photos on the cafe walls and it had an old aviation theme to it, and from the window we could watch the planes. This might not seem such a big deal, but I had never been in an airport before, nor had I been on a plane. Except when I was three months old, and that doesn't count because I don't remember too much about it. It isn't as though I was scared of going in a plane. Okay, maybe a little, but that wasn't the reason. The real reason I had never flown is that we had a caravan, and before that, a tent. And apart from that, there was this budget thing going on, about keeping the cost of holidays down to less than staying at home.

But now it was different. We weren't so poor. In my day-job life I had become an accountant for reasons of self-preservation, because accountants seemed to get more money than bus schedulers. So maybe now we *could* afford to go on a plane.

We sat in a line on one side of our dining table, munching on cheese sandwiches, and watching the little Cessnas and Pipers and Beechcrafts rolling and bouncing along the grass, then leaping into the air. This looked like fun. Above the window was a sign.

Pleasure flights around Land's End: £25

Whenever a plane took off or landed, then passed out of sight, my eyes strayed to the sign.

"See that?" I said.

"Mm," said Sarah.

"Mm," said Amanda.

"We could do that."

"Mm."

"Mm."

"What do you think?"

"If that's what you'd like to do," said Sarah.

"Well. What would *you* like to do?"

"Don't mind. If you want to go in a plane, we'll go in a plane."

"You'd do it?"

"If *you* want to do it."

I thought about it.

"Don't know," I said.

We munched on our sandwiches for a while more.

"Might be fun," I said.

"Might be," said Sarah.

The conversation went around and around.

"Lot of money, though," I said.

"Mmm."

A minute passed.

"Maybe we should do it," I said.

"Maybe we should," said Sarah.

Another minute.

"I wonder how long the flight is."

"Twenty minutes," said Amanda. She pointed to a notice by the booking desk.

"Mm," I said.

"Do you want to go on a plane, or do you want to go on *this* kind of plane?" said Sarah.

We watched as a little plane bounced over the field, dipping a wing and rolling in the turbulence.

"Not sure I want to go on *any* plane," I said.

"So why the conversation?"

"Just thinking about it."

"Look, if you want to go on a plane we'll go on a plane," said Sarah.

"Seems wrong," I said.

"Why wrong?"

"Kevin's not with us. We've always done everything together. We should do our first plane trip together. Wouldn't be right to do it without him."

"So," said Amanda. "You're scared to go on a plane."

"I'm not scared."

"Sounds like it."

"Sounds like it to me, too," said Sarah.

"It's just… Kevin. It's wrong to go without Kevin."

The argument was flawed, really, because within a year Kevin would fly to the Dominican Republic and Amanda would fly to Majorca. Here was my chance to be first. But I didn't know this.

"I feel like we're cheating Kevin," I said.

"Well, just go on your own. That way you're not singling him out. Or just take Amanda. I don't mind not flying. I'll watch from here."

"No. That wouldn't be fair on you. You'd have to come."

"Don't mind. Really," said Sarah.

"Mm," I said, and took the last bite of my sandwich.

And that was how we didn't go on a plane.

WE MOVED AGAIN the next morning, to Harlan Bay, near Padstow. This time our location was another temporary site. Again, we wondered if it would still be there after all the rain a few days earlier. We needn't have worried. The site was there and it was good. We could walk to the beach. We tried. We paddled, and again the water was fearsome cold.

Every village in the area had seaside shops selling surf boards and wetsuits. We came to a decision. There must be something in this wetsuit business. Perhaps now was the time to find out. One thing was for sure. This was a holiday for going in the sea and as things stood we wouldn't be going beyond our knees unless the water succumbed to a sudden and unlikely fifteen-degree temperature surge.

Amanda stayed in her tent and read Harry Potter. Sarah and I went shopping for wetsuits.

It is a hard thing, when you're not late teens, early twenties, when you don't have a six-pack stomach and when you are unlikely ever to be accepted for a Speedo advertisement, to go shopping for wetsuits. The sales teams are young dudes straight off *Bay Watch*. They have sun-bleached hair and a surfer-dude drawl. They are confident in their bodies. I too would be confident in their bodies, but sadly I have to make do with my own body.

A wetsuit salesman eyed me up and down and appraised my physique, clearly unimpressed with what he saw.

"Hmm," said the wetsuit salesman… salesteenager… saleschild.

Sarah went upstairs, to the ladies department. Her tale, told a half hour later, was similar to my own.

"A wetsuit has to fit. It has to be snug. Try this one," said the teenager.

I looked at the wetsuit. I looked down at my stomach. We clearly had a size differential going on here. I took it into the changing cubicle and began to struggle.

Climbing into a wetsuit is an art. I'd never tried before. The first time, I put it on backwards, with the zip down the front. I realised my mistake before trying to pull it up my torso and before going outside, as instructed, to have the sales child appraise my physique. I pulled it off, turned it around and tried again. The legs alone were tricky enough; with my flabby white flesh it was a little like trying to put toothpaste back in the tube.

Legs in place, I heaved it up over the waist then tried to figure out how to get my arms in the sleeves that hung down behind me. Do I go both together or one at a time? And was that clicking sound a harbinger of impending shoulder dislocation? The grunts and cries coming from inside my changing cubicle must have sounded like sea lions having sex.

Zipping up the back was the final challenge. There's a long tape attached to the zipper and this has to be pulled up over one shoulder. A lot of shrugging and flexing is needed to settle the suit across the chest, but I managed and felt quite proud for someone who has trouble scrubbing his own back.

I went outside feeling very self-conscious.

The sales child looked at me and shook his head. He walked around me and tutted, making me feel like bad meat.

"No," he said. "See here, under the arms?" He pulled. "Way too big."

"I try to watch what I eat," I said, feeling chastised.

"No, no," he laughed. "The suit. A size smaller I think." He took another from a rack and handed it to me.

"Smaller?" I squeaked the word. "I can barely breathe as it is."

"You'll thank me," he said. "There're gaps all over the place. It has to be tight. You'll get used to it."

It has to be tight, he'd said. I already felt as though an elephant was sitting on my chest. I returned to the changing cubicle. Now I had to unseal the "too-big" suit. I felt joints popping and muscles straining just reaching for the tape to pull down the zipper. As the zipper released there was blessed relief as my chest expanded and I drew air back into my lungs. How the hell was I going to get into a *smaller* suit?

I set about trying. Legs first. Oh my God, then the waist. How could I even manage to pull the thing over my backside? And that was the easy part.

I put my arms in the sleeves and wriggled and fought and took time out for a rest, then began the struggle once again, dipping first one shoulder then another, working it higher and higher. Without the chest zipped it felt as though my back was resisting a powerful spring that threatened, in a moment's lost concentration, to fold my spine into two. Then the chest. Flex, stretch, reach. I felt muscles tearing and straining. I pressed my shoulder blades together and zipped. Success. But I'd stopped breathing. Had anyone died before, zipping themselves into a wetsuit? Would I be the first? I flexed my shoulders some more and worked my arms and felt a moment of slippage and relief. I drew in air.

Again I stepped outside.

"Perfect," he said. "Look."

He took me to find a mirror. The mirror was on the other side of the shop, so I had to do the walk of shame through all the hordes of young surfer dudes with their blond hair, California tans and gleaming white teeth. What were they thinking? Had they ever seen anything like it? I must have looked like a vacuum-packed chicken leg in a Morrisons cold cabinet.

In the mirror I saw a different me. Not exactly lean, but certainly not as bulbous. I feared for all the internal organs that had been compressed to nothing inside. They just weren't used to living in such cosy proximity. But I looked, *almost*, like a surfer. Or at least one that hadn't been out much. I wondered if I could get away with wearing it under a business suit. I'd look better at the office. So long as I didn't try to sit down.

"How's that feel?"

"Tight," I said.

"Good. That's how it should feel. It will loosen up in the water, but not so much you lose the benefit."

"I'll take it," I said.

I returned to the cubicle for another ten-minute bout as I enacted my escape. With a fancy surf-shop bag in hand I met Sarah out front. She had a bag, too.

"How was it for you?" I asked.

Her smile and single head-shake said it all.

So now we had to try them out. We collected Amanda and headed for the beach in the rain. Didn't care about the rain. We had wetsuits. Rain all you like.

Climbing into a wetsuit is hard in a shop's changing cubicle. Try it on a beach with a small towel for modesty. There are no hand rails for balance while doing the flamingo hop. And there is another factor. There's sand. Sand means friction. Oh! My! God!

But we managed. We helped each other. We cursed each other. We fell over a lot. And eventually we got into the sea. Okay, so it was still agony on the feet and hands, but that's all. None of the gasping, sobbing pain when the waves hit your stomach. This could be fun. The sea could be enjoyable.

We ached a bit the next day. We don't know if the aching came from the swimming or from the struggles in and out of our wetsuits. Getting out of the suits when wet is even harder, and in the end we left them on, deciding to do the unrobing in the privacy of the caravan. It worked fine except for all the sand. Sand everywhere. The inside of the caravan came to look like a sand silo at a builder's yard, but it was worth every struggle and protest. We are, officially, surfer dudes. Except we don't have surfboards, just daft polystyrene things that little kids use.

Cornwall was a success. The weather behaved, by and large, and it became our place.

Amanda came with us to Cornwall again in 2005.

"They do surfing lessons," she said.

"I'm too old for surfing lessons," I said.

We watched one. There were surf students who were older than me. I thought about how cool it might be to surf on a proper surf board, one that didn't come from the beach-toy section of the shop. One that didn't have a My Little Pony sticker on the deck.

We signed up. Thirty-five quid seemed fair for a full-day course.

Our instructor was Australian. She was blond and lean and tanned and must have found the grey skies and ice waters of England a bit of a comedown from Bondi Beach, but she hid it well. Who knows, maybe she enjoyed not having to dodge great white sharks and venomous sea snakes.

She spent the first part of the lesson on the beach, showing us how to paddle by scooping and throwing sand. Then we learned how to look backwards for a wave then jump up on the board and balance. I thought it seemed easy, except we were still surfing the beach.

Then she took us in the water.

I always thought the hard part was standing up and balancing. Wrong. You push your board out until the water is chest deep, then you clamber onto it, lie down and paddle. Clambering onto it, *that's* the hard part. Because you do it again and again and again. You point the board towards the beach and you wait. A wave. Paddle like hell. It passes by. Dismount, push the board back out, clamber back on, and repeat. Once every ten waves you get it right, the wave picks you up and you're moving, and it is the most amazing rush. You try to stand up, fall off…

And push the board back into the waves.

We all managed to stand up a few times. Not for long, just seconds, but the sense of pride, the massive smiles. We loved it. Couldn't get enough. Had to go back and try again.

All afternoon.

Hours.

And then it was over. Time to come out of the water.

I'm a science fiction fan. I read sci-fi. I write sci-fi. (This is relevant. Stay with me.) One of the themes that often comes around again and again, is that astronauts who spend long months in space feel weak when they return to Earth. They feel the brutal pull of gravity in every fibre of their being. I'd written about it. I'd never empathised with it. Yes, I felt sure that it could be a bit hard, but these astronauts are strong, fit people. They'd get over it.

That afternoon, at about five PM on Watergate Beach, I found my empathy with the returning spacemen, as I walked out of the sea, and with each step, as the supporting water level moved lower down my body, and the relentless pull of Earth's gravity increased, I felt my own mass. On the edge of the sea, supporting my full body weight, my legs collapsed beneath me and I fell to the sand.

"Come on, up!" our instructor shouted in her Australian accent. "Bring your boards."

We'd been shown how to carry the boards, in twos, one in front, the other behind, with a board under each arm. I looked across at my board-carrying partner, who also lay on the beach, not enough strength to lift her head out of the wet sand.

"I can't get up," said Sarah.

"I can't even speak," I said.

We dug deep. We fought against the mass of Mother Earth and we dragged ourselves a little way up the gravity well, until we were again standing on two legs. The boards felt as though they were made from lead. Each step up the beach was a massive effort.

Our campsite was on the top of the cliff. We'd walked down. It didn't seem far. Now we had to do something amazing with our legs. We had to use them to drag the weight of our bodies and the heavy, soaking-wet wetsuits, to the top of that cliff. Five hundred feet. They were the last five hundred feet to the summit of Everest. Each step was a battle against a giant hand that tried to crush us against the surface of the road.

Surf lessons dominated the rest of the holiday. No, we didn't do it again. We just suffered from it. Every joint, every muscle screamed and ached. Never, *ever*, have I felt so stiff.

"What shall we do for tea?"

"Chippy."

"Fair enough."

But that meant going in the car. It was hard opening the car door. It was hard getting out of the car. Cornwall 2005 was the year of the big ache.

But also, it was the year of change.

We had plenty of other weekends, both 2004 and 2005, but the dynamic was changing. Once, in the Lakes, Kevin joined us again. He didn't come with us; he drove up a day later, pitched his tent nearby and joined us for meals and hikes. We were just getting used to the idea of three in a 'van when Amanda, now working as a legal secretary, also began to follow us to our destinations in *her* car when late finishes at work prevented her from travelling with us. More and more Sarah and I went as a couple, met one or other or both kids while we were away, then came home as a couple. Things move on. Families grow and drift.

Every May for the last ten years we had gone to Rhayader. The place we all loved. The place with ley lines.

In 2005 Kevin came to join us for one night. He brought his girlfriend. Sometimes a girlfriend becomes part of a family. Sometimes a son becomes part of the girl's family.

2005, Rhayader, was the last time we camped as a complete family unit. It wasn't Kevin's last time in the caravan. He came with us for a weekend in Ruthin at the tail end of the summer, but a new change was taking place, because on that occasion it was Amanda who stayed home.

In August of that year we went for a weekend near Lake Brenig. Kevin was in Turkey. Amanda was in a youth hostel in the Lakes.

Now we were Two in a Box.

2006: LONDON

At the time of writing it is autumn, and I note the appearance of a new sign: SKID RISK! It's next to the one that's been there for years, that says FLOOD RISK! because of all the blocked drains.

Wouldn't it be cheaper just to sweep up the leaves?

—*No. 92 from the Moanicles of Michael.*

We started 2006 with a trip to London. In mid-February. This was the earliest we'd ever dared to go away. We'd started to trust our caravan. Yes, in February it would keep us warm.

We were going for the best part of a week and we were two in a box. It felt strange. The caravan felt big. It also felt just a little bit liberating. Because this time in London we could do the art galleries, and do them right. The full works. And we could spend as much time in each as we wanted.

We went to the Caravan Club site at Abbey Wood.

Now, just because there were only two of us, the mojo of a typical Wood holiday didn't change. We hit traffic on the M25. All the M25. The queue began as we left the M1 and continued without respite until after the Dartford crossing. The forty miles of M25 around London took us longer than the entire two hundred miles of getting to the M25 from home.

"What time is it?" I said.

Sarah pointed to the clock on the dashboard.

"They don't allow new arrivals after eight at night," I said, with an edge of tension creeping into my voice.

"I know," she said.

"We're not going to get onto the site. This is ridiculous. We left home after breakfast."

"I'll ring them." She tried her mobile. "No signal."

"What? London. One of the biggest cities in the world, and they don't have a mobile signal?"

It is amazing how expectations change. A few years ago nobody had mobile phones. Now it had become almost criminal to have places that didn't have a signal. But this was the M25, and it *did* go round London and it *didn't* have a mobile signal and it *was* criminal and I slapped the steering wheel and had a little paddy for the umpteenth time in the last thirty miles.

I won't labour the point though. We made it. We queued on every one of the last forty miles to Abbey Wood, but we pulled through the gates with minutes to spare. What would we have done if the site had closed its doors? I don't know. Gone home perhaps. Through the night. The biggest sulk ever known to mankind would have been a certainty.

It was of course dark at the campsite. We'd have to wait until morning to see what it was like here.

Morning arrived and the site was good. Happy. We caught the train into London and did the whole art thing.

First destination was the Victoria and Albert Museum

where Sarah wanted to see a painting she'd loved for a long time. It's a Victorian narrative painting called *Recalling the Past* by the artist Carlton Alfred Smith. She asked the girl at the enquiry desk where she might find it.

"That's in the special collection," said the girl. "It isn't on public display. But you can request to see it. Except today is Sunday and we don't do special viewings on Sunday."

"I could come tomorrow."

"Monday? I'm sorry. No special viewings on Monday either."

Sarah looked at me with puppy-dog eyes.

"Can we see it on Tuesday, then?" I asked.

"Yes. Would you like me to make an appointment?"

It was done. We were coming back into London on Tuesday anyway, because Tuesday was theatre day. I had something special that I'd booked.

So we continued our full immersion art tour with visits to the National Gallery and the National Portrait Gallery, then got soaking wet in the rain and returned to the caravan. Monday took us to Tate Britain, then lunch, then Tate Modern, where we sniggered and ranted at the crappy modern art. We are not lovers of modern art. We are not even lukewarm about modern art. Staring at a long crack in the floor, or a pile of bricks, or a canvas that looks as though it was left out in the yard for the local strays to mark their territory would be funny except for the vast sums of money that seem to change hands over these pieces of tomfoolery, and the constant hoodwinking that says if you don't like it then you are just not intellectual enough to appreciate it. Well, I don't mind saying it's bollocks. I'm happy to stand in a gallery and say it's bollocks, and I'm happy for the intellectuals with their red corduroy trousers and their crumpled, ill-fitting canvas jackets to hear me say it's bollocks.

We left before I got us thrown out.

Across the Millennium Bridge to Somerset House and the Courtauld Gallery and this was more like it. If you want to see some of the best French Impressionist masters in one place, then this is the place, though it felt a little uncomfortable seeing them here and not in Paris.

Also on the agenda was Stanfords map shop. Sarah has to prepare me for a visit there. Pockets sewn closed, wallet emptied of all cash and credit cards, then, with an allowed budget folded in my hand, I can enter in safety. I wanted IGN maps, the blue ones, of Brittany. We had a plan for the summer. There are a lot of blue IGN maps covering a country the size of France. I have to be controlled.

"Look at this. They have an offer on maps around Provence."

"We're not going to Provence."

"But they're cheap. A really good price."

"You've only got two weeks' holiday. We discussed it."

"I know, but for another time?"

"Which ones do you want?"

"I don't know. I could do with all of them."

"But we're not going anywhere near Provence."

"I know but…"

My lip came out and pouted. But she was right. The old urge was back.

"Here's a map of Rouen," she said.

"Rouen's in Normandy."

"Yes, but think, you could write all about it. The Road to Rouen."

"Ha, ha."

We had tea in a fancy restaurant in the city, called McDonalds.

Then came Tuesday, our last day. Our big Theatre Day. But before the theatre we had that appointment with a painting. We headed for the Victoria and Albert. We were directed to an upstairs room where Sarah handed a chit to a man in a white lab coat with white gloves.

"Through this way, please."

He took us into a room. No paintings on the wall, but wide desks around the sides. Standing on the floor, propped up against a cupboard, was a rough wooden storage frame enclosing the painting Sarah had come to see.

Recalling the Past, by Alfred Carlton Smith, painted in 1888.

"There you are," he said. "Just let me know when you're done." He left us to it.

"So, there you go. What do you think?" I said.

"Lovely. Smaller than I expected."

The picture shows a young lady or girl, in a pink dress, sitting at a desk with her head laid on her forearm which rests on the arm of the chair. Her attitude is one of despair. There is paper screwed up by a wastepaper basket and an opened envelope on the carpet. The room is bare. The carpet is faded. There are dead or dying flowers in a vase. A dead stag's head on a cupboard. Symbology all over the place. Perhaps her lover has left her, or he is sick or dying.

Or he's dead. Or maybe she works in an accounts office and it's Monday morning. Who knows?

"Look at that," said Sarah. "The picture's damaged. There's a section that's been inserted."

"Hmm."

We both looked at the picture.

There was activity around us as people worked on documents at wide desks and scribbled notes on pads or on laptops.

Two minutes went by. A clock ticked on the wall.

"I feel I should be doing something," said Sarah.

"Yeah. Write in your notebook."

She took out her notebook and clicked open her pen.

"What should I write?"

"Don't know."

"How long do you think is normal to look at a painting?"

"Well, they've gone to all the effort of reaching it out for you. More than two minutes I'd think."

"Okay. A little longer."

We looked at the painting for a little longer.

"Do you think that's long enough?"

"Everyone else is still looking at their pictures."

"They're working. At things."

"Yeah. Well, any time you're ready."

"Another minute."

"Your call."

"I know."

We looked at the painting and listened to the scratching

and tapping of notes being scribbled and typed all around us. We hoped someone else might be first to leave.

"They look as though they're staying all day," said Sarah.

"You need to do something scholarly," I said.

She opened her notebook and wrote for a while. I was impressed.

"What did you write?"

"We need eggs and cereal, for breakfast."

"Okay."

We waited another minute, staring at the picture.

"Right," said Sarah.

"Right."

We thanked the man in the lab coat and left.

"Okay?" I asked as we went down the stairs.

"Yes. I'm happy I've seen it. Bit awkward though, wasn't it?"

"A bit. Cup of tea?"

We headed for the basement cafe.

OUR OTHER APPOINTMENT was with the Queen's Theatre in the evening. I might have mentioned before, I'm a clarinet and saxophone player. I play in a big band, but I also like to do pit work for amateur operatic companies around and about the Wirral. I have some particular favourite shows that I've played in: *West Side Story*, *Copacabana*, *Singing in the Rain*, *Sweeny Todd*… the list goes on. One show that I'd love to do, but isn't on the amateur circuit yet, is Les Misérables. I know and love the music but I wanted to see the show, and in 2006 the film of the musical was years away from appearing in cinemas. I'd read the Victor Hugo book and loved it, and couldn't imagine how they could turn such an epic into a two-hour story with songs. Many friends and fellow musicians, though, had raved about this show. *You must see Les Mis,* they'd say. *You must see it.*

We knew weeks earlier that we would be in London. Just the two of us. *Les Mis* was one of the huge, long-running shows in town, and so I booked tickets. I wanted to see it properly too, not just from cheap seats in the gods where you need oxygen and you get to sit behind a pillar. So I took us on the crumbling, unsafe footpath to the cliff edge of bankruptcy. These seats were expensive. I'd be paying for years, but I was *finally* going to see *Les Mis*, after so many years of wishing. The whole evening would be a special treat. It wasn't my birthday. It wasn't Sarah's birthday. Our anniversary was months away. We'd have to justify it some-how, but… ah well.

We went for a pre-show meal. Somewhere fancy, at least fancy for us, fancier than the previous night. It might be classed as fast food to everyone else though: a chain pizza/pasta place on Trafalgar Square.

We went too early. The restaurant was empty and had all the atmosphere of a closed hospital ward. Our table faced away from the window and away from the other diners – there were only two of them. The only thing nearby was the cold draught from under the door. Our meals came quickly, were only warm, and we couldn't afford dessert, so we found ourselves back on the street after twenty-five minutes, with two hours still to go. It was an inauspicious start.

We wandered around the West End killing time. We rehearsed the walk from the theatre to Charing Cross Station, to time it. This might be important. I'd checked on what time the show ended because we had a last train to catch just after eleven. We could not miss that last train because it is a long way to Abbey Wood by taxi – sixteen miles and probably more than an hour. It would cost a small fortune. Cheaper to buy the taxi. But it would not be an issue. We'd have plenty of time, more than half an hour, and after practicing, it was only a ten-minute trot to the station.

We went into the theatre as soon as they opened the doors. This was February. Cold. I bought a souvenir programme. Cost a fortune. Had nothing inside of any interest, just a bunch of adverts for Hatton Garden jewellers and fancy hotels. It was too big to put in a bag or a pocket so it just became this big, awkward thing we had to lug around. But the useless programme and the tepid meal would not spoil this evening. It is not often you get to have one of those once-in-a-lifetime moments. The night would be wonderful, I knew it.

I looked with interest into the orchestra pit. A *professional* pit. Okay, a bit disappointing. I'd heard rumours they'd reduced the orchestra size to save money, and gone more for synthesisers and stuff. The rumours were true. I'd played in bigger orchestras for amateur shows. Oh well, stay with the mood. I was here to see *Les Mis*. For real.

The overture started. The band were good. Top notch. Very tight. But you'll notice they were now "the band" rather than "the orchestra". Hey ho.

The curtain lifted and I was entranced. What a fabulous show, the music, the acting, the effects, the constant movement and colour. I even managed to forgive the small band, because they were so polished. All of this magic lasted for about forty minutes.

Scene change.

Long pause.

I could hear the band doing little vamping games, extending phrases, doing repeats, and repeats of repeats. Some of the audience began to grumble. The band reached a point where they could no longer get away with the vamping. So they stopped, and I could hear rustling as the wind players shared a packet of jelly babies. This I knew: wind players do not eat jelly babies unless there's a long time before they have to blow again. It's to do with saliva.

We waited, looking at the closed curtain.

A man in a dinner jacket appeared onstage looking frazzled.

"Ladies and gentlemen, I apologise. We have a slight problem. We'll continue with the show as soon as possible."

He disappeared again. From behind the curtain came the sounds of industry. Someone was beating all buggery out of something with a big hammer. The hammering went on for several minutes. The man in the bow tie reappeared. His bow tie was crooked, and his face appeared flushed, as though he'd been fighting.

"I'm sorry, ladies and gentlemen. We are going to take

an additional interval, to allow time for us to clear the stage. We have some heavy props, several tons in weight, and they have to be moved. One of the props has broken and will need to be craned off. Again we do apologise. In the entire twenty-two-year run of this show, both here in London and on Broadway in New York, this has only ever happened once before. Please be patient. There will be a fifteen-minute interval."

The house lights came up.

We got up and walked around, kind of aimless, but we didn't want a drink or ice cream, we wanted information. I had another issue, too, and it made me more and more agitated. The delay had lasted ten or fifteen minutes. Add another fifteen minutes for the extra interval, and we'd be cutting things very tight for catching our last train to Abbey Wood. I mentioned it to Sarah.

"How long will we have?"

"Should be okay. Twenty minutes, less than the ten minutes it takes to walk to the station. So long as nothing else happens and they restart on time."

We returned to our seats and watched the fifteen-minute interval become twenty minutes. Now we had only a five-minute cushion. Catching or missing our last train might hinge upon the unknowable – the time it might take to leave the theatre and cross the road through the traffic outside the station.

The curtain went up. No scenery. The entire cast were seated on chairs in a line along the stage. They sang the songs, taking it in turn to stand centre stage to perform. This was rubbish. I might as well just listen to the CD.

Where was the drama? Where was the spectacle? I couldn't believe it. I'd waited for eight years to see *Les Mis*, and this was it?

I only had to endure ten minutes because the real interval followed.

As we left the auditorium, the theatre staff were handing out printed sheets that they'd dashed off in a hurry.

The theatre apologised for the cast having to perform the concert version of the production. Unforeseen circumstances, blah blah blah. Yes, we'd guessed. We'd heard the hammering. Fair play, though, if we called in at the box office we would be given complimentary tickets for an alternative night, depending on availability.

But we were leaving London the next morning. We couldn't just trip along to the theatre any old night they happened to have spare seats. We lived two hundred miles away. We'd need accommodation, and time off work.

We didn't know what to do. Should we stay and see it through, and thus forgo the offer of replacement tickets, and watch a bunch of people sitting on an empty stage singing? We'd paid over a hundred quid for our tickets. It would not do. There again if we left now, we would miss the rest of the show that we'd already paid to see, and had no chance of getting back down to London to see it another time.

In the end circumstances decided it for us. The interval ran long. We soon reached the point where it became obvious that we'd have to leave before the end anyway. Or walk back to Abbey Wood, sixteen miles, through the East End of London, at night.

We left.

Outside, it was raining. Very heavy rain. Lots of puddles. We had no raincoats but it felt right and proper. It put the icing on the cake. A horrible night. The thirty-minute train journey back to the campsite was *so* depressing. The dark. The rain. The loss.

Les Misérables. That was us.

As an afterword, though, I have to say the theatre acted with decency. I wrote to them. They understood our position as out-of-towners and refunded the cost of our tickets in full and without quibble.

But.

I still haven't seen *Les Mis*. I've seen forty minutes of it. We have been back to London. We have often wanted to see a show, we've thought about it, but do we want to pay all that money when we've already seen most of the first half? Or should we just see a fresh show? Each time it is the latter argument that wins. I have a suspicion that I'll never get to see the rest of *Les Mis*.

Later in 2006: HAY-ON-WYE

You're in a strange town, approaching traffic lights. There are two long lanes of stationary traffic and there are no road signs. Do you choose the left lane or the right lane? Well, of course you choose the left lane because you are towing a caravan and you are a patient and sensible fellow.

The lights change to green and the traffic begins to move forward. The cars ahead spread out and now you can see the paint on the road. Lane arrows. The right-hand lane is ahead only. Your lane, the left-hand lane, is left turn only.

Into Sainsbury's car park.

So you indicate right and everyone in the outside lane closes ranks because they hate you. You're a stupid caravan that tried to be clever and got in the wrong lane. You can't turn left because Sainsbury's car park is not a good place for a caravan, and so you're trapped, and now everyone behind you hates you too, because they want to be in Sainsbury's and you are spoiling their day. You stare into your wing mirror, but whenever a gap opens in the traffic on your right, someone nips out quickly from behind.

The lights turn red. You're first in line but still in the wrong lane, signalling right. Will the person beside you show mercy and let you in when the lights change again? You try to catch their eye. You note the set of their jaw and the death grip they have on the wheel and you realise you are engaged in psychological warfare: a game of chicken.

The lights turn green.

—No. 93 from the Moanicles of Michael.

Despite the last, depressing day, we had enjoyed London. We were getting used to doing holidays on our own. We'd reached the point where we told the children we were going in the caravan, rather than asking if they wanted to come, because they usually didn't, or if they wanted to come they couldn't because they both had work and other interests, and coordination became difficult, even at weekends.

Weekends for two became the norm, but as May approached, the empty nest syndrome began to tell once more, as we considered Rhayader.

Rhayader was our family place. We had joint ownership on finding the Elan Valley, and for ten years there had been no question of our going anywhere else over the May bank holiday. But would it be the same with just two of us? Would we spend our weekend strolling by the River Wye, remembering the skimming contests we had there, or cycling up the valley past all the dams and remembering when there were four of us? Was this, perhaps, a good time to break with a family tradition and go somewhere else?

It just so happened there was another place we could try, and I'd been putting off even suggesting it for a couple of years because it always clashed with our Spring bank holiday weekend in Rhayader.

John, a colleague at work, had been to the Hay Literary Festival a couple of years earlier. I remember how he came straight up to my desk on the Tuesday after the long weekend.

"Mike, did you have a good weekend in the caravan?" I sensed he didn't want to know, it was just an opening. He had news.

"Hi, John, yeah, a very good weekend. We went to mid-Wales again and—"

"We went to the Hay Festival. Brilliant! You'd love it."

"The Hay Festival? I think I've heard of it."

"Mike, let me tell you. You'd *love* it. Really. The whole weekend is about books. There're writers and publishers and... well, there're talks and events. Clever people, you know, ageing hippies and academics and bookish people. And cheap books of course. You. Would. Love it!" He punctuated the last bit with a punch on the shoulder after each word. John's a very touchy, feely, punchy kind of person. "You've got to go. Honest. Brilliant."

A year later. We'd been to Rhayader again. I was in the office kitchen making a brew and I felt two hands grip my shoulders. I knew it was John.

"Mike. Honest. Hay Festival. You would *love* the Hay Festival." He hadn't even gone through the preamble of asking about my own weekend. When John gets enthusiastic about something it can be kind of infectious. He knew I wrote a bit in my spare time, and that I'd had the odd story published. He hated that it was mainly science fiction – he's not a sci-fi reader – but you can't win them all. He knew I had a passion for books though. He really wanted me to go to this festival thing. I would have given it a try, but the dates were all wrong. Spring bank holiday was Rhayader weekend.

But not this year. This year we felt the need for something different.

Sarah brought it up first.

"Do we want to go to Rhayader again this year? Won't it be... I don't know, a bit sad?"

So I mentioned an alternative. "Well, there is something. A festival, a little further south. Hay-on-Wye. Still mid-Wales, but... You know John, at work. He reckons we'd love it."

"What, like a pop festival?"

"No. Books. Authors."

"How does that work?"

"Don't know."

"Okay then."

We sent for a brochure. We found a site nearby. We booked the site for three nights and we booked some events.

We weren't sure though. A festival? Was it us?

We drove down through Wales in glorious sunshine. In Newtown we hit traffic and queued for ages but this was the same queue we'd crawled through for the past ten years. It felt a little strange because the route was the same one we'd always travelled, only when we came to the roundabout where we always turned right to Rhayader, we kept straight on. Somehow this felt like a betrayal. Nuts, I know.

We passed through Builth Wells and came to another halt. The road ahead was blocked. A car had left the road and taken out a wooden telegraph pole. Snapped it in two. The driver was okay, but there was debris and wires everywhere. It was that kind of journey again. Now we just needed rain. So it rained. Not heavy rain, just grey drizzle. The kind that weighs heavily on your soul.

We arrived at the site and hated it. Sometimes it happens. The ley lines are wrong, or whatever. This site was not *our* site. Our site was the lovely Gigrin Farm in Rhayader, with views of the mountains and the Elan Valley. This site was close to a road that sounded like a racetrack. There were random derelict clapboard buildings in the field, held together with tar paper. We didn't have a view, just the back of a tar paper building, with a pile of rusty wheelbarrows stacked up in front. The ground itself was muddy, in a way that suggested it would remain muddy throughout a long summer drought, the way the sea stayed wet. There were dogs. Not happy, intelligent farm dogs, but the kind of dogs that foamed at the mouth and would have looked more at home behind a chain-link fence and answering to curses from owners called Jed and Luke.

"I think we should move," said Sarah.

"So do I," I said. "But where?"

"Anywhere. Rhayader."

"Everywhere else is full. And we can't go back to Rhayader, we've already booked festival events."

"We can't stay here."

"I know, but we have to."

"We don't have to."

It was a long conversation that went nowhere. The Hay Festival, it turns out, is popular with more than just John at work. Other people come here too. And accommodation is impossible. Every site we called was full, weeks in advance.

Some site owners laughed. They'd been booked all year and were already booked for next year. People daisy-chain their bookings; each year they pay deposits for the next year.

So when we secured a booking for this site so easily only a few weeks earlier, we should have been suspicious.

"Yes, of course, we have plenty of room."

There might have been a clue in there, somewhere.

It went dark. Even with the lights on and the curtains drawn we could feel the bad vibes from the site around us. I keep a diary in the caravan where I record all the impressions I have from places we've stayed. My entry, that night, for Hay-on-Wye says: *We won't be back!*

We had breakfast staring at the rain running off the tar paper shed, then drove into Hay-on-Wye. Our site was too far outside Hay to walk.

There were car parks in fields, but the rain was bad and Sarah suggested we park in the town and walk back along the road to the festival site. It turned out to be an inspired move because later we saw how cars had problems getting out of the official festival car parks, mired in mud.

We still weren't getting it. The Hay Festival. What was so good about the place? Rain, mud, mad dogs. Horrible!

Then we walked into the town of Hay-on-Wye.

A town of books.

A bookshop on every road, on every corner. An old cinema converted into… a bookshop. The books were second-hand and cheap. Books I'd read as a child and lost. Books I'd never seen before or heard of before. We had an hour before our first festival event and I just wanted to stay and buy books.

We dropped off our bags of books in the car and walked back to the festival site. The Hay Festival was a tent city in a farmer's field. There were marquees and awnings and circus-sized tents. There were coffee shops and eateries and... book shops. The atmosphere amongst the tents was one of excitement and passion for anything with pages. Everyone carried canvas carrier bags that came with a *Guardian* newspaper in it, so we bought one. The bag was useful; we put more books in it.

Our first event was a talk with Chris Stewart, whose travel book, *Driving Over Lemons*, I'd read only a few months earlier and thought was just brilliant. He was here to talk about his new book, *The Parrot in the Pepper Tree*. Nearly an hour listening to insightful questions and entertaining answers about process and technique and hilarious anecdotes about living the good life in Andalusia, and I was buzzing. I hadn't been to an event like this ever before and I lapped it up.

We came out of the tent hyper. I wanted more. I wanted to settle into one of the on-site coffee shops and reflect on the last hour, but there wasn't time, we had another event in fifteen minutes back in the town.

The road running from Hay to the festival site was crammed with two-way foot traffic, all trying not to fall into the road under the wheels of the cars and buses and rickshaws that like to use the road, too.

The next event was in The Swan Hotel. It was a BBC recording of *The Verb*. Its presenter, Ian McMillan, the Bard of Barnsley, chatted with us on our way in, in his broad

Yorkshire accent. He does that. He makes you feel like you're his best friend. He's brilliant.

We found a seat and caught our breath and two other people came and sat next to us. I looked over at them.

"Hi," said Chris Stewart. He was a little out of breath having half-run from the last event. *His* event.

"Oh, hi," I said. I shook his hand. "Er, we just came from your talk. Loved the book."

"You did?" He beamed. He introduced me to the lady he was with, his agent.

We talked for a few minutes. Chatted. Me, and Sarah, with a *real* writer and a *real* agent. Then *The Verb* started, and I just let the show wash around me, brilliant witty writing, thumping performance poetry, and I felt my grin widening so much it threatened to lop off the top of my head.

The Hay Festival, I thought. *What the hell have I been missing?*

The show finished. I said goodbye to "my friend" Chris Stewart, and we went into the town to find a place to eat. The rain had stopped. In the square there was live music. A folk band with a pounding jazz-like beat. Around the corner, a man on stilts.

"Are you leaving? Please don't leave."

"We're not leaving."

He wiped away a theatrical tear of joy.

We stumbled into a restaurant called The Granary. Home-cooked food. Lots of veggie options. There are low beams and old farming equipment hanging from the walls. Seating is at long wooden benches, with a few small tables here and there. Sarah went upstairs to bag a table while I waited in the queue to order food.

Upstairs I found Sarah in deep conversation with a young guy. They were discussing the Al Gore interview, for which we hadn't bought tickets, about his book, The Assault on Reason, all about the environment and stuff. We came to realise there were too many things we wanted to see. I joined in their conversation until our food arrived, then we wished each other a good festival and he left us to eat.

Sarah was beaming.

"I love this place," she said. "People are so *interesting*. They just come up and talk to you. It's just… it's wonderful."

The food was gorgeous. Perfect.

We strolled back through the town, still busy, still hopping. We collected our car and drove back to the campsite. Somehow the tar paper sheds looked more… rustic. The dogs seemed playful, not sinister. The traffic noise… what traffic noise? That was just the buzz of anticipation.

The next day, Sunday, we had more events. At one of them I found myself standing in a queue and spotted a familiar face under a familiar black hat a few places back. Terry Pratchett! We saw him on a panel with Jasper Fforde (another writing hero of mine) an hour or so later.

It went like this all weekend. So many events. Our heads filled with new knowledge − history, politics, science, art − until it dribbled out of our ears. We both walked around with beaming smiles, spotting the famous writers in the crowd.

At the end of the second day my caravan diary entry was a little different.

Love the Hay Festival! Sad that we have to go home so soon, but have already booked the caravan site for next year.

Our two-in-a-box adventures were taking off. Our next outing beckoned. I had the plan. I had the IGN maps. Our sights were set on Brittany.

Further into 2006: BRITTANY

Referring to Moanicle 93 (also 94 and 95, not shared here) regarding the liberal use of paint on the road. It's no longer liberal, it's all rubbed off. Ever since Austerity began, the authorities have stopped touching up the road paint. Many complex junctions have now moved toward the French anarchy model of free-for-all traffic management, and we Brits are just not used to it. We manage okay if we stay local, and memory helps to fill in the gaps, but as soon as we venture afar we're expected to adopt lane discipline by using psychic powers. It can be disconcerting to find oneself adrift with a caravan in a sea of tarmac, with only the odd dot of remaining paint to suggest which way the road is meant to go. And my, how the locals love you for it.

—No. 105 from the Moanicles of Michael.

The last light was fading from the sky by the time we began boarding the Brittany Ferries ship to Roscoff. You've already heard about our journey south to Plymouth, and our GPS antics across the fields of Devon. That was a misadventure we'd put behind us, along with the need to find a Halfords in Plymouth to get the brakes fixed, but that's not so interesting. No, we were ready for real adventure.

We had a night-time sailing, with our own cabin. This was going to feel like a proper ocean cruise. For many hours we'd be out of sight of any land. Way more serious than a Dover-to-Calais hop.

We took special care when we left the car and caravan down in the hold. I made sure the vibration sensor was disabled. I didn't fancy having the car alarm barking away all night when people upstairs were trying to sleep – done that before. Also the fridge. We checked that it was empty and switched off the power so it wouldn't feed off the car battery for twelve hours. That wouldn't be good.

We went looking for our cabin, through a maze of identical corridors and turns. My sense of direction evaporated. The only clues were the wall plates with cabin numbers and arrows, left, right, right, straight on, left… and we twisted and turned deeper into the depths of the ship.

The cabin was small. I've always been impressed by caravans, the way their designers conserve space by making every fitting do double duty, then fold away when no longer required. The nautical designers of our cabin could have done with a few lessons from caravan designers. The cabin seemed small even before we extended the bunks. Being in the centre of the ferry, far from the outside, it also felt confined and claustrophobic, something we've never felt in a caravan, even the old two-berth Sprite with four adults packed inside.

We decided it was too early to sleep, so we went for a coffee, to be with other people, and to watch Plymouth slip away into the night. I was surprised to see that Plymouth had already slipped away into the night; I hadn't realised we'd left the dock. Just a slight vibration and nothing more. Once clear of Plymouth Sound though, we knew we were at sea. Not rough or even choppy, but… movement. Rocking and undulating. I have to admit I'd had conversations with myself about this part of the journey. I had a track record when it came to ships.

When Sarah and I were girlfriend and boyfriend, during our first, teenaged summer together, I wanted to take her to the Isle of Man. I am Manx, born in Douglas, and proud of it. I wanted to show off my homeland. I only learned later that Sarah, although born on the Wirral, has a long and noble Manx heritage, being related to a famous seafarer and poet. But that is another tale.

We planned a day trip to the island, a long day since it was a four-hour crossing each way, with twelve hours on the island. We took the midnight sailing and arrived shortly after four AM. We had planned to find a cosy corner of the ship, stretch out and try to sleep, but the ferry was full and we had trouble even finding anywhere to sit, so we wandered aimlessly around the boat for hours. As exhaustion threatened to wipe us out, a row of empty seats appeared before us. We grabbed them, and settled down to get some sleep, but two minutes later a crew member hauled us back from the edge of oblivion, and told us to move. We'd arrived in Douglas and hadn't realised. This, of course, explained the sudden abundance of empty seats; our fellow travellers had already disembarked.

So we spent the day on the island, doing all the sights: Douglas, the Laxey Wheel, Snaefell – there's nowhere else quite like it, this island was and remains gorgeous. On our way back to Douglas, tired and happy, we rounded Onchan Head on the electric tramway and I saw something different on the sea. White caps. The wind was up and waves were crashing on the beach.

"Brilliant!" I shouted. "A rough sea. It will make the trip back more exciting." I meant it. I thought it would be exciting.

Sarah was less enthusiastic. "Oh dear. I don't like the idea of it being rough. I hope it's not too bad. What if we get sick?"

"You won't get sick. I've been over loads of times in rough sea. It isn't a problem at all, trust me."

The last time I'd crossed to the Isle of Man I'd been four and a half years old.

So we caught the ferry, the *King Orry*, and as she backed out of Douglas Harbour, there was a bit of rocking.

"Uh-oh," said Sarah.

"It's fine," I said.

People laughed, constrained and nervous chuckles, all around us, and as the ship lurched a few inches the cups and saucers in the coffee bar gave a little tinkle. But we hadn't yet left the harbour.

The *King Orry* turned. And swayed.

Then she headed out to sea and the rolling movement began. I lasted two minutes. I groped my way out of the coffee bar and dashed for the rail. I won't go into the specifics of an extended five-and-a-half-hour crossing, with waves taller than houses rearing up all around us, and passengers jostling for space at the rail to put in their shift at the vomit factory. The ship ran out of paper bags. I have never felt so ill. It was, and remains the longest five and a half hours in my life.

Sarah just watched. Unfazed. Every now and again she asked if I was okay and I said *urrgh*. She suffered not the slightest queasiness. She thought the wind and spray nothing worse than bracing, while all around her an epic puke-fest was in full swing. We'd only been going out with each other for a few months. It's a wonder she still wanted any part of me after that day. But here's the thing: I've never been allowed to forget it. On the *Royal Iris* across the Mersey, on one-hundred-yard chain-ferry crossings in Devon, on kiddies' paddle boats, she's always reminded me of that day.

So, on the Brittany Ferries' *Pont L'Abbé*, we drank our coffee, tried to relax, and felt that… swaying movement.

"You okay?" said Sarah.

"Yeah, yeah."

"Are you sure?"

"Yeah, I'm sure. I'm fine."

"Because, you remember that time we sailed back from the Isle of Man?"

"It was thirty years ago."

"Yes, but… You were fine then, until—"

"I'm fine. Really."

I was fine. No problem. It wasn't rough. Not at all. Nothing like the Isle of Man crossing. This was just a swell that was, well, unsettling. I'd worried about it. Sarah had worried about it, for me. I felt okay, fine, but I thought, you know, it might be better lying down. So we returned through the maze of blue-carpeted corridors to our cabin where we followed the printed instructions on how to unfold the bunks.

"I'll take the top bunk," I said.

Sarah laughed. "You have got to be kidding me. You are not going up there, above me. If you start throwing up, I want you as near to the ground as possible."

"Fair enough," I said. She had a point. "But… just something to consider. What if *you're* sick?"

She gave me a look and a tilt of the head. She didn't need to say it. Isle of Man.

I wasn't ill, I was fine. The guy in the next-door cabin though. Man, he was a long way from fine. He started being ill soon after we settled in our bunks. The walls were thin. His woes were very audible. Every ten minutes we heard the toilet flush and the cycle would begin again. It was hard to sleep. Impossible.

And the *swaying*. You wonder how babies ever sleep with all that rocking and swaying they have to endure. It wasn't regular, either. You'd lie there, unmoving, nodding off. Then a slight movement and whoa! A drop off a cliff, albeit a cliff only a few inches tall, but that first half inch has you convinced you're going a long way down. Your eyes pop open and you stare, and become aware of being right in the centre of the ship, with all those corridors to negotiate. We didn't want to end up like Leonardo DiCaprio and Kate Winslet, hanging onto some plank in the ocean. If this sucker went down, we wanted seats in the lifeboat.

Here's how confident we felt: We slept in our clothes; neither of us fancied clambering into a lifeboat in our jammies. Our coats and shoes were laid out close to hand, and we rehearsed the route to the muster station three or four times so we could do it in the dark, fast. We tried it a few times late at night, too. It seemed a good way to pass the long hours of wakefulness. I also had a hankering to see the magnificence of the night sky from far out to sea with zero light pollution, and so, in search of respite from the vomiting soundtrack of our next-door neighbour, we took to frequent late-night wandering. I didn't get to see the night sky because the ship had lots of lights blazing and the sky was overcast. But at least we found respite away from Mr Mal de Mer, next door.

We left the ship in Roscoff. When we had planned this trip, we felt it would be good to start our road journey after a restful night at sea, and to begin the day refreshed and ready to go. Congratulations to anyone who manages it. We started the day knackered. I suppose this was one disadvantage about pre-planning the holiday. We were tied to the caravan site we'd booked and paid for, a hundred and fifty miles away. At this point I'd have been happy to roll up at the nearest municipal campsite, drop the legs and flop into an unmoving bed.

There's a delay on a car ferry where everyone waits in their cars. You can see nothing except the back of the lorry or motorhome in front, and your only clue as to what's going on is the clashing and rattling of chains and the occasional orange strobe light and siren that means something to someone and hopefully isn't an indication that the ship is going down. We were ordered down to the car deck long before the ship even arrived in port, so we had no idea whether we were still at sea, with ages to wait, or mere seconds from the mad scramble off the boat.

I used this downtime to set Sarah up with the essential tools of the navigator's trade. You remember? I've mentioned them before: Laptop, handheld satnav, lots of wires. I also had comprehensive route instructions that I'd handwritten, and the orange Michelin road atlas that is so big when opened it could cover the entire windscreen if you allowed it to get away from you.

"I don't need the laptop. I'll just read the map," said Sarah.

I felt affronted. The laptop wheeze was my foolproof hi-tech solution.

"Remember last time in France, how we kept getting lost?" I said.

"It didn't work in Plymouth," said Sarah.

"We found the campsite didn't we?"

"*I* found the campsite. You couldn't find it even when we were parked in the entrance."

"France is different. It's complex. We need help. This is the modern way. Technology. We'll always know exactly where we are."

"Well you'd better have a word with the ship's captain, because right now the technology says we're still in Plymouth."

I looked at the laptop.

"Yeah. Okay, but we need line of sight with the satellites. We're still in the bowels of the ship. It *will* work, as soon as we're outside."

"And how long before the laptop shuts down?"

"I've sorted that. It won't shut down. Trust me."

And there was no time for further comment. Engines roared. Daylight ahead. I started the engine and followed the motorhome in front. I still find it all a bit frantic, this process of leaving a car ferry. The long spell of inactivity, then sudden overload of sensory input. Go! *Aller!* A new country, drive on the other side of the road, foreign languages on the signs, dock workers in high-vis vests, waving and directing. There is no customs control in France, it's all done on the English side, so there's no opportunity to join a traffic queue and gather your wits. Before you know it you are propelled onto the open road and there always seems to be a peer-pressure urgency from other travellers to get the hell out of town as fast as possible. Junctions come at you without warning. Crossroads with irrational traffic lights, wrong-way-round roundabouts, urgent-looking hash marks painted on the road with no obvious purpose. Gendarmes with guns and spot-fine lust in their eyes.

"Junction ahead. Which way?" I tried to keep my voice calm.

"Don't know. Still in Plymouth. Acquiring satellites."

"Well… Er… Roscoff Centre or Morlaix?" Becoming less calm.

"Don't know. Not Roscoff Centre. Middle of a town. With a caravan. Go the other way."

"Oh. T-junction. D58. Left or right?"

"Still in Plymouth."

The motorhome ahead turned left, so I followed, fighting the urge to do the British thing and swing into the left-hand lane. I only managed it because the motorhome got it right.

"He must be going somewhere out of town too," I said, proud of my sharp reactions. "If I follow him—"

The motorhome slowed and took a right into a narrow side street.

"—He might ask us to his home for breakfast," said Sarah.

Now I was on my own. This road looked nothing like a through road from a major ferry port ought to look.

Beside me, plugs were being unplugged, wires tossed onto the car floor, and with an uncomplimentary adjective, Sarah frisbee'd the laptop onto the back seat.

"I'll use the map. Where are we?"

"D58."

"No. What page?"

"I don't know. The one with Roscoff on it."

The Michelin Road Atlas is a big book with a lot of big pages, like reading the *Sunday Times* or the *Telegraph* in annual omnibus editions. I heard a rustling and tearing of paper. I stared ahead, saying my little survival mantra over and over.

Drive on the right. Drive on the right.

Roundabout. Left or right? Right. Feels wrong. Bugger! Cool it – must be right. Okay, signal. Exit.

"Okay, we just did a roundabout. How are we doing?"

"I've found the page. Which exit did you take?"

"I don't know. I just… picked."

"So we don't know where we are?"

"No idea. I'll just drive until we come to something."

A sign beside the road. We were on the D58. We'd taken all the correct turns. By some miracle we weren't lost.

Sarah read the map and followed my written instructions and we were fine.

Some time later we missed a turn, and drove through the town of Landivisiau several times. This time I was map-reading and Sarah was driving. Somehow we went around in circles and kept coming back onto a long, straight road with speed bumps. Speed bumps are horrible in a caravan.

But we got out of it. I reworked the route to take into account our being in a completely different part of Brittany to the one I'd planned, and we had no more issues. It took us both about an hour, and fifty miles, for our blood pressures to return to normal. By then it was time for a break.

We stopped in a big parking area and ate a sandwich we'd bought at a petrol station. The only other vehicle in the park was a huge artic with GB plates. The driver saw us and wandered over for a chat.

"You heading home or just arriving?" he asked.

"Came over to Roscoff this morning," I said. "Heading down towards Vannes."

He cocked his head to one side, thought about it, then said, "Interesting route choice. Taking the scenic route?"

"We missed a turn," I said. "Hard to turn with a caravan."

"I guess," he said.

I looked over his shoulder at the sixteen-wheeler he'd walked from and supposed he thought I was an idiot.

"Bit harder in that thing," I said.

"Nah, it's easy," he said. "I'm on my way back. Been

over here for four or five weeks. Looking forward to getting home."

"What, like one trip?"

"No, you do a delivery, pick up another load, take it somewhere else, and then take another load. I can be over here for months at a time."

"And you live in the truck?"

"Yeah. Proper home from home in there. You're a caravanner, you'll appreciate it. Come and have a look."

He walked us over to his truck. We both climbed up into his cab. Higher in the air than I expected. Lovely comfy driving seat. A bunk bed in the back with a small cooker and a TV. It was homely. I thought, *I could do this*. Then I thought about how many times I could get lost in Europe and how hard it might be backing this thing out of a cul-de-sac, and decided I'd leave long-distance lorry driving to others.

He also showed us the trailer, empty for the first time in weeks, and I was astounded at how big it looked inside. We see them every day on the roads but we don't really see them. These things are massive. I couldn't imagine the responsibility of driving one of them around full of expensive goods: designer clothes one day, oranges the next, bottles of wine another.

We spent maybe an hour chatting. We told him about places we'd been, places where we'd been lost. He'd hauled goods to all of them. We had a fascinating hour.

We bid farewell and got back on the road, heading for Vannes, then south onto Presqu'île de Rhuys, below the

Morbihan Gulf. Our campsite was close to the village of La Saline.

I had no worries about language here. This was a big site, with "English spoken". I tried, as always, though, to speak French. The receptionist was either a non-English speaker and my French had become fabulous, full of dazzling wit and subtlety, or she was very polite and humoured me, allowing me to stumble along while she smiled and nodded without understanding a word of what I was saying.

We were allowed to select our own pitch, one with its own tap and, I was relieved to see, its own drainage grid. And that was that. We had arrived. Minimum fuss. No drama. Not very entertaining, from a story-telling perspective. The site was quiet. There were more than two hundred pitches, but only a dozen or so were occupied, and all of them by Brits. I wondered what had happened to the locals.

It was early afternoon, so we got the bikes off the back of the car and went for a cycle. There are miles of cycle paths on the peninsula, and even in those places where we had to use the road, the traffic was minimal to zero. All the cafes and bars were closed. We reached the beach and it was empty. No life at all. This was beyond quiet; it had the aura of death about it. The weather, too. What was all that about? We'd come a long way south and felt chilled. We needed our coats. Our spirits began to sag a little. This was not what we expected. On another day we'd have been delighted by quiet beaches, but we'd come a long way for good weather and a European holiday, and this felt like… well, like Southport and the Lancashire coast. Don't get me wrong. There's nothing overly unpleasant about Southport. But it's only a forty-minute drive from home. We'd come a bit further. Brittany just didn't seem special enough.

Back at the campsite we treated ourselves to a pizza in the site restaurant. A very good pizza, but we were the only guests. I'm uncomfortable in empty restaurants. It makes conversation awkward. The restaurant manager came over.

"You enjoy the pizza?"

"Yes. Thank you."

"This is off season, so things are closed. The pool, the shop, the clubhouse. But tonight, England playing Sweden, *le Coupe du Monde*, yes? I tell other English campers. Tonight I will open the club and you watch football on television, yes?"

So there was the answer. Off season. The French don't do holidays in June, and that's why everywhere was deserted. We felt we ought to go and watch the match since they were opening the club just for us, so we had a surreal evening sitting in a bar in Brittany, occupied exclusively by English caravanners, watching our home team playing Sweden in the World Cup in Germany, with French commentary.

A draw, by the way. Two all. It summed up our initial feelings about Brittany. Neither good nor bad, just… a draw.

THE NEXT FEW days were better. The sun appeared. We cycled everywhere, exploring all the quiet little villages, noting how all the houses were shuttered up for the winter. By the third day the sun was strong. Sarah fell off her bike and skinned her knee, and a very nice French lady who'd been trimming her hedge rushed out of the garden to help, and bathe the wound. Later, Sarah realised the sun was stronger than she thought. She'd been cycling in shorts and her legs went bright scarlet. She spent the night howling and rubbing in Savlon.

We were going through a gradual shift in Brittany. The holiday began with mild disappointment, but slowly the Frenchness began to cast a spell. We began to feel less like we were on holiday and more like we lived here. People spoke to us. They spoke in French and didn't seem to mind our stumbling responses at all. We noticed how, in restaurants, other diners would shout *bon appétit* and raise a glass, with a smile, just as we were about to eat. I loved that. One day we were on a bench about to eat a sandwich when a couple of young boys, no more than ten or eleven years old, cycled past and shouted *bon appétit*. My instinct almost prompted me to shout back a retort, like *up yours, too*, except I realised what they'd said and that they'd been sincere. They meant it. They'd seen us eating and wished us a good meal. Back home, ten-year-olds on bikes were more likely to shout *eff off* and cycle away guffawing at their own delightful wit. This was so different. We began to feel welcomed, with genuine warmth, into a community. It was a most uncommon feeling. The Breton's natural tendency seemed to be inclusion, to wrap their arms around us in friendship, no matter who we were. I felt a tingling inside, a sense of belonging, and it was good.

～

WE HAD a day out in the car. Our fourth day at Presqu'île de Rhuys, and it was the first time we'd felt moved to drive anywhere other than the supermarket.

I'd seen pictures of Josselin and the chateaux that stands high above the Oust Valley. Of all images this was the one that had most prompted us to try Brittany as our destination for a confidence-building return to Europe. The pointed medieval turrets were the stuff of fantasy and legend, and so unlike our own dour and forbidding castles. We wanted to see it first-hand.

It took under an hour to drive, and I quite enjoyed the chance of motoring through France without the 'van on the back. Now we could go wrong as many times as we liked, and doing so would be discovery rather than disaster. We didn't go wrong though. We found a car park in Josselin, strolled into town and fell in love with the place.

There was more to Josselin than the chateau. The old medieval buildings, the cobbled square, the flowers on the bridge. But also, yes, the chateau.

Looking from the river, the chateau rose high above the road, with three circular towers capped by circular pointed roofs. There was another tower, standing alone behind the castle. The main towers were joined by walls topped by battlements, with a pitched roof and six tall and elegant gable windows. Josselin was, in every way, a fairytale castle.

To enter the chateau, we approached from the rear, through typically French-style ornate gardens, and the whole character of the building changed, because the courtyard was set much higher up the castle walls, so from behind, the walls were only half as tall as from the river side, and nothing like as imposing. From this vantage point the chateau looked more like a home. It was a home – the Rohan family had lived in it for centuries.

We booked a tour, and were taken around the castle by a lovely guide whose English was perfect, and yet this session was the first time she'd ever done the tour in English, and she admitted to being a little nervous about it. We didn't notice. There were about eight or ten in our party and our guide had a way of involving us all and making every detail fascinating.

We spent another hour or so exploring Josselin, then back to the car and headed for Carnac.

I wanted to see the "alignments".

The standing stones in Carnac, the menhirs, are arranged in alignments, long straight rows of evenly spaced stones. Ten thousand of them. Why? Who knows? They are believed to have been erected around 3000 BC. They are not that big, not by Stonehenge standards, but still, they're big enough. You'd need a crane to move one. And yes, there are over ten thousand.

We took a land train that drove around the various groups of alignments and they were astounding. What on Earth compelled the people of Neolithic Brittany to gather ten thousand humongous rocks and line them all up? There must have been a good reason because it looked like a lot of hard work.

One of the popular ideas is that they were assembled over a long period of time, and that families would erect a stone to honour their ancestors. I suppose it was a little like the modern tradition of couples declaring their undying love for each other by attaching padlocks to various bridges. Just as modern padlock salesmen do very well out of the activity, there was probably a brisk local trade in big rocks at the time. You can just see the rock sellers calling out to tourists. "Buy your ten-ton rock here! Best deal in Carnac! Black Friday specials, delivery charges not included!"

Carnac had a nice beach too. I also fancied a drive down the Quiberon Peninsula that sticks out about eight miles into the sea, but it was more of a "because it looks good on the map" sort of a whim, so we drove back to the campsite instead. There was more to see. We had a list and the Quiberon Peninsula was further down than other attractions.

High on our list was a tour of the Morbihan Gulf, the vast inland sea that is peppered with islands and is tidally connected to the ocean via a narrow channel at Port Navalo. All the tour-boat options were pricey, though, and we were enjoying the simple pleasure of cycling; we'd never known such excellent traffic-free routes. On one day we cycled over thirty-five miles and found a chateau at Suscinio that was marked on the map as being a ruin, but turned out to be one of the best castles we've ever seen, with a full moat and everything.

But as our week passed by, and our enthusiasm for the area grew, we felt it would be wrong to leave the Morbihan without seeing the main attraction, so we cycled into Port Navalo and caught a Novix tour boat around the gulf, always expecting it to be a bit of a let-down. Something to moan about.

The Gulf of Morbihan has about forty islands, many of which cease to be islands at low tide because all the water drains out. Two of the larger islands can be visited and these were included on our tour.

The boat took us first to the town of Vannes, but only to pick up more passengers. Then we returned to the gulf and were taken to our first island, Isle d'Arze, where we had about three hours to explore. It felt remote and peaceful walking around the island, which is about two miles in length and has a single village in the centre. Then we boarded a different tour boat for another sail around the little islands, then to the larger, Isle aux Moins. We had an hour and a half to visit this one. Again, remote, peaceful… an island.

Here's the thing about visiting islands, though: You are told when to be back at the harbour. You try to explore in a random, easy-going fashion but you're always aware that you have to get back. You set a time limit. You do not want to spend the night here having missed your boat. I'm sure we'd be fine, benighted on such a lovely island. I'm sure there'd be accommodation and places to eat. I'm also sure you'd have to pay for it, and a night on idyllic peaceful islands such as these would not come cheap. In short, we did not want to be left behind. So, on both islands we reached a point in our explorations where we felt we ought to head back. The walk back would be in a straight line, not meandering loops with stops to see interesting things, so for both island visits we found ourselves back at the harbour long before the boat was due to collect us. An hour early on Isle d'Arze and half an hour on Isle aux Moins. It's a long time to wait for a boat, but not long enough to go back and explore something else.

So when the boat came at last, we were done. Eight hours. Brilliant value for money. But done. We wanted to return to Port Navalo, not go on another tour of the gulf. Maybe we'd have been more engaged if our French had been better. We tried to follow the commentary. I picked up *à gauche* and *à droite*. In fact, I had these words drilled into my skull, because each time the commentary said *à gauche*, every head swivelled left with unquestioned obedience. Likewise for *à droite* when heads turned right. They were the only words I understood. Had my French deteriorated or was my brain ill-tuned to the heavy Breton accent? Whatever, I couldn't follow the commentary. It must have been fascinating because the others in the tour, the French tourists, hung onto every word, transfixed. I know that some of the islands in the Morbihan Gulf are owned by famous celebrities, and which ones and by whom would have been interesting trivia to learn about, if that's what was in the commentary. But we'll never know.

The tour cost us the equivalent of about thirty pounds for the two of us, and it was excellent value for a full eight-hour day and three boats. But by the end we were exhausted. Happy but knackered. It was about five miles to cycle back to the caravan site, not far, but it felt a long way.

∾

WE WERE sad to leave the Morbihan, but the time had come to return to Roscoff. The plan was good. We would spend the second week of our holiday close to the ferry terminal, so that, on our final day, we wouldn't have any stress from driving to catch the one sailing per day. It's all very well having a long drive to Calais, because ferries sail every hour. If you miss one you drop back a sailing. If you're early, they'll often push you forward. But one per day from Roscoff was something not to be messed with, so we chose to eliminate the risk. It worked. Our return was stress free. But before then we had a week in northern Brittany to look forward to.

Our route back involved retracing our steps, or nearly. This time we took the proper route. Sarah used the map. My laptop stayed in the boot of the car. We headed for a site near Plougoulm, a gorgeous location overlooking a river estuary, the Anse du Guillec. Our pitch was in an open field, all on our own. We set up the caravan then headed off to do a food shop at an E.Leclerc.

This was the biggest supermarket I'd ever seen. The parking had a canopy to shade the cars so they wouldn't get too hot from the sun. Isn't that a thoughtful touch? Inside we were boggle eyed at the array of goods on offer, like cycle hats for nine euros. We'd just paid close on forty quid for ours back home. In a centre aisle a stack of boxed wine bottles stood, and seemed very popular with the locals.

"These are a good price," I said.

"Are they? How much would they cost at home?" said Sarah.

"I've no idea."

"Then how do you know they're a good price?"

"Because all wine is a good price in France."

"Doesn't sound like a very good argument for these bottles in particular." She had a point.

"But look at the other shoppers. Loading their trolleys. The French know wine. They seem attentive to these bottles. They know a good bargain."

"How do you know the other shoppers are French? They could be gullible British tourists like you, drawn to a shiny pile of goodies," said Sarah. But she said it with a smile. We were the only Brits in the shop.

"If you think they're a good wine, then buy them," she said. "I'm not bothered; I don't drink; I won't be drinking them. You can keep them with the bottles you bought in Joinville, six years ago."

"Yeah, those bottles weren't so good," I said.

"And these are? You know this?"

"I don't know. It's just… a hunch."

I lifted a box into the trolley. I admit, I know nothing of wine. Sarah doesn't drink at all, wine or anything, so when it came to consuming the stuff I'd be on my own. And she was right. I still had bottles of the stuff left over from Joinville, lying in a corner of the garage with a covering of dust that made them look like expensive wine bottles rather than unloved and abandoned wine bottles. Was *this* wine a bargain? Was it a better quality? I had no idea.

We continued our tour of the shop: chocolate bars, DIY equipment, clothing. It was nothing like Asda, Morrison's, Sainsbury's or Tesco. We were fascinated, again, by the words on the labels, the mystery of what lay behind those labels. *Vive la différence.*

In fact, we were so engrossed in our study of all the wonders and special offers and prices, that the shop closed, and a polite young man asked us to make our way to the checkout before we'd had a chance to buy any food. All we had in our basket was the box of wine bottles, a bag of lentils, a chocolate bar and yesterday's *Le Monde*. I always like to buy a French newspaper in France and pretend to myself that I can read it.

We were the last car in the car park. Our first night in Plougoulm, we dined on lentil stew and chocolate.

WHEN WE ARRIVED in Roscoff on the ferry, a week earlier, we were suffering from a combination of panic, drive-on-the-right disorientation, and sleep deprivation, so we managed to drive right through without seeing either Roscoff or its near neighbour Saint-Pol-du-Léon. We decided to rectify this and drove into Roscoff. The most distinctive feature of the town, that could be seen from all over, was the bell tower of the church, Notre Dame de Croaz-Batz. Very gothic. Lots of columns and arches, and the bells, which hung not in the tower, but out in the open.

The sea front included an old harbour, and from the harbour wall there was a concrete pier, l'Estacade, from where the ferry could be caught, which sailed to the island Île de Batz. It was a long pier, and neither of us can resist walking to the end of a pier. About halfway along we were tempted to think we might be walking all the way out to the island itself and that the ferry had become redundant. Looking behind us, Roscoff seemed tiny and partly obscured by the horizon.

A nearby attraction, around the headland from Roscoff town and on the other side of the ferry terminal was a botanic garden, the Jardin Exotique. This was just like stepping into South Africa or Australia. All the plants were from tropical Southern Hemisphere locations, and all kept outdoors. We had a hot day with clear blue skies when we visited and it seemed strange to be visiting another country, France, while feeling as though we were visiting another continent.

This characterised our entire stay in northern Brittany. We pottered around, sometimes on foot, sometimes on our bikes. There were things we'd never seen, like zillion-acre artichoke fields, and one-per-day tides that denied us a decent view of the sea, because the tide only ever came in at night. I couldn't figure out how this worked at all. We were only on the other side of the English Channel and yet the laws of nature were different. Other things defied understanding, too. One day we'd been riding our bikes in the heat and decided to stop for lunch at a cafe. It was closed for lunch. The owner was coming out of the door as we passed.

"Excusez-moi, monsieur. A quelle heures le café est ouvert?"

"Non. Fermé. Demain, peut-être."

"What did he say?" said Sarah.

"I think he said he might be open tomorrow."

"I thought that's what I heard. Might be? Doesn't he know?"

"I don't think he's bothered," I said. I watched as he jumped onto a clapped-out old bike and tottered up the road, weaving from side to side.

The only other place we thought we might find food nearby was a dusty little shop called *8 à Huit*, a little further up the road.

"That means eight till eight doesn't it?" said Sarah.

I nodded and watched as the shopkeeper closed the front door and twisted the little card sign round from *ouvert* to *fermé*. I looked at my watch. It was twelve thirty.

"Maybe it means eight at night until eight in the morning," I said.

We went without lunch that day and made sure to bring sandwiches from then on.

But for all the quaint reluctance to serve food at mealtimes, we loved this part of France. Again, like in the Morbihan, the people were friendly and relaxed with us. They treated us like their own, not like tourists. This was demonstrated in abundance midway through our holiday when I had a hankering to do something a bit mad.

"Let's go to the pictures," I said.

"Why?"

"I don't know. It'll be fun."

"We don't speak French," said Sarah. "It's not like there'll be subtitles or anything. We'll be clueless."

"Oh, I don't know. We've picked a bit up here and there."

"Unless the film is all about ordering croissants and

coffee – and it'll be boring if it is – I suspect we might struggle," she said.

"I suppose."

"But you're right. It does sound fun. Quirky. I think we should try it."

We'd been into Saint-Pol-de-Léon a few times and found it to be a charming and friendly little town. It had a cinema, in Place Michel Colombe, next door to a hearing-aid shop. The Cinéma Majestic. This was no multiplex. There was an arch leading into a small courtyard called Centre Michel Colombe, and beside a low stone building, not unlike a stable, was the tiniest cinema. I didn't expect much. With only one screen, they provided variety by showing different films on different nights. That night's offering was a children's cartoon called *Cars*. We'd seen *The Da Vinci Code*, the next night's film, and even though the thought of watching Tom Hanks running around the Louvre, speaking American French that had been subtitled into American English and then dubbed back into voice-over French held a certain appeal for its manic complexity alone, it was still not what I was looking for. But the third night offered a French film called *Quatre Étoiles*. This looked promising. It starred José Garcia, Isabelle Carré and François Cluzet, none of whom I'd ever heard of, but they had the right kind of names. I was choosing a film using the same kind of criteria I used for choosing wine. We vowed to return in three days.

In the meantime we cycled around the artichoke fields, visited chateaus, paddled in the sea and fell ever deeper in love with Brittany and its people. Three days were enough. Three days allowed our excitement to build to a peak. We were going to the cinema, and we were going to do it just like French people do it. No subtitles. No fake actors' voices. No safety net. Any more of this and I'd be wearing a beret and singing La Marseillaise.

We dressed up. At least as near as we could get to dressing up in a caravan, by making the best of the clothes we hadn't worn yet. If I'd had a gig, I could have worn my tux and dicky bow, but then I'd have probably ended up collecting tickets at the door. But I found a shirt that looked okay, at least it had a collar, and Sarah found a dress she'd brought just in case we did something posh, and we drove into night-time Saint-Pol-du-Léon, parked the car in a cobbled square and went to the cinema.

It was good we'd made an effort. Others arrived in long dresses and the men wore ties. To the *cinema!*

I asked for *"Deux billets, s'il vous plaît"* at a little ticket kiosk reminiscent of cinemas from my childhood, from when going to the cinema was an event, rather than just having the sort of ticket price that made it feel like it *should* be an event.

The man in the kiosk made pleasant small talk, unaware that I had exhausted my French after the *s'il vous plaît.* Why should he think otherwise? We were coming to watch a French film. We must have *some* knowledge of his language. I didn't want to rob him of the illusion, because then he'd have just thought we were nuts, so I smiled and nodded in what seemed like the right places and said *bon* and *oui* a few times and I seemed to have passed the test. He handed me the tickets, and we moved down to a curtained doorway, less than three yards along from the kiosk where a lady in a ballgown collected our tickets. This seemed like chronic over-manning to me, but perhaps they saved costs by having the lady pass our tickets back to the kiosk for the kiosk man to sell to the next customers, thereby operating the entire cinema with only two tickets, recycled time and again. It didn't matter. I thought it was lovely. Personal. I felt like a guest.

The lady in the ballgown engaged us in small talk, and once more we bluffed and blagged, and smiled and nodded our way past and into the cinema. She must have been impressed. I bet there aren't too many English tourists who know enough French to visit their cinema.

Now, in years gone by, in Wallasey, the town where Sarah and I once lived, there were a couple of small cinemas not unlike this one, at least from the outside. They were small establishments and they ran on a shoestring. Shoestrings were important, or at least shoe *laces*, because upon entering you had to make sure your shoes were well fastened or you might walk out of them once the sticky carpet took hold. They called these places flea pits, but that was unfair because they never had fleas. Fleas preferred to live in the coats of mangy stray dogs rather than risk the seats in our local cinema. These were seats with less knee room than a Mercury space capsule, and the springs would offer so little resistance you often found yourself suspended with your buttocks just three inches above the carpet, strug-gling to see over the back of the seat in front.

The Cinéma Majestic was not like that at all. For one thing it was much bigger than I expected. The carpet was red and so deep you wanted to kick your shoes off and run your toes through it. The curtains were of rich, red velvet, with tasteful purple uplighting that added class and a touch of opulence. Then the seats, oh the seats! Deep armchairs, with room to stretch. Plush red upholstery. My goodness, this was how a cinema should look. A beautiful cinema.

The other unexpected aspect came from the other customers. As we walked down the aisle, they turned in their seats to watch us approach, then smiled and nodded and whispered a respectful *bonsoir*. Let me stress, this wasn't just one or two customers. There were about twenty already seated, and every single one of them greeted us as we entered. We nodded back, mirrored their greetings and took our seats. When new customers entered we all, ourselves now included, went through the same polite and remarkable routine.

"What?" Sarah asked.

"Mmm?" I said.

"You're smiling. Beaming. What is it?"

"This place," I said. "I love this cinema. The seats, the staff… the people."

"I know. It's amazing," said Sarah.

"I don't know about you. I don't care how the film turns out. I'm going to enjoy it because… well, all this." I indicated around me. "It's brilliant."

The lights dimmed. The curtains opened. The film started.

And it scared the bejesus out of us.

It wasn't the main feature. It took us a while to latch on to this fact. They were showing a B-movie first. The way it used to be in the good old days. You'd get a B-movie, then a break for ice cream, then a news reel, maybe even a cartoon before kid's films, and then, when you were good and ready and receptive to anything, they'd roll the main feature. That was how it used to be in the sixties. That was how it *should* be. And that was how it was in 2006 Saint-Pol-du-Léon. Fabulous. Except the B-movie, as I said, was some surreal avant-garde freak of cinematic weirdness, full of dark figures in raincoats wearing goggles and gas masks and doing unspeakable things, to a brutal music soundtrack that would make Karlheinz Stockhausen scratch his head. It lasted for about twenty minutes. We watched with our mouths open and our eyes agog. I can't tell you what it was about, just… weird and dark!

The main film was better. The locations in the south of France, mainly Cannes, were gorgeous and colourful, and more than once I found my mind wandering and thinking how that place, Cannes, was just a drive of a few hundred miles south of where we were sitting at that moment. Driving to Cannes would be like, well, driving from home to Brighton. Okay, a bit further, but it made you think.

Anyway, back to the film. The story line was just about decipherable from the occasional key words we managed to translate. There were things that were, well, culturally different. It seemed acceptable at one point for the male lead to break the female lead's arm and yet not appear to suffer too much loss of sympathy for his actions. He lost it from us, we thought he was a total bastard, but then maybe we weren't exactly picking up all the nuances.

The film seemed to have an upbeat ending, though I couldn't tell you what happened. Everyone else in the audience seemed to enjoy it, so we absorbed all the satisfaction from them, and left the theatre laughing along with everyone else. We all parted as lifelong friends, wishing each other *bonne nuit*.

In some ways it was better than watching a film in English. A lot of the films I've seen lately have been shallow, with plots as thin as wet newspaper, have zero subtext, and are good for about forty seconds of post-movie analysis. This one had us talking all the way home then on and off for most of the next day as we tried to unwrap, interpret and understand what we had seen. It was an experience, and a worthy means of bringing our Brittany holiday to a close.

We'd managed our first foreign excursion as a couple. We'd hardly thought about the children – no more than once or twice a day.

The next morning we packed, hitched up, then drove the short twenty-minute route to the ferry terminal for a seven-hour daytime crossing aboard the *Pont-Aven*. No cabin this time. We left before lunch and arrived in Plymouth early on Sunday evening, having dined aboard the ship, just like being on a cruise but without the stage shows, or Ernest Borgnine and Shelley Winters.

Driving from the ferry into Plymouth, it might have been tempting to think we'd arrived home. Not so. It was Sunday evening. I had to be back at work on Monday morning, and we had that small matter of a three-hundred-mile night-time drive along roads with cars, cones, road closures, diversions and boredom, before getting to our beds.

And it took over an hour and a half just to get out of Plymouth Dock.

"Passports?"

She could have said please.

"Do you have any illegal immigrants in your caravan? Have you checked in the caravan toilet?"

"In the *toilet*? No, I emptied it before we left."

The customs officer fixed me with a hard glare while she decided if she should arrest me for being flippant.

"Okay, but I need to look," she said.

I showed her. She was thorough. Methodical. She even looked in the overhead lockers.

Sigh!

The drive home was worse than I expected. Returning to work after two hours' sleep was horrible.

But it was all worth it.

Brittany: I hinted at the significance of this trip at the start of the book because yes, it was a milestone. A key event. Well, we'd done it. Success.

So what next?

2007/2008: TWO YEARS IN THE RAIN

Electric cars. Oh, I could turn out a whole book about electric cars, so let's skip the bit about people in tower blocks having to drape three-hundred-foot extension leads out of their windows or the trip hazards along terraced streets, and turn instead to the fact that we once had perfectly good electric vehicles: milk floats. Whatever happened to electric milk floats? And before milk floats, we had something even more ecological: horse-drawn carts. For fuel they ran on grass, and much of the time, a century before Google cars, they operated as driverless autonomous vehicles. The milkman walked down the road whistling a happy tune while the cart followed at just the right pace, stopping and starting whenever necessary. Exhaust emissions? Okay, there were some, but put them on your roses and you wouldn't have to spend a fortune down at the garden centre on Sunday afternoons.

These days our milk comes in diesel vans.

We call it progress.

—No. 107 from the Moanicles of Michael.

"Y ou remember that film we saw in Brittany?"

"Quatre Étoiles?"

"Yeah. Remember Cannes? It looked lovely."

I was working up to my punchline. Coming at it from sideways.

"We could do Cannes. South of France. In the caravan." Okay, so I abandoned the oblique approach as soon as my excitement got the better of me.

I pressed on. "We've never been to the South of France."

"For a reason," said Sarah.

"What reason?"

"It's too far."

"No, no, it's doable."

"You're only allowed two weeks' holiday."

"Ah, but! I have an itinerary. A plan."

I showed Sarah my plan. It was hard. A grueller. Three hundred miles per day. More. But possible.

Sarah looked at it. "We spend every day on the road," she said.

"Not every day."

"No. But nearly. Two weeks. Four days on the Riviera. The rest in the car. No."

"I can stretch my days. If I include a bank holiday, pinch a couple of extra days at the start… I'm sure I could swing it."

"It's not only that," said Sarah. "What would a trip like that do to the car? Your plan's a brute. The poor car needs sympathy and tenderness. She's fifteen years old. She's in her 'ageing gracefully' period."

I shook my head. "Okay, and, well, she's twenty-two, actually. She was fifteen years old when we bought her, seven years ago." I said this with the conviction in my voice falling, all the enthusiasm leaking out. I'd lost, I knew. Because Sarah was right. You don't take a twenty-two-year-old car one thousand miles, over mountains, through forty-degree temperatures, all the way to the South of France and not expect to become acquainted with mechanics and garage owners. We hadn't avoided a car-repair business in the last seven or eight years of holidaying, and we hadn't been further than Cornwall. Oh, wait…

"What about Chamonix?" I said, before thinking it through.

"What *about* Chamonix?" said Sarah.

"Well, the Alps were more than halfway down to—"

"And we lost the exhaust in Belgium on the way back."

"Oh, yeah." I'd forgotten. And then there'd been Brittany, a motoring triumph, except for needing to find a Halfords in Plymouth before even boarding the ferry, to buy something important to make the brakes work.

"When we get a newer car, we'll go to the South of France," said Sarah.

She was right. Our car had allowed age to creep up on her. I couldn't offer a compelling argument that made sense. Was that the death knell for Milan, too? We'd often spoken about Milan, not as a destination but as a metaphor for the next big Adventure: South of France, Austria, Italy. Because we both knew we'd never be able to afford a car reliable enough for that kind of trip. Not this year, anyway, because we had another matter to deal with this year.

"Look," said Sarah. "The car's on her last legs now.

She'll struggle to get through the MOT next time or the year after. So after that, when we start looking for another car, why don't we up our budget a bit? Maybe we can find something more reliable."

"I suppose." I was unconvinced. When we bought cars, we bought them for hundreds, not thousands, of pounds, and the only difference between a five-hundred-pound car and a nine-hundred-pound car, apart from four hundred quid, was that when it broke down, there was more to cry about.

"There's nothing wrong with having our holidays in Britain," said Sarah. "If the weather's good we're fine. And there are so many places we still haven't seen."

She was right again. We'd travelled all over Britain and I now felt a sense of loss whenever I noted a place, in a book or magazine or on TV, that we hadn't visited before. There were towns to see. Cities, countryside, coastlines, mountains. But then what about that other thing she'd said, too. *If the weather is good.*

But even there our jinx was expunged. We'd had a long run of horrible weather, and this had played a large part in driving us south of the Channel. But in recent years our weather luck had turned. We'd had some good holidays. We'd spotted a big, round, yellow thing hanging in the sky, a thing I'd come to believe only existed in foreign parts. I allowed my enthusiasm to show. I'm good at rationalising when I set my mind to it.

In 2007, though, our travels were on hold. Our daughter Amanda was getting married at Easter.

The build-up to the wedding was as hectic as wedding plans can be. Sarah took it all in her stride by compiling lists, filling her Filofax, and assuming calm control while everyone else slid into panic mode. I did as I was told and wrote cheques and flashed the plastic because I found this was by far the best way for the Father of the Bride to remain on speaking terms with the rest of the family. A week before the wedding it snowed. This was apparently of some significance because, as I was often reminded, the bride and bridesmaids would all be wearing off-the-shoulder dresses. But then the snow cleared, the sun came out and we enjoyed the first bright, sunny, and warm Easter for years. This was clearly a sign that the Wood family weather jinx was broken.

It is normal to admit to a wedding being a stressful and terrible ordeal for the father. But this wasn't the case. I enjoyed it all. Amanda looked gorgeous. So too did Sarah. Our new son-in-law, Jules, told us he had plans to take Amanda camping. We already liked him but on learning this piece of news he gained maximum points on the approval rating.

The ceremony went off without a hitch. The reception was a triumph. I occasionally play weddings in the two big bands I belong to, so it was a proud moment for me when I could, for once, invite one of those bands to play for my daughter's wedding, and I even got a chance myself to play on some of the numbers.

The house felt empty afterwards. Irrational, because both Amanda and Kevin had moved out some months earlier, and we'd done our Brittany holiday alone so we knew all about operating as a twosome. This emptiness felt different though. There was a permanence about it. How could we fix it? How could we heal the gap that had opened up in our lives?

We needed a caravan holiday.

But first the car needed an MOT. It failed. Oh my, did it fail. It failed bad.

"How much?" I asked the mechanic.

He laughed. "Oh, it's not a matter of how much," he said. "Cheaper to buy a new car."

"What? Really?"

"Oh, yes."

We'd had that conversation about buying a better car. Buying a reliable car. A car that might take us to the Riviera.

But we'd just paid for a wedding.

So we bought a cheap car. A very cheap car. It was brown and it had a full MOT. The MOT bit was all that mattered.

"If we can just coax a year out of her," I said. "One year. Then we'll see where we are."

I had a good idea I knew where we'd be. Mired in the old crap-car cycle.

Around about this time I had an interesting turn of fortune in my writing ambitions. I'd been writing for years. I sent stories off to science fiction magazines and had given up counting the rejections that came back. I didn't mind the rejections. Sometimes the editors said encouraging things that suggested they had read beyond paragraph one, and I was cheered by this. It is always good when someone reads what you have written. I preferred it when they took a long time to reject stories because then I could dream for a little longer. On rare occasions though, I got emails that said they *liked* the story and they would publish it, and I would do a little happy dance. I'd had a couple of minor science fiction sales this way, and once I even sold a *travel* story to the Camping and Caravanning Magazine for which payment came in the form of a gas barbecue. I was delighted, even though we were vegetarians, and the only thing we ever managed to do to vegetables, on a barbecue, was set fire to them.

On this day I found an email in my inbox with a subject line that said, "Congratulations!" and this was normally a reason to delete the email, because emails with "Congratulations" in the header usually involve a Nigerian prince and a request for bank account details in exchange for untold wealth. But I didn't delete it, I read it. I'd entered a writing competition, weeks earlier, the Jim Baen Memorial competition. The congratulations were genuine, from Bill Ledbetter, the contest administrator. I had won the contest. First place. I did more than a happy dance. The prize was good. Publication in a *professional* market, *Jim Baen's Universe*. There was a trophy. They also gave me a full year's membership to the NSS, the National Space Society, and... the prize was to be presented at the International Space Development Conference. I checked online and found out all about the International Space Development Conference. I looked at the guest list. It was filled with rocket scientists and names I knew, like Buzz Aldrin. And I had

been invited to attend as a guest, my convention membership already paid. I would meet these luminaries of space
exploration. I would chat to them. I would get the tee shirt.
The tee shirt, in fact, had already been reserved for me,
they just needed to know my size. I was amazed and
stunned and starry-eyed. Part of the pack that arrived in
the post soon after included copies of the *Ad Astra* magazine
that I would get for free for a year, and in the *Ad Astra* was a
write-up about the ISDC 2007 describing all the things I
would see, and even a section talking about how the winner
of the Jim Baen Memorial contest would be presented his
prize. That person was me. All I had to do was get
myself to…

Dallas.

In three weeks.

Ah.

There were problems, not least of which was the day
job, and accounting month-end. The date coincided with
Spring bank holiday week, a week I'd never been allowed to
take off work, despite trying. As an accountant I was tied to
the accounting calendar and it was not negotiable. I could
have any other week off, but not *that* week. I'd wanted it for
the week-long holiday site in Rhayader. I'd wanted it for the
full Hay Festival week. But no. No exceptions. Not for the
Hay Festival and not for a trip to Dallas to collect a trophy
and meet the second man on the moon.

Oh and the other problems: I'd never been on a plane. I
didn't have a US visa – didn't even know if I needed one.
We'd just paid for a wedding, and then, with the rag end of
the money we had left over, we'd bought a car.

I googled the cost of flights. I looked at the cost of hotels near the convention centre. I shed a tear.

"You could go on your own," said Sarah. "It's not so much for just one."

"I don't want to go alone."

"Why not? You've been away alone before."

"That was for work. One night in Leicester. And Dallas is further than Leicester. Anyway, what's the point in getting presented a prize when *you're* not there to see it? I'd hate that."

It was a moot point, anyway. Day job. And I couldn't afford the trip even for me alone. Even if I rowed a boat across the Atlantic and hitch-hiked my way to Dallas. Because I wouldn't be able to afford the boat. Or the oars.

So, three weeks later, instead of going to Dallas, we took our new brown car to Hay-on-Wye, to the Hay Festival — the weekend, not the week. And as we passed though Builth Wells the sun went out. The clouds became portentous. The sky darkened. The first drops of rain, big drops, struck the roof of the car, then apocalypse, as though a giant had upended a bucket the size of the North Sea, right onto our car.

I looked at my watch as we aquaplaned onto the site.

"I suppose they'll be awarding the prize right about now," I said. "There'll be an empty seat between Buzz and Bill."

Sarah reached over and squeezed my hand. All the words had been said. We'd done what we always did. We'd rationalised. *Dallas would have been too hot. We'd have hated the heat.*

"It'll happen again," said Sarah. "You'll win another contest in America. Next time we'll go."

I shrugged. I'm a realist. I knew all about my past success rate. Another contest? Yeah, wishful thinking on a grand scale, like winning two lotteries in a row. I put it out of my mind. I tried to repress the image of Buzz Aldrin shaking my hand. I tried not to think about all the panels and lectures by rocket scientists. What was wrong with me? We were in *Hay*. Clever people came to Hay. Academics, writers, agents, publishers. I would become clever by just being here. I would become clever through osmosis.

The campsite was just as we remembered it from the previous year. Wet. I didn't mind the rain. I didn't mind the crappy campsite we'd vowed never to revisit. I didn't mind sloshing about the muddy field in my trainers because I'd forgotten to pack the wellies. Because I loved Hay last year and it *would* be just as good this time. I felt the excitement. I worked hard at my mental health and somehow managed to lock the images of Dallas in a box, and set them aside.

I took a breath and moved on.

Before I could empty the car I had to take down the bikes from the cycle carrier. Yes, we'd brought bikes with us. So much better to cycle into the town than to drive and pay for parking. So much greener, too. Gaia, Mother Earth, would love me for it. I can say here and now, though, that the bikes never turned a wheel; you can't carry an umbrella on a bike. But Gaia remained safe. We walked.

We walked to our first Friday evening event. A forty-minute hike. The umbrellas failed. Most of the rain came through. The rain that didn't come through bounced off the road and came up at us from the tarmac. We'd chosen to take a more circuitous route to the festival site, one that took us along quiet lanes away from the speeding, spray-blinded traffic. The few cars that did pass threw up lesser plumes of spray, but succeeded, with help from the developing gale-force winds, to reduce our umbrellas to mere wire frames and fabric.

Our shoes squelched. Our waterproofs… weren't.

We sat inside the marquee, shivering, while the rain thundered down on the roof. We could hear the wind getting stronger. The aluminium support frames creaked and groaned in an effort to keep it all together. Canvas flapped. We tried to listen to the discussion against the cacophony of wind and rain, but became increasingly distracted by the cold. Our clothes remained wet. Evening temperatures dropped, and we squirmed in the cold, hard, unforgiving plastic seats. The wind began to reach inside the tent, and inside our clothes.

We had hot chocolate in one of the festival coffee bars afterwards. The drinks went cold before we'd even carried them back to our seats.

We returned to the caravan. An epic walk. Forty minutes in driving rain, probing wind and sodden wet clothes. And it was full dark, too. No moon. The only thing that warned us off wandering into the deep roadside gullies was the playful sound of all the water, gurgling and frothing down there.

Now you might think we were hating this. You might think we'd be saying things like "stuff it" and "never again" or even "we should have gone to Dallas". But no, this was Hay. This shared sense of adversity, of university types thrown into a mixing pot filled with mud, was what it was all about. We loved it. We also loved having a caravan with a gas heater, above which we could hang all our wet clothes while coaxing warmth into bodies with dangerously lowered core temperatures. We talked. We'd heard a fascinating panel discussion and we were buzzing. We talked until late while the rain hammered down on the roof. We talked in the cosy warm cocoon of our caravan, with the duvet pulled up under our chins. We talked until our throats hurt and not once did we mention Dallas.

In the morning we had breakfast, pulled on clothes that had dried stiff overnight, and set out into the rain for more. We did it again the next day, too, realising the value in no longer having umbrellas, because we needed both hands to carry the heavy bags full of secondhand books.

We drove home from Hay-on-Wye, content and happy. Perhaps now and again I lapsed into contemplative silence while I drove. I tried not to let it show.

Alas, though, we'd set a pattern for the year.

It rained in Pembrokeshire. It rained in Cheshire. It rained in Yorkshire.

IT IS SAID that the Inuit have fifty words for snow. I guess they know snow. Well, by the following year, Easter 2008, I had acquired a similar vocabulary for rain. I'd seen a lot of it. In fact, as Sarah and I ventured out onto each successive outing in the caravan we came to sample pretty much every imaginable variant of rain. We had rain on every single holiday, short break, weekend and the occasional night away. A whole year. Rain.

So to anyone who knows a thing or two about weather patterns, Scotland might seem to have been something of an unwise choice for an Easter holiday. I blame the milkman. He'd been to Culzean Castle.

"You really should go," he said. "We had gorgeous weather up there. It's a lovely site and not as far as you'd think."

We went along with his recommendation. And hey, he was right about the second thing, Culzean Castle *is* a lovely site. But the first part, about the gorgeous weather? Well, bully for him. And the distance? Oh, he lied. Culzean Castle is a hell of a journey, especially for just a short Easter weekend. In a blizzard. Or three blizzards if you count them as separate events between the five-minute respites.

We set off early on Good Friday, in clear, bright, hurricane conditions, and that didn't help. No, we hadn't planned on an early, stupid o'clock start, but the hurricane roared throughout Thursday night and what with the sound of bins blowing down the road and fence panels ripping free and flying, and things breaking, sleep became... elusive. So at five AM, in total darkness and with total bad tempers, we crawled out of bed.

Our Avondale caravan was designed to be slippery. She had a streamlined low profile shape to help her slice through the air. But in the face of a seventy-miles-per-hour northerly, the aerodynamics didn't seem to work so well. It felt as though we were towing a three-masted schooner under full sail, head to the wind. But who's to know without the benefit of comparison? If we'd been travelling north in the old Sprite, we might well have ended our journey in Brighton.

It wasn't so bad at first as we headed east. Just a tendency to swap lanes with an unexpected snap now and again. But as soon as we hit the M6 and pointed north it was like rounding Cape Horn. We became engaged in a bitter duel with nature. We jigged and turned and tacked and slowed. With my foot hard down on the accelerator I couldn't maintain fourth gear for more than a few seconds at a time. Over and again I had to change down to third, sometimes even second to keep the revs up. My speed dropped. Now and again, with a bit of downhill to help, we started to motor, and I'd whoop for joy each time we attained forty miles per hour. Then we'd reach the bottom and have to crawl up the other side. If I'd managed to catch the slipstream of a truck now and again it would have helped, but those few trucks on the road – it was an Easter holiday – were being blown onto the verges on their sides, so it felt safer keeping away from them.

I stopped at every service station for fuel. Tears of wind chill, and frustration, and escalating poverty came to my eyes each time I pumped gallons more into the tank. At this rate the journey would use more fuel than a road trip to Gdańsk.

We stopped for a late lunch in Tebay, Westmorland services. It had taken us *hours* to get this far and we were still in England. A stop at Tebay should have been one of the treats on a trip to Scotland. It's without doubt the best services on the whole motorway network. Tebay isn't just acceptable, it is a pleasure to visit. The food in the restaurant is excellent. The surroundings are wonderful. The ceiling is supported by pillars of rustic drystone walling. There are expansive views from the windows. There's even a little stream running through the restaurant, with a stone bridge to cross to the other side. Why is this? Why is Tebay so good? I'm not suggesting Tebay is a *bit* better than other service areas. The comparison is like a Mercedes S-class vs a used Lada. All the other motorway services, at least all the ones I've visited, and that's a lot, are horrible. They are not places where you can relax, they are places where you go to weep.

We had lunch. Very nice. Didn't enjoy it. The luncheon experience was spoiled by concerns over lengthening journey time. I jollied Sarah along, urging her to eat faster, shepherding her back out to the car before we'd finished. It was as though I *wanted* to get back outside into the elements. I felt the imperative of reaching Scotland before dark.

The M6 is exposed at Westmorland. The full wrath of the wind came unimpeded across Shap Fell and scoured the shine off our paintwork. Progress became slower.

I always feel, going north, that the journey is uphill. It's psychological, and to do with the way we print all our maps with north at the top. This felt far more than psychological though. Britain had tilted and Scotland lay at the top of a very steep slope. We refuelled, *again*, at Penrith and continued on towards Carlisle, and then at last, Scotland. We bade farewell to the M6 soon after Gretna Green and angled northwest towards Dumfries where the wind dropped to only gale force. I allowed hope to find a place in my heart.

That's when we drove into the blizzard.

There is something hypnotic about driving into falling snow. The flakes form white lines and become a tunnel to infinity, and your eyes are drawn to a perspective vanishing point. I found myself having to blink and slap myself across the face to stay awake. It wasn't heavy snow and it wasn't sticking, but that was the only good news. Time marched on. The A76. Thornhill. Mennock, just a bridge over a wee burn – see that? Wee burn? I'm thinking like a Scotsman. The English me would have thought "babbling brook" or "bit of a stream". The Scots me also thought, "Bloody hell, only half a tank, and och, look at the price of the petrol up here. Are they noo having a sale?"

Now we passed through Sanquhar, a row of low single-storey cottages built squat and low to resist the wind, and with big chimneys to shift all the smoke that came from when they had to burn a ton of peat to keep warm.

Tea time came and went. No time to stop. No time to eat. We had to reach our campsite before eight, because at eight came the stigma of "late arrivals".

The late-arrivals park is a caravan park for undesirables; the underclasses who can't get themselves to a site at the proper time; the reprobates who have to be segregated until next morning so they don't disturb the "good" campers. I didn't want to be a late arrival. I didn't want to be one of the naughty campers, and sleep in the car park, and drag water for miles, and have to go through the whole process of pitching, sleeping, unpitching and driving two hundred yards onto the site the next morning, all for the same price. We only had three days. I didn't want to waste one of them micro-touring.

Through Maybole. Dark now. Nothing to see. Closed. Desolate empty streets, frost-glistening streets. Nobody about. Then beyond the town onto more empty roads.

Nearly eight o'clock. Five to.

And then we were there. Culzean Castle Campsite.

We clambered out of the car, stiff and hungry and... *Hell's teeth it is cold.* Easter in Scotland. No need to bring sun block.

The site managers booked us in and showed us to our pitch. This next part is the bit where I always want to relax and unwind but can't because there is work to do. We have each evolved our roles. We know them and we set about our tasks without discussion. Sarah does things inside the 'van. I get the water.

Getting water involves standing beside a tap for fifteen minutes while the Aquaroll fills, getting a feel for the local scenery and the local climate. In this case there was no local scenery, it was dark. And the local climate was passing straight through the weave of my woolly hat without impediment, making my brain go numb. When I'd finished I lurched into the caravan and dropped onto a bunk, hoping to recover feeling in my feet, and not to have to lose a toe.

SATURDAY DAWNED, and we got our first proper look at where we'd be staying for the next couple of days. Andy the milkman had not sold us short. From our caravan window we could see right across the Firth of Clyde to the mountains of Arran. They were white. The sea was a shimmering slate grey. The clouds were puffy and stuffed brimful of new snow. Yes, Andy the milkman, it was a beautiful view, but one best seen from indoors. We had showers. The Aquaroll ran dry. On cue the clouds emptied their load of snow, which fell sideways.

Cabin fever set in after an hour or so. I didn't fancy the walk to the castle before acclimatising to the arctic, so we decided to take the brown car for a drive to Ayr. Besides, there was something I wanted to see. The road from Culzean Castle to Ayr crosses Electric Brae.

Electric Brae is a hill on the A719. It is an uphill section where, if you stop and take the brakes off, your car will roll up the hill. Who could resist such a thing?

It is a phenomenon known as a gravity hill. An optical illusion. There are others elsewhere in the world, but Electric Brae is the most famous. During the war, Eisenhower – *the* Eisenhower, Dwight D – had an apartment near the castle, and would bring visiting guests to the Brae to experience the magic.

I drove. We took it slow, looking for a heavy stone marker at the side of the road. There used to be metal signs but people kept stealing them. A couple of times we stopped beside a rock, but each time it was just a rock. I even tried taking the brakes off at one such rock, because we were clearly on a hill, but the car rolled backwards, down the hill.

At last we found the right rock, a stone marker with clear instructions as to what to do. It's an ordinary road that comes out from some trees and goes up an ordinary hill. I stopped the car. Looked over at Sarah, who just wasn't getting it. I had my boyish grin in full-on mode because I knew we were about to see something extraordinary. I rubbed my hands together.

"Right, watch this," I said.

"What's going to happen?" said Sarah.

"Just wait and see. Magic."

"Go on then."

I switched off the engine.

"You see the hill?"

"Yes."

"You see how I turned the engine off."

"Yes." Actually, she sighed at this point. I don't think I had the timing right in my magician's patter. I was foreshadowing, trying to build anticipation.

"Well, watch as I release the handbrake."

I released the handbrake with a flourish.

Nothing happened.

"Well?"

"We're meant to roll up the hill."

"Why?"

"It's Electric Brae. It's famous."

"Okay. But we're not moving."

"I'll give the car a push."

"Doesn't that defeat the object?"

"To get it started, that's all."

I jumped out and pushed the car. It moved forward, up the hill, and stopped. It was bloody cold outside so I jumped back in.

"So?" Sarah was clearly unimpressed.

"Did you see it roll? Up."

"I saw you push it. Up."

"It's meant to roll."

"Are we done? Can we go now?"

I felt crushed. Electric Brae had been high on my to-do list. Maybe I needed a better car, one with less rust, that rolled more freely. Or maybe I needed to come on a day when there wasn't a fifty mph headwind.

I drove on towards Ayr in a mood that I liked to think was reflective, but others might have interpreted as a sulk. At least we could have a towny visit in Ayr.

Ayr was closed.

I exaggerate. Not closed but… battened down. In defensive trim. Wintering. On the face of it, Ayr seemed an agreeable enough town, except there was nothing much to see except big old grey houses. There was a dour grey river with a grey concrete harbour wall that blended seamlessly with the grey sky. There may have been colour and signs of ornamentation elsewhere in the town had we been brave enough to clamber out of the car for more than a few minutes at a time, but from what we could see, Ayr was grey. So we drove back to the campsite. We drove back over Electric Brae, and I felt a moment of inspiration.

"Maybe we did it the wrong way," I said. "Maybe we should have been going in this direction."

So we tried it again and it still didn't work, so I sulked again and we went back to the caravan for a sandwich and I felt better.

In the afternoon we made a decision. We put on layers.

We dressed in pretty much every item of clothing we possessed, and we set out, walking like teddy bears, to see the castle.

It isn't a long walk, but setting out in the cold wind felt like an act of bravery, or insanity. One of those. There is a long approach down an avenue of trees and this leads to a courtyard with information and a coffee shop. We were late in the afternoon so the coffee shop was closing. We saw that they had what looked like rather good scones, so we promised ourselves we'd treat ourselves when we came back the next day. We knew we'd be back; we'd seen the castle and knew we'd need a full day to explore. For now we clambered down to the stony beach and admired the fortifications, standing high above us on imposing cliffs, a wonderful sight.

There were lumps of ice floating in the sea and it triggered a mental image. I'd been reading about Shackleton's South Pole expedition, and from our position on the grey beach, looking across towards the rugged, snow-covered peaks on Arran, feeling the pellets of frozen sea water driven in on the wind and watching how the waves moved with that slow, lazy, state-shifting swell, it wasn't hard to imagine ourselves on the shores of Bear Island, after a meal of whale blubber or penguin. The word bleak became overused, but we continued to use it again and again for want of a better one.

≈

NEXT DAY the sun came out. The wind dropped, the clouds became fluffy islands in a sky of blue, and with a little imagination we could envisage ourselves heading out wearing only a vest, a tee shirt, a single jumper, a fleece and a Gore-Tex jacket for protection. Oh, and the hats and gloves. We tried it. We survived.

We went back to Culzean Castle and explored. By lunchtime we were each carrying a jacket, a fleece and a jumper, with hats and gloves stuffed into our pockets. All around us visitors emerged from their cars wearing only tee shirts and shorts, as if they'd known in advance.

It was a long walk to the castle so we headed first to the coffee shop where we'd seen those rather excellent scones the previous day. We found a table and waited with mounting anticipation for our turn to be served.

"Sorry, we're out of scones."

We had tea and some sort of speciality biscuit that had all the flavour and consistency of a tongue depressor. The castle was fantastic though. It kept us occupied for the whole day. The gardens were lovely, and probably amazing in the summer, and we walked for miles around the country park.

Our brief return to Scotland, though, was over. I'm looking at the caravan diary that I keep wherever we go, and cannot understand why we took a full week's holiday, drove all the way up into Scotland, then only stayed for three days before driving back down to Keswick. What were we thinking? I haven't written down our reasoning, and the plan seems just a bit loony. But we have done our fair share of loony things over the years, and maybe on this occasion our reasoning was sound. Whatever, we drove halfway home and spent the rest of the holiday at a site we'd been to many times before.

The first thing we did after siting the caravan was walk into Keswick and head straight to Main Street. We'd been stiffed out of our scone in Culzean so we set this right in Bryson's tea rooms.

Bryson's is special. There's a fabulous bakery on the ground floor, and upstairs, if you're lucky enough to get a table, there is a tea room. It has a Victorian feel. There are potted palms and chandeliers and service comes from ladies in black dresses with little white aprons. If there were room for a palm court orchestra, I'm sure they'd provide one. Sarah had a conventional scone while I had a date and treacle scone. It sounded fabulous, and yes, it tasted okay, but was half the size of Sarah's. So I had to watch her savour every last crumb while I felt I was still owed half of my special treat.

Another special treat I was looking forward to in Keswick, was going to a play in the Theatre by the Lake. I'd booked tickets in advance. The idea of walking from our caravan along the shores of Derwent Water to have a night at the theatre appealed to me. And the thought of returning in the dark, cutting through Crow Park with the waves lapping on the beach and sparkling in the moonlight, seemed all very magical. We'd done it before, a few years earlier, and we desired an encore.

My enthusiasm, though, was tempered with a smattering of caution. We'd been having an unfortunate run of stupidity with some of our live theatre excursions. Over the past few years

we'd developed a love for the theatre and had been to productions at Theatre Clwyd, near Mold, with increasing regularity,
and that was fine. But then there'd been our half-Misérables
experience in London, but that wasn't my fault. Not like Guys
and Dolls. I'd bought tickets for the Liverpool Empire, the
previous January. I booked online. I was fast. I didn't hang
about. Click, click, click. I liked to do my online transactions
with speed, mainly because Sarah is slow and methodical, and
it always gets me agitated watching every line being read and
checked. So I was, I suppose, showing off. Anyway, we got the
tickets, got ourselves all gussied up, and drove to Liverpool. We
got to the theatre at around seven and the ticket collector took
our tickets, shook his head and looked sorrowful.

"These were for the matinee performance, this afternoon. I'm sorry."

"No, that's not right, I—"

He showed me the tickets, underlining the performance
time with his thumb, and gave that sad little smile again.

"Can we change them?"

Of course not. The evening performance was a sell-out.
I'd been looking forward to it. Guys and Dolls was one of
many shows I'd wanted to see from the audience. I've played
for it in orchestra pits a couple of times, and that's all very
well but you don't get to see the musical numbers, apart
from the bits where you have a few bars' rest.

We came away feeling foolish and deprived of theatre
once more.

So you understand, I'd become a bit antsy about theatre
trips.

"Let's just check the tickets again, hey?"

Sarah reached them out of her purse.

"It does say evening?" I asked.

"Seven-thirty start. We're good."

We left the 'van and headed out for an evening of culture. The weather hadn't been too good of late, so our walk across Crow Park was precarious, lots of mud and some low-friction spots that threatened to send unwary theatregoers skiing into the lake, but we did that part without mishap.

The mishap occurred inside the theatre foyer.

"I'm sorry, those tickets were for last night's performance," said the usher.

"No," I said. "They're for tonight, Wednesday. I checked." There was a stroppy edge to my voice.

"Tonight is Thursday," said the usher.

"Thursday? No it's not. It's…" I stood for a while, blinking and flapping my jaw while I reran the film reel of our week in my head. Friday, went to Scotland. Saturday, the grey place, Ayr. Sunday, the castle, didn't have scones. Monday, came to Keswick, had a Bryson's scone. Tuesday, tried to walk, rained, another scone. Then… Wednesday. Oh. Rain. Yesterday was Wednesday. We did the laundry. So today is…

"Sorry," I said, with a rictus smile. We turned and tried to blend in with the mingling theatre set.

"We've done it again," said Sarah.

"*I've* done it again," I said. "I'm an idiot. A buffoon. A pillock."

"You're not an idiot," said Sarah. "Let's try the box office."

There were no more tickets. I didn't mention why I was asking. I pretended to be an impulse buyer.

"Do you have any for tomorrow night?" I asked.

"Yes, we have some."

"Two, please."

Back in the foyer, Sarah was laughing. "You realise that makes it more expensive than a London theatre night?" she said.

I grimaced with the pain of it. The expense. The shame. The stupidity.

Kevin rang us the next day.

"How was the theatre?" He was interested. Since leaving school he'd turned a work experience job into a full time job working for a theatre supplies company, and in his spare time he was a lighting technician for the Gladstone Theatre, a local enterprise run by volunteers who staged professional-standard productions. Kevin was into theatre in a big way. He wanted all the details.

"It's not until tonight," I said.

"Says Wednesday on the wall calendar," said Kevin.

"Really? Must be a mistake."

"Check the tickets," he said. He still remembered my last mistake.

"I will," I said.

We chatted and I handed him over to Sarah. They chatted. At one point I heard her say, "Yes, I know, Dad's going to check them."

"Check the tickets again," said Sarah after she'd hung

up. "Make sure they're not for the afternoon, or a week Friday, or…"

I didn't argue. I checked the tickets. Three times.

"On the bright side," I said. "We'll get to do the magical walk back from the theatre to the caravan through Crow Park with the waves lapping on the beach and sparkling in the moonlight."

"True," said Sarah.

Not true. Outside, it was raining. The kind of rain you photograph and share with your friends for the shock value.

I should mention, for the sake of completeness, that we did see the play the next night. It was called Our Country's Good. It was excellent. We didn't get the moonlight walk though. The photogenic rain that started Wednesday evening was still falling.

We commented on it on Friday morning, over breakfast.

"Still raining."

"Yeah."

"What shall we do today?"

"Can't go walking."

"Nah."

We turned to the leaflets. That thing you do on holiday – pick up all the leaflets in tourist information offices for all the attractions you can't afford to visit, then stash them in the caravan. They only ever do leaflets for the things you have to pay to go in. Economics. Here's a strange thing, though. There's always a leaflet for Wookey Hole. Doesn't matter where you are in the country, they always have a Wookey Hole leaflet, even though it's down in Wells, south of Bristol. They probably had one in the

Tourist Information in Ayr, in Scotland, but I'm just guessing; we didn't go inside because that would have meant getting out of the car and stepping into the ice wind without a survival suit.

Anyway, we didn't plan on driving six hundred miles for a round trip to Wookey Hole – we also have a basic understanding of economics – so I picked up the leaflet for Rheged instead. For some odd reason, Rheged was free. I'd thrown money at our theatre problem. I didn't want to throw money at anything else. It seems they built Rheged because it rains in the Lake District now and again.

On the face of it, Rheged was good. It was undercover. It had one of those turf roofs that had become fashionable amongst corduroy-trousered ecologicals. There were shops with the kind of stock that looked good in the display cabinets but you'd never think to *buy* any of it. There was an IMAX cinema so we watched the film about climbing Everest. We'd seen it before; it's a good watch, and there's something about high-definition images showing life in the death zone that puts a few days of Lakeland rain into perspective. I'd noticed in our leaflet, too, that the National Mountaineering Exhibition was here, the film was part of it. That sounded good. We followed the signs but the exhibition was closed. No explanations. It looked as though it was closed forever.

"Let's have something to eat," I said. "It will pass the time."

There was a stylish restaurant in Rheged, the kind with three wine glasses at every place-setting and a veritable armoury of cutlery, so we knew long before taking a cursory glance at the menu prices that eating here was never going to happen.

We drove to Penrith and had omelette and chips in Morrisons' supermarket cafe. Don't get me wrong, I'm not knocking it. We enjoyed our lunch probably more than we would have enjoyed the exclusive dining in Rheged. We eat in a lot of supermarket cafes. The food's good, someone else does the dishes, and there's no angst over tipping. What's there to dislike?

We walked in the rain in the afternoon, up to the waterfall, Aira Force, near Ullswater. We walked about a mile and a half. With all the rain, the waterfall was spectacular, but... a mile and a half. That's all the walking we'd done in the Lake District in five days since getting here. It felt wrong. I wanted to go up into the mountains, but that would have been folly. So we did what motor-tourists do. We drove to something and walked a mile and a half. It made me feel shallow and unsatisfied. Then after tea, that's when we went for our double-priced theatre evening, so at least I got some culture.

THIS IS BEGINNING to read like *Blade Runner* (the film) in that it seems to be raining a lot. If I give that impression, it's because yes, it rained a lot. We had a weekend in Bethesda, right in the heart of Snowdonia, in an effort to do some mountain walking. The forecast was good. Sunny. But it rained. It started the moment we arrived, it kept us out of the mountains, but it turned out the rain wasn't all bad news. Sarah wanted to paint. More and more she'd been concentrating on flowers rather than landscapes. There's a National Trust property near Bethesda – Penrhyn Castle and gardens, and so she wrapped her paintbox in a plastic bag and we caught the bus from Bethesda village which stops right outside the castle. It's a good walk through the grounds from the bus stop, though, and we'd dressed for a stately home visit rather than for mountaineering, so by the time we reached the gardens our shoes were squelching and the water had percolated upwards to reach the knees of our jeans.

"Sorry, babe. A bit wet for painting," I said. "We can look around the castle, though."

"You go and look around the castle," said Sarah. "Try out the tea room. I've come here to paint. A bit of rain's not going to stop me."

I'd have felt guilty inside, wrapped around a warm cup of coffee, knowing she was sitting outside in a monsoon, so I followed her over the hill and down into the garden. She took out her watercolours – *watercolours!* – and perched beside a bush. There were no flowers, they'd been beaten off the stems by the deluge and turned to mulch, so she painted the wet leaves. I held the umbrella. I didn't argue. She had that look of steel that I'd come to know well. When the wind came I held the umbrella with two hands, not over the two of us but over the paper. She painted for an hour.

A watercolour takes longer than an hour. In Sarah's case, the detailed ones can take twenty or thirty, but she managed a wet leaf with all the detail, then took some photographs so she could finish later.

"Let's go to the cafe," she said. We had soup. And cake, too.

You'd have thought this exercise of bloody mindedness would have been futile, Sarah thumbing her nose at the elements and nothing more. In fact it was a turning point. That was the day Sarah discovered a style that she has honed and developed and stayed with to this day. She finished the painting and on its first hanging, sold it. There was something about the dark and the wet leaves and the stray shafts of occasional sunshine that lit it all up. That was a significant day, and there have been many more like it since. Painting in the rain has become her thing.

We had a few sunny weekends, but in each case life got in the way and we had to stay home. On one such sunny weekend we turned traitor and stayed in a hotel, with a pool and a gym and a flushing toilet.

Here's my excuse. We went to London to see the Osmonds. Yes, *those* Osmonds, the ones who smile a lot. They were playing a farewell concert at Wembley Arena and my way of accumulating a *massive* brownie-point balance was to surprise Sarah by booking tickets. We'd seen Donny Osmond in Merthyr Tydfil the previous year, the first time Sarah had seen her girlhood idol live, and she'd enjoyed it so much, even after standing in a field in Wales in torrential rain for eleven hours, that I knew she'd want to see the whole band on their last tour together. I'll admit to this, too. I enjoyed it myself, even though I was pretty much the only male in the whole of Wembley Arena, not counting the six up onstage. Imagine it, me and twelve thousand purple-clad, screaming, fifty-something-year-old teenyboppers. A surreal night. And as I say, we stayed in a posh hotel so the rain wouldn't spoil it. And the sun shone all the time.

The Hay Festival was looming and the May sunshine had given us hope. We had a desperate yearning to visit Hay-on-Wye in dry weather. All the photographs in the brochure showed happy visitors reclining on deckchairs under blue skies, reading books and smiling. Were these just clever artists' impressions, mashed together on Photoshop? No. They *must* have had sunshine once. So was it us? Had we jinxed it? Would someone find out and ban us from attending?

Despite the Wembley sunshine we upgraded our water-proof clothing. We bought Gore-Tex. We bought over-trousers. We decided to reverse-engineer the weather processes and challenge Fate, head on. If we bought all this wet-weather clothing, if we left the shorts and tee shirts at home, then surely, *surely* the contrary actions of Fate would intervene and we'd have blistering, end-to-end sunshine. And if not, well, we were at least prepared.

The Hay Festival would be so much better this year, too, for another reason. I would not be distracted by the anguish about that missed trip to America. A year had passed since that disappointment and time is a great healer.

We set an alarm for an early start.

The phone rang before the alarm.

It was six in the morning and nobody rings at six in the morning. Not unless someone's ill, or has died, so straight away I was flustered and on edge.

Sarah answered. "Hello? Yes?" She looked over at me. "Yes, he's here."

She passed me the phone with a quizzical expression.

"For you. An American lady."

I mouthed *who?* She shrugged.

"Hello?"

"Hi, Mike? Mike Wood? I have some really good news for you."

I didn't reply straight away. My brain was trying to dust away the cobwebs of six-in-the-morning torpor, while at the same time throwing all the possible scenarios into the mix: What good news? She didn't sound like a Nigerian prince, and I didn't know any Americans, so what new phone-based scam was this? Actually I did know an American: Mimi, she's married to Sarah's cousin, but we both knew Mimi's voice. Could it be someone who knew Mimi? Why would they ask for me?

All of this thinking takes time and I realised I'd been holding the phone in silence for too long. Sarah, too, was mouthing *what?* and spreading her hands and shaking her head. I was getting more confused.

"Hello? Hello, Mike? Are you still there?"

"Oh, sorry, yes. Still here. Who's this?"

"This is Joni, from Writers of the Future. Wait for it, Mike... *You're a finalist in this quarter's competition.*" She sounded very excited. I got the impression she wanted me to be excited too. I must have been a disappointment to her because I didn't say anything. I was trying to work out if this was something I *ought* to get excited about, and why. I knew about Writers of the Future, or at least a little bit, like the mailing address. It was a market that I had on my list of places to send science fiction stories. I didn't know much else. I had about a dozen short stories out in the slush piles of various magazines and anthologies at the time, just waiting to be converted into rejections and sent back. This didn't sound like a rejection. But *finalist* didn't sound like an acceptance, either. What I couldn't get my head around was why someone was making the effort to phone me, all the way from America.

"That sounds good," I said, with hesitancy and a heavy ladling of caution in my voice. I was still waiting to be asked for money.

"It *is* good," said Joni. "There are only twelve finalists. I loved your story and I'm rooting for it."

"That's great," I said. I had no idea which story she was talking about, so anything I said about it had to be concealed in generic references. "I, er… I enjoyed writing it."

"How do you pronounce the story name?" she said.

Right, so much for generic ambiguity. I supposed I'd better come clean.

"Er… remind me. Which story did I send you?"

I felt the disappointment coming through the phone, undiminished by ten thousand miles and a barnacle-encrusted trans-Atlantic cable.

"It's just, it's early here. I haven't woken up yet. Still processing this… news."

"Of course, yes. Your story was Risqueman. Is that Reesk-man, or is it, Risqué-man?"

"Oh, right. It's pronounced Risk-man," I said. I remembered that story. I wrote most of it in the caravan in South Wales, the previous summer, while it rained, so most of the setting is around Swansea and Cardiff, and in the first draft there was rain. I took the rain out later when it got me depressed. I sent the story to Writers of the Future because it turned out to be a long short story, and they were one of the few markets that would consider that length.

"Have you been entering the competition for long? Do you enter every quarter? You must be really excited."

"Well, this is the first time I've—"

"Really? First time? That's awesome. You know, some people enter stories every quarter, four times a year, year after year, and long to get even an honourable mention."

"I didn't know that."

"Oh yes. So, Mike, is there anything you want to ask?"

I always hate being asked if there's anything I want to ask, because I usually say, "No, that's alright," then remember all the things I wished I'd asked about five minutes later. Clearly there was a whole heap of things I needed to ask in this case because I knew nothing. What did she mean, *finalist*? When would I move from *finalist* to whatever happened after *finalist*? Was publication or money involved? I needed to ask these questions in a way that gave the impression of knowing something. That I wasn't some naïve out-of-towner. Which I was.

"What happens next, then?" I was proud of this question. It was a catch-all place-marker that permitted the chance that I knew all about the competition – and in truth I'd only learned it *was* a competition in the last thirty seconds, as against a regular anthology market. Joni went on to explain how a panel of judges would choose three winners from the twelve finalists, and she'd let me know the outcome in the next few weeks. All this time I'd been allowing my excitement to build, because the tone of Joni's voice suggested this was a thing of great magnitude, and I really should be excited. But then, with those words, *three winners*, it all collapsed in the way that a week-old saggy party balloon goes into a farting kind of decline when you pop it. Three winners out of twelve. That was that, then.

I kept up an act, trying to sound upbeat, while Joni went through the good wishes and goodbyes, then hung up the phone.

"Well, what was that all about?" said Sarah.

"Just a story market. Not a sale or anything. Might win some competition, but I'm twelfth, and there are only three winners, so…"

"It was a long phone call just to tell you that you hadn't won a competition."

"I'm not out of it yet. Just… probably."

"What's the prize?"

"Don't know. Publication, I suppose."

"They wouldn't ring you if you had zero chance."

"I don't know. Anyway, focus. Hay Festival. We need to shower, get packed, and go."

I tried to build up the excitement again. I'd been dragged from sleep, pumped up to delirious, high-pressure bursting point. Deflated. Now it was time to build the excitement again. But ups and downs are hard. In my mind was the question: So what is Writers of the Future? I couldn't resist. While Sarah was in the shower I googled it.

It takes about three-and-a-half hours to drive to Hay-on-Wye. We'd done the journey a few times, so we knew what to expect. We knew where the traffic congestion hot-spots lay in wait. We reached our first after an hour and began to crawl. We'd already discussed the panels and events that we'd booked to see, and we'd talked about the weather, that was still dry. So we lapsed into silence for about ten minutes until Sarah brought up the thing we'd been thinking about for the last hour or so.

"What did you find out about Writers of the Future?"

"Hmm?"

"Come on. You've googled it. I know you have."

"Okay, well, the story gets published in a book and... you have to go for a couple of days to do a workshop."

"Couple of days?"

"Hmm, a week, actually."

"Where?"

"Los Angeles."

This led to another silence.

"Sounds expensive."

"Not so much. They pay. At least, they pay for me. We'd have to pay for you, but that's only one ticket."

"So we'd go to California?"

"Yep."

And the conversation moved along like this. Cagey. Nonchalant. As though it was no big deal. Apart from the fact of maybe winning what was clearly a massive writing prize – and meeting mega-star sci-fi writers, and being in Hollywood – there were other factors. Sarah's cousin, Mal, and his wife, Mimi, whom I've already mentioned, lived in California. Visiting them would be a huge thing, a thing we'd both wanted to do without any hope of ever doing so, because, you know, *California*. It's a little further than Wales.

The questions came fast. The workshop was for one week; could we go for three weeks? Could we drive from LA to San Francisco where her cousin and his wife lived? Could we afford the extra ticket? Could we hire a car? What about hotels? More questions that I should have asked of Joni, and many more we needed to ask ourselves.

Except for the central problem: Twelve finalists. Three winners.

For the second year our Hay Festival became dominated by what-ifs. We tried not to do it. We tried so hard, because the more we built it up the greater would be the crash when the call or email came to destroy the dream. But we couldn't stop. Every panel had something to remind us. A writer from California. A film director from Hollywood. Someone talking about motivational psychology and saying how it was good to dream big. A debate about the US election.

On things Hay-related: I forgot to bring the bike lock away with us, so we worried about cycling to the festival in case someone nicked the bikes. On the Saturday, we walked into Hay-on-Wye, in bright sunshine, and bought a fancy new lock in a chandlers-that-has-everything, and on the walk back the rain started again. It became too wet to cycle, so we decided not to use the bikes until the weather cheered up again. The bikes stood rim-deep and rusting, in a puddle, lashed to the caravan with their new bike lock for the rest of the festival. The rain was extra special this year. The local fire brigade were brought in to pump water off the festival site as it threatened to overwhelm the whole event. We were okay. We had our Gore-Tex and our over-trousers. We wore heavy walking boots and socks to keep our feet warm and felt smug and properly equipped for a literary festival, unlike those in deck shoes, straw boaters, corduroys and canvas jackets. A few times I wondered what I'd wear in California. It doesn't rain there. But that brought to mind the certainty of the crushing disappointment to come, which I felt prepared me, mentally, for the inevitable phone call. I wished it would come soon. Better to get the crushing disappointment out of the way early.

2008: IT'S GRIM UP NORTH

~

I'm told by the light of my life that this is all getting a little dark, so enough with the moanicles and the negative posicles. In the interests of avoiding divorce I shall face the fate of UK roads and shambolic UK politics with a firm jaw, a stiff upper lip, shoulders back and a positive mental attitude. I can do it. I can fake it till I make it. Never again will you hear me uttering these words: It's all turning to crap.

At least, not in print.

~

"Oliver, come out of the water!"

"Oliver!"

I nudged Sarah and winked. People watching could be so rewarding at times. We tuned in again as the couple resumed their noisy and enigmatic conversation. Oliver continued his aquatic adventures, oblivious to the shouts from the man and woman who might be his parents.

"What's that?" said the man. "Is that Pinot Grigio you're drinking? Would you like another? Do you usually drink that?"

"Yeah, I'll have another," said the woman. "Thanks."

"I'm thinking of buying a different car. Not happy with the— *Oliver!* —with the Jag."

For an hour Sarah and I hadn't spoken to each other. We sipped our tea and coffee and listened, fascinated, to the loud conversation between Oliver's supposed parents. Now and again Oliver distracted us by venturing deeper into Coniston Water, fully dressed. The water had gone well over, and filled, his wellingtons. His jeans – some children's designer label, like Snot-Noze-Brat – were soaked to the waist. I wondered how they'd approach the upcoming problem of inserting Oliver into the father's Jag; even though he was unhappy with the car he'd probably care about the fate of his calf-hide seats. I mentioned this to Sarah.

She shook her head. "That's not his father. He's just a guy who's here with Oliver's mother. She has no claim to the Jag. She's more the BMW type."

"You're wrong," I said. "She can't be his mother. It's Jag-man who's doing all the shouting. She isn't even acknowledging the kid. Jag-man's divorced. Brought Oliver up to the Lakes for a weekend of father-son bonding, and met the woman here."

"Liz," said Sarah. "Her name's Liz. And Oliver called her Mum."

"No way."

"Yes way."

"When did that happen?"

"When he demanded ice cream."

"I missed that."

"So did Liz. She ignored him so he went back into the lake."

We watched and listened. Their voices, especially Jag-man's, had a klaxon-like quality that echoed off the Coniston fells.

We were sitting outside the Bluebird Café, right by the water's edge. It was August. We'd had a few weekend excursions in the months since Hay, but now we had embarked on our main summer holiday tour. Our Grand Tour of the North.

The cafe was the old, wooden Bluebird Café, before the flood and the rebuild. It was one of our favourite places then, the remodelled cafe still is now. A lovely place to relax and study the water and the mountains and Oliver and his parent(s). The cafe is integral to the story of Donald Campbell and the water speed records he set on Coniston back in the sixties, and ultimately the tragic accident that claimed his life in 1967, and there are photographs and memorabilia everywhere.

"You want another coffee?" said Sarah.

"Hmm. I'd better have a decaf. It's my third."

She stood. "Keep me posted."

A minute later. "Oliver still in the lake?"

"Yeah," I said. "Shirt's all wet now."

"Cool."

"Jag-man's just been telling Liz about his apartment in Spain."

"As if she doesn't know about it? That would mean he *is* Oliver's dad. He's not the dad. Can't be," said Sarah.

Oliver chose that moment to quit the lake and slosh up the beach.

"Daddy, I want an ice cream. Now!"

We both looked around for Daddy, left and right along

the shore. There was nobody else within earshot. Jag-man *was* the father. Liz *was* the mother.

"But they don't know each other," I said. "At all. He's been hitting on her with pickup lines all morning. He's done nothing but tell her how much money he has."

"And she doesn't care what Oliver's doing, not a jot."

"I'm still banking on Oliver going for full immersion," I said, as the boy stomped a foot and returned to the water. "That'll tell us. There's bound to be some reaction. I've put away three coffees waiting for the big reveal. Can't handle any more. Come on, Oliver, go for it."

"Don't be mean," said Sarah. "What if he drowns?"

"One of them will fish him out. I'm betting the one who goes in after him is the real Monday-to-Friday parent. They—"

Oliver chose that moment to do what I'd been willing him to do for over an hour. Right under, head and all. Marvellous. He came up all in a flap, bawling and coughing. Neither adult moved. Jag-man was in the middle of a monologue, listing the AIM shares he'd been buying lately to boost his portfolio. He'd been getting into a small group of ethical companies that promised strong returns. Without pausing in his monologue about share prices and financial instruments, he stood, strolled down to the water's edge, and beckoned Oliver to come out. He led the wet and wailing boy off to the car park. Liz, the one that Oliver had called Mum, didn't even watch them go. She sipped her Pinot Grigio with a look of contentment and peace as she took in the glorious lakeside panorama.

"Well?" said Sarah.

"Dunno," I said.

Oliver and Jag-man never returned. The relationship remains, to this day, one of the great Lakeland mysteries.

We spent three more days in the Lakes during which we stayed drier than Oliver, but not by much. The wettest day came when we moved on to our next destination of the Grand Tour. The Kielder Forest.

We queued to get onto the M6. We were going north, others were heading south, everyone was getting out, and choking the roads in their haste to do so. Sarah noticed water coming into the footwell every time I braked.

"There's a little waterfall down here. Whenever you slow down, water pours out from under the dashboard."

This didn't sound like good news; there was electricity under the dashboard. Fuses could blow. But I couldn't do anything. I wasn't stepping out of the car to investigate, that was for sure. We might have a waterfall in the footwell but there was worse outside. Sarah emptied her shoes and sat cross-legged to avoid further soaking.

"Is the carpet wet?" I said.

"Well, yeah. I suppose. I can't *see* the carpet, you know, under the water."

I couldn't look. The car windscreen had steamed up and I had the heater on full to try to clear it. This was August. We didn't enjoy having the heater running in August. The car felt like the tropical house at Kew.

The rain eased. We stopped in Westmorland services to mop out with towels. The rain turned to that fine, soaking mist, and we pressed on. We left the M6 and headed east.

I'm sure the countryside would have been lovely if we'd have been able to see it.

"HOW LONG ARE YOU STAYING?"

"We've booked for four nights," I said.

"Four nights? Well, you'll need to weaponise."

The warden at the Kielder caravan site had the demeanour of an army colonel, square jawed, with a grim, mirthless smile, and a fatalist respect for his enemy. He regarded us both as raw recruits from School for Softies. He gave a curt nod then turned to his shelves of supplies and began pulling boxes down and slamming them on the counter, piling them high. This didn't feel like arriving for a holiday. This felt like a visit to the quarter-master's store before a tour of duty on the front line.

"The midge, here in Kielder, is a special kind of enemy. Treat him with respect. Take all precautions or the little bastards will eat you alive."

I laughed but it was the wrong response.

"I'm serious. Do not go out after dark. Best to make sure you have all the water you need before 5 PM. If you stand by the tap for more than a few minutes in the evening, yon midge'll strip you down to bleached bones before you know it. We've had people hauled out of here in a state of anaphylactic shock. Tongues swelling, eyes goggling, wheezing, coughing. This is not a laughing matter."

I nodded, chastised.

"We have fly nets," said Sarah.

Colonel Death gave a barking laugh.

"Fly nets? These buggers'll get through your fly nets. They'll get through the rubber seals on your windows. They'll come in under the doors, through the roof lights, through the vents in the back of your fridge." He looked around, as though walls, or midges, might have ears. "But you can beat them," he said, in a conspiratorial voice.

"Do not go outside after dark, and keep your lights off in the caravan. No point advertising your presence. Windows closed tight, you hear? *Always* keep the door closed. And you'll be needing these…"

He gathered the products he'd placed on the counter into a taller pile, so just his eyes could be seen. Toxic candles. Carbolic soap. Exterminator plug-in repellant. As he listed each item, he took it from his pile and placed it in a new pile in front of us.

"Best of all," he said. "This one you won't find in the survival magazines, but it works…"

He smacked his last item down on the counter. His secret weapon. A pink, plastic bottle.

"Avon skin lotion."

Ha! Really? Is this what it's all about? He's plugging Avon products? Mind you, he was the meanest, toughest Avon Lady I'd ever seen.

"This is my secret. Has to be this brand. They hate it. Trust me, it works."

He sprayed some on his forearms, rubbed it in and sniffed. "It'll make you smell nice, too. I'd suggest a couple of bottles. You need it all over. Not just exposed skin."

He booked us onto the site and relieved us of a further twenty quid for all the biological warfare kit.

On the bright side, the rain had stopped.

We sat in the dark at three o'clock in the afternoon looking out of the caravan windows. The clouds were heavy and black. The surrounding evergreen forest dripped and slimed. There was an oppressive, soaking mist outside, cloaking the enemy's presence. I sang a chorus of "I'm H-A-P-P-Y," in the miserable Figgis voice, the theme tune from the sitcom, *Only When I Laugh*. We'd been using it as our holiday soundtrack for some years, but these days we saved it up for special circumstances.

"It's three o'clock," I said. "Two hours to curfew. Shall we go out and look around?"

"Do we have to?"

"We need to know what's out there."

We took a bottle of Avon skin lotion each and prepared for extravehicular activity.

Why had we come to Kielder Water? There had been several reasons. It was known for dark skies, so the star gazing at night was meant to be exceptional. I was beginning to forget what a starry sky looked like, and even wondered if I'd ever, truly, seen a real one. I hadn't expected dark skies at three in the afternoon, though, so I suspected someone hadn't read the script. This was also supposed to be a good area for cycling, there being a path around the lake, but so much was under water, and when I thought about that cold wet stripe down my back from un-mudguarded tyres, fine when I was in the mood for dirt and adventure, but I'll admit it just didn't do it for me here. Somehow I couldn't get in the mood. I liked the idea of peace and quiet, and in this at least, Kielder was delivering. Walking around the site and beyond, in the middle of August, I got the sense we were the only souls brave enough, or stupid enough, to venture outside.

Right, I don't want to spoil Kielder for others. I'm sure it's a beautiful place when the sun is shining and the sky is clear. I'm sure the dreaded midge would move on under such conditions and find a nice damp field full of tasty cattle. The miles of off-road cycling tracks would be a delight on a better day. But our minds were not open to this possibility. We saw no end to the damp and the gloom and the insects that were salivating for our blood. We went outside with closed minds. Nothing we saw would please us on this day. We walked over to a lakeside complex that was coffee shop/restaurant/bar/shop/ice rink, and were not at all surprised to learn that only the coffee shop part was open. We had coffee. In paper cups. Nothing special. Today we felt we needed "special" with knobs on.

Back at the caravan, Sarah went inside to prepare a cheerless evening meal – the shop had been closed, it being Sunday, and we were down to tomatoes and lentils – while I stayed outside to do the chores before the evening lockdown. I emptied the rubbish and waste water, and this proved very popular with the midges, who saw it as a fine appetiser before turning to the main course.

Said main course then set about filling the Aquarolls, and here the warden had been correct. Standing by the tap was bad, even with a good protective layer of Avon skin lotion. Perhaps it put some of them off, but enough midges had developed a tolerance to give me misery. I was surprised by the midge. I expected something robust and muscular. Something I could fight and swat with my Swiss-patented wasp swatter. Not so. These midges were microscopic, like dust. No wonder the fly screens were useless. They only became visible when they stuck to the lotion on my arms and accumulated in large enough numbers.

Inside the caravan the midges appeared to have the run of the place, passing in and out as though the walls were mere holographic light tricks.

"We're going to have to use the equipment," I said.

"I don't know, I'm not too happy about filling the caravan with poisonous fumes," said Sarah, while scratching at her arms, her shoulders, her scalp.

I already had the plug-in Exterminator out of the box, and I poured over the instructions while scratching my head hard enough to rake bald patches. There was a bottle of some liquid, I didn't want to read the small print. This fitted into a plug socket. We'd been sold two. The warden wanted us to buy three, but we explained we only had two power sockets, so he'd made a hissing noise while shaking his head, and sold us a couple of toxic candles as backup.

So this was our holiday. This was the only time on our tour that we'd have electrics, and we couldn't use them. We sat in darkness, trying to read by toxic candlelight. The weather might have been dull but it was still August and so very warm and humid, especially with the heat from the candle flames topping it up. The caravan smelt like a fume cupboard in a chemistry lab. We sweated and scratched and moaned a lot. I had my laptop, but with all the power sockets put to alternate use the battery died after only twenty minutes. I'd wanted to check my emails, because, although I tried to put it out of my mind, there was still that outstanding matter of California to resolve.

"I'm not going to hear anything now," I said, several times a day. "They wouldn't take so long. They'll have told the winners, I'm sure. Maybe someone tried to ring us at home while we've been away. If I'd won they'd have emailed."

But I couldn't check. The laptop lay on the table cold and dead.

In the back of my locker I found a sheet map of France. I unfolded it.

"What are you doing?" said Sarah. "Be careful of the candles."

I couldn't read it, anyway. Not in this light. My use of the map was symbolic.

"I'm thinking about next summer," I said. "We're not doing this again. I don't care if the car's old. I don't care about the money. I don't care how long we have to drive. Night and day."

"Sounds like a song coming on."

I shushed her. I had my Mr Serious expression all over my face.

"We're going to the sun. Next year. South of France."

Sarah moved to speak again but I cut her off. I wasn't in the mood for discouragement.

"This," I said, holding up my hands, waving them around, sniffing a good draught of poisonous gas. "This is not going to happen again. Enough's enough. Just think, we could be lying by the pool, sipping drinks with fruit on sticks. We could be swimming. We could be wearing shorts." I held up a finger. "One thing I swear. Next year we're going to the Riviera."

BUT NEXT YEAR was next year, and this year was still this year, and so the following morning, despite having paid for four nights' pitch fees and four nights' supply of biological weapons, we rose early, wound up the legs, and drove.

The Cheviots are a wilderness. There were gunnery ranges and red flags and moorland. It's beautiful moorland and I'm sure there are safe paths in amongst the live-round military zones, but this was not for us. Not this time. We headed for the Northumberland coast.

I'd been to Northumberland as a child and I remembered wide empty beaches and castles. My strongest memory of Northumberland was not related to the scenery though. It involved some friends of my parents with whom they had decided we should share our holiday. There was me and my brother, Andy; my mum and dad, and there was Jim and Irene and their daughter Diane and son Phillip, all of us in two large frame tents and several smaller pup tents in an arrangement that made our corner of the field look like a Bedouin camp.

Jim was a keen swimmer. Every morning he would take his swimming costume and towel and drive to one of the nearby beaches, five or six miles away, where he'd go for a long swim in the icy North Sea. We all found this to be a pretty impressive regime. He usually got back from his swim before most of us had climbed out of our sleeping bags.

On one morning, though, he was late returning. When after over an hour he still hadn't returned, the adults began to worry. I was still a child, so beyond worry, outside of meal times (not enough) and wash times (too many). But I picked up on the general atmosphere of potential tragedy. The campsite owner was told and the police and coastguard were called. There were gatherings of all the campers in the field, worried conferences and soon cars were heading out, up and down the coast, to check the nearby beaches.

Jim arrived back at the site an hour or so later, on foot, wearing only his towel and a sheepish expression. He'd apparently driven to his usual beach, stripped off behind the car and thrown his clothes into the car boot. He'd realised, just as he slammed the boot lid closed that his car keys were in the pocket of his trousers. His swimming trunks were still in the car. He'd had to walk back. Five miles, cross-country to hide his shame. A decent hike, naked apart from the towel and in bare feet.

The story didn't end there, because the keys were his only keys, and once dressed, the remaining drama of he and my dad searching for a mechanic willing to break into a parked car was not so exciting, at least to me. And that is pretty much all I remembered from my only childhood visit to Northumberland.

We headed towards a temporary campsite near Bamburgh Castle. There are usually roadside signs pointing the way to temporary sites, but on this occasion there were none. We turned in the road twice, not easy with a caravan, until on the third pass, using an Ordnance Survey map and the six-digit map reference that we should have used in the first place, we found the track where the site ought to have been. I chose not to drive down the track. Had I done so, this paragraph would have turned into a chapter all its own. We left the car and caravan behind and reconnoitred on foot. Fifty yards along the track, and already knee-deep in mud, we came to a long, steep, muddy descent to a field in a picturesque hollow, with a loose collection of caravans and motorhomes that are probably still buried to this day. The mud down there was insane. These vehicles were going nowhere. Now we understood why the road signs had been removed; they wouldn't be pleased to welcome another problem slithering down into their mud bath.

We debated talking to the stranded folk below, but it was hard to stand upright at it was. There's every reason to believe that the people down there, and any that joined them, would not even be able to walk out of the site. We returned to the car.

I muttered a few more things about the South of France, next year, but Sarah took me in hand and told me to focus. Right now we needed an alternative. Northumberland is a popular destination, and there were two other temporary sites we could try that year, so we drove to the next, at Beadnell Bay, with low expectations.

And here the drama came to an end. The site was muddy but flat. We were welcomed, we pitched, and the sun came out.

Northumberland. Beadnell Bay. A new love affair had begun. We walked into Seahouses, a couple of miles along the beach and over the headland. We noticed, entering the picturesque fishing village, a kind of embankment with twenty or thirty wooden benches filled with people. Was it some kind of ceremony? No, they were eating fish and chips. Seahouses has some of the best fish and chip shops and restaurants in the world, and they have the foresight to provide outdoor seating where a daily battle of wits is enacted between chip-eaters and seagulls. We chose to eat inside – we'd come second to seagulls before – and we picked a fish and chip establishment at random. Was it the best in Seahouses? Who knows, but we saw no reason to try the others because it's hard to see how they could be any better. Now, when we are thinking about a holiday, we might often say, "How about some fish and chips in Seahouses?" as a reason for the five-hundred-mile round trip.

Another thing we found, apart from the wide, empty, golden, beautiful beaches and the fabulous castles on every headland, and the fish and chips, was the town of Alnwick. There's a castle, of course, with an uncanny resemblance to Hogwarts, because they used it in the film. And there's a secondhand bookshop, Barter Books. It used to be a railway station, but fell under the Beeching axe in 1968. There's still a train there, but it's a little toy train that runs around on top of the bookshelves. We'd only recently been to Hay-on-Wye of course, so you'd think we'd have had our fill of secondhand books, but after a full afternoon amongst the shelves I emerged with a lighter wallet and several bags. Okay, I admit it, I'm a nut.

It gets worse because I found a branch of Barter Books

in a side street in Seahouses a couple of days later in the holiday. I didn't buy so many there, though, because we were cycling and it can become dangerous with a few kilos of ballast swinging around on the end of your handlebars.

WE CONTINUED our Tour of the North by moving inland to Barnard Castle, a town we chose for no other reason than that it lay at a convenient point on our route home. It's an historic market town – they'd had a French market the weekend before, a pity we'd missed that. There's also a castle that stands high over the River Tees. Very picturesque and a good base for touring. And it had a car accessory shop, very handy for buying some power steering fluid when I noticed how the brown car had become unwilling to go around corners soon after we left Northumberland. A red light in the shape of a steering wheel had appeared on the dashboard, flashing with stop-or-die urgency.

"You know," I said to Sarah, as we sat in the castle grounds, in the rain, eating a sandwich. "I thought we might get through this holiday without a mechanical problem."

"Aren't you forgetting about Niagara Falls in the passenger footwell?"

"That's not mechanical. That's just… you know…"

"The car falling to bits?" she finished.

"No, it just needs a bit of car body filler, that's all. To keep the weather out. I'll sort it when we get home."

"And the steering? You still have a thing about driving

all the way to the South of France? You're going to pick a route with straight motorways?"

"She'd be fine, you know. She's a good car deep down." I believed it. The steering fluid did the trick. She needed a bit more before we got home, but I'd only had to use half of the bottle we bought in Barnard Castle, so we were good.

We paid for an afternoon in the town car park. There was a good mobile signal so we called the kids, hands-free, to tell them about the repair to the brown car. Kevin was at work painting barn doors. I needed an explanation after jumping to the conclusion he'd made a career switch into agriculture. Barn doors, he told me, were the flaps that are fitted around theatre lanterns. He had fifty that had to be painted black. He also needed to find a rag and wipe the fingerprints of black paint off his mobile. I took the hint, wished him a good day and left him to get on with it. We called Amanda. She was at work, too, as a legal secretary. We could hear her typing as she spoke, and we sensed the distracted tone of someone multitasking but too nice to say she was busy. We called both our parents. The two conversations were similar.

"What's that noise?"

"It's rain," I said. "On the car roof."

"Really? It's lovely here. Sunny."

We pulled on our waterproofs and ventured out into the summer. We saw the castle and looked at the historic market cross, and to escape the rain, we found a tourist information office and did the leaflet thing again.

There was a museum in Barnard Castle, called the Bowes Museum. I didn't expect much. A converted shop, perhaps, with some dusty old cases filled with dead animals and broken pots. But it would be dry.

We followed directions out of the town, along a quiet road, through some ornamental gates, to… a magnificent French chateau. We stopped in our tracks. In front of us stood a massive building that wouldn't have looked out of place in the Loire. It was designed by a French architect and was apparently based on the town hall at Le Havre.

There was an entry fee, and I grumbled a bit about this, but it wasn't a lot and within minutes I'd stopped muttering, because I'd become captivated by one of the most fascinating museums I'd ever seen. The varied collections of art included original Sisley landscapes, paintings by Goya and Canaletto, and a mind-blowing collection of strange and arcane items from all over the world. The information panels, too, were worth reading. Usually my brain skips off with information panels. I'm not gripped. In the Bowes Museum, however, I hung on every word. There were even hands-on exhibits that were as much for adults as for children. We loved it all. We stayed until they had to throw us out at closing time.

There was one regret. In amongst all the fabulous items, their star exhibit, an automaton silver swan, was closed to visitors during refurbishment. Our site warden got all excited about it, later. The automaton swan was the must-see object at the Bowes Museum. I found it hard to imagine that anything could top what we'd already seen, but we made a note that one day we would return and experience the silver swan.

We had one more day at the Barnard Castle campsite.

The Met Office promised more rain. They got it right. I don't give the Met Office any gold stars for that; they have a £97 million Cray T3E supercomputer they can use. I came up with the same forecast by standing outside the caravan and looking up at the sky.

There was one other outing I very much wanted to do and had wanted to do since we visited Teesdale back in the old Sprite Alpine days. I'd seen a postcard in a shop, a wide, panoramic postcard that showed a view of a landscape feature called High Cup Nick. The name had been on the back of the card and I'd stored it away in my memory amongst all the other places I had to go and see with my own eyes. High Cup Nick is a valley; a perfect "U" shape with vertical walls at the top, and it's green. All of it. Even the vertical walls. I don't do it justice with description. See for yourself. Google "High Cup Nick", select "images", and prepare to be awed.

Few people know about it in the UK and yet it is as dramatic as the Grand Canyon, or at least it is for someone who's never seen the Grand Canyon.

If this landscape feature is so amazing, then why isn't it better known? The answer is simple. You can't drive there. It's a bit of a walk. More than a bit, it's fourteen miles there and back, over rough ground. Rain or shine though, I had to see it. We couldn't just pop up there on a fine weekend. It's far away in the woolly north, and who knew when we'd be able to come back to Teesdale.

We started out early. The sky was the colour of our grey-water tank.

We drove to the car park at Cow Green Reservoir, a

bleak and lonely place, especially with louring cloud and seep-into-your-socks drizzle. Creeping out from the car, we abandoned the only safe haven for miles, and it was hard not to feel a growing knot of anxiety when the drizzle turned to rain, the kind that comes down in straight lines set at a jaunty angle.

Our path took us to Cauldron Snout. A boiling, urgent, barging-with-elbows waterfall. Cauldron Snout – what a perfect name.

Sarah was impressed. "Is this High Cup Nick? It's fabulous."

I didn't want to break it to her. Half a mile walked, seven to go.

"Ah, bit further, yet," I said. I was getting the hang of Yorkshire understatement.

We tramped on, mile after mile. The rain fell. But we had good waterproofs, and it was okay, apart from the odd halt for some necessary spectacle-polishing, and the occasional peat-bog moment when a boot would get sucked deep, to knee level, and fill with water. Overall, though, we enjoyed the walk – the wildness and utter desolation of it all.

The rain eased to a fine drizzle. Sometimes it stopped altogether. We pulled back our hoods and enjoyed the cool air and the sound of our boots sloshing and sheep crying across the moor. Then moments later the rain returned and we pulled up our hoods and closed out the world, back to our personal sound-deadened universes. In our packs we had sandwiches for lunch but I resisted the temptation to stop and eat. On a there-and-back walk we didn't want to eat too early, it would only make the return more gruelling than need be. So we walked on and ignored our growling stomachs.

I checked the map. I checked my hand-held GPS. Together they told me we should be there, and yet all I could see was bracken and moorland and low cloud. Where was High Cup Nick? Had I gone wrong? Was this becoming a marriage-threatening fiasco? A five-hour walk in the rain, through sodden peat-bog, for nothing?

But then magic happened.

Two more steps? Three? I don't recall, but an instant later we saw a line in the mist, then an edge. We stepped to the edge and there, spread out before and below us in a sweeping arc, was a valley – perfect curves, lush green colours, and with immaculate timing, a shaft of sunlight to add perfection. High Cup Nick. I gasped. Sarah gasped.

Our vantage point could not have been better. We stood right on the centre line. Mirror symmetry to right and left. And a handy rock on which to sit and munch our tuna sandwiches with smiles of contentment. No anxiety over the right amount of time to look at the view this time. We took a long lunch.

WE MOVED SOUTH, to a canal-side site near Ripon. Only a one-nighter, just to minimise the time spent queuing along the roads to York, our ultimate destination. I didn't expect Ripon would offer much in the way of tourist attractions, but when we walked into the town we found it to be attractive and interesting, with a large and open market square with an elegant column in the centre. We found a good pizza restaurant, too, which was cheap and excellent and had the kind of ambience that transformed it into "our place" within minutes. One night extended to two. We even changed the terminology; a two-night stay became a two-pizza stay.

Then we learned about a French market in the town square on the coming Saturday. The French market would be run by French stallholders selling French cheese and French bread and French pastries. The concept of a *three*-pizza stay emerged. I had visions of strolling into town, wandering amongst the stalls, speaking French… The rain wouldn't be an issue. It rains in France, too, sometimes. At least in Northern France. We've seen it.

This would mean, though, that our plan to linger at a temporary site in York to end our tour would have to be revised. We'd both been looking forward to this, but York wasn't removed from our itinerary. Ripon was only thirty miles away. We took the car and visited York for a day, using the Park and Ride.

The bus route into York passes the cricket club where our next site was to have been. It looked a perfect spot beside the river and as we approached, we wondered if we'd been a little rash in extending our stay in Ripon, just for some fleeting gastronomic temptations of pizza and French patisseries. But then we noticed how the river seemed to be lapping up to the side of the road, sometimes across it, and all that could be seen of the cricket club was the top half of the white sight screens that poked out of the water in mockery of the English summer game. Our Park and Ride bus was morphing into a Park and Ride/Float with every mile. We smiled at each other. We'd won one. Had we departed Ripon after the one night per our schedule, we'd have probably had to go home. There would have been no turning back to Ripon, either, because the "site full" notices had gone up soon after we'd arrived. We'd never seen a temporary site become full and closed to new arrivals before, and we'd been surprised. But now we knew the reason why. The York monsoons had brought us an influx of caravan refugees.

York is a beautiful city. We'd been before, we've been back since and there will be many times when we'll visit again. The York Minster stands tall and dominates every sight line. Riverside walks are usually a feature, but not on this day, with all the paths under a foot of water, hiding the real edge of the river from view.

We found ourselves drawn to the secondhand book shops. There are many. Sarah struck lucky. She found a copy of The Hound of the Baskervilles written entirely in Pitman's shorthand. She bought this for her mum, who collects such books so she can translate them back into alphabetical English to keep her shorthand skills sharp. We look out for them whenever we're in a new town that has antiquarian and used bookshops. It has become something of a quest. I'm quite envious of her shorthand skills. It must make note-taking a doddle. I write notes longhand and I defy anyone, myself included, to be able to read them afterwards.

I also found an especially useful prize to help my own translation efforts, *The Penguin Parallel Text*. It's a book of

French short stories, in French on one side of the page with the English translation on the other. It's to help English-speaking students of French to develop their language skills. It was way more advanced than the level I had reached. I needed pictures and a story that went something like, "This is Jack, this is Jill, this is Spot the dog. They ask for a coffee and a tea please." But I felt that every little bit might help, especially with our upcoming visit to Ripon Riviera's French market. I wanted to be able to do better than ask for "*Un pain et un* lump of *fromage, s'il vous plaît*".

I found a map, too. Only twenty pence. I bought it but didn't tell Sarah. The right moment would come, but it wasn't here yet.

York has another institution, Betty's Tea Rooms. One day we'll go there and find out what all the fuss is about. It wouldn't be on this day though. A hundred and fifty others were there before us and they were already queuing outside in the rain. I accepted that I'd have to live without my tea being served up by a girl in a Victorian dress and white pinafore. Maybe it's more to do with the fancy cakes that come with the tea? So we Park/Rode/Floated back to the car then called in at Tesco for a bag of scones and took them back to the caravan.

That evening I lay in bed and read a French short story from my new book. It was called *La Plage*. Very minimalist. Something to do with three children walking on a beach. Then I read *The Beach*, in English, and hey, it was about three children who go walking on a beach, and… well, that's about it. They didn't even ask for a tea and a coffee. But I'd absorbed a lot of French words during the process, and I awoke the next morning inspired and ready to dazzle the French market stall owners of Ripon with some deep philosophical insights into the subject of bread, cheese and, with luck, those fabulous *tarte Tatins* we'd sampled in Brittany a couple of years earlier. We headed into town. Phrases like *Bonjour, comment allez-vous?* and *Deux tarte Tatins s'il vous plaît* rattled around inside my head. I'm always surprised at how much better these words sound when they stay inside my head. Once past my lips they always somehow manage to disappoint. But not today. I had this. I'd read *La Plage* and even understood some of it.

We left the site, crossed the canal bridge and headed into town past the industrial park where I'd noticed a branch of ATS, tyres, exhausts and batteries when we first arrived, where I'd felt that familiar glow of reassurance I always get when finding such places on our holidays. We have a mental checklist for every new town: car repairers, hospital out-patients and supermarkets, in that order.

We passed our home-from-home pizza parlour, in which we were playing such a large part in keeping financially afloat, then turned into Ripon market square.

We stopped. Where were the flying tricolours? Where was the pungent aroma of cheese? The wheezing sound of accordions? Berets and striped tee shirts? The sound of old men playing boules – thud, clack, "*tsk*", "*merde!*"

I checked my watch. Ten o'clock. There should be a market. The square was empty.

I lie, the square wasn't entirely empty. At the far end was a single stall selling hats and bags. I walked over.

"Bonjour," I said.

"How-do," said the stall owner.

"I thought this was a French market," I said.

"Nay lad. Next wikend. Ey up, 'ow's t'at? Need a new 'un?" he asked, pointing to the black cowboy hat I was wearing to keep the rain off. It was the one I'm wearing on the cover illustration of this book. I'd bought it from a stall at Skipton Market years earlier.

"Looks like wun o' me-un," he said, with a laugh. "Got wun jus' la-ak it. Do it yer for fa-ave pun?"

I wasn't sure what he'd said. I'd have understood more if he'd spoken in French.

We walked back to the caravan, me wearing a new hat that I didn't need. Sarah wore the old one. It helped to keep the rain off.

BACK IN THE VAN, with the rain playing drum rolls on the roof, we made tea and finished off the scones we'd bought in York.

"*Tarte Tatin* would have been nicer," I said.

I decided this was the moment to reveal the other thing I'd bought in York. I pulled it out with a flourish.

"What've you got?" said Sarah.

"A map," I said. "South of France."

I spread it out on the table. I didn't speak straight away. I wanted it to sink in. I wanted her to see how blue the sea looked. It wasn't any bluer than the sea on a map of Hull, or Bridlington, but when you have words scattered about, like Provence and Nice and Monaco, it's amazing how powerful psychology can be in affecting things like colour perception. I noticed Sarah's eyes flick away from the map to the caravan window – nothing to see out there, just blurry caravan shapes and streaming water – then back to the map.

"You're talking about next summer?"

I nodded. Then I pressed home the arguments.

"Remember the swimming pool in that hotel we stayed at, for the Osmonds concert?" I'd unleashed the nuclear option with my first preemptive strike. I'd mentioned *Osmonds* and *swimming pool*, all in the very first sentence.

"Just think, we could have a swimming pool to come back to every evening after a hard day in the sun. Right by the caravan. Open air."

I watched her eyes as the thoughts churned, back and forth: sunshine, pool. But then: cost, clapped-out old car.

"We've talked about it before. Sounds great. But the brown car. She's old."

"The car would love it," I said. "She'd lap it up. Two weeks in the sun. The carpets might even dry out. We'll buy the best European breakdown cover we can get. If she breaks down, they'll come out and fix her. Hell, she'd come home in better shape than she left."

Sarah nodded. "But the cost."

"We can afford it. We have savings. I'm an accountant now."

This was true, despite my unwillingness to job-hop – because I was in a good, final salary pension scheme and didn't want to screw it up – which meant I was still on a pittance compared to others who came in and did the same job. But I wasn't bitter. Well, not much.

Sarah was weakening, I could tell, but she still had an arsenal of solid, counterstrike arguments to work through. "I'm not sure I could take the heat. Could you?" She nodded to the window where the rain was coming down hard enough to take the song and dance out of Gene Kelly. "We're just not used to it," she said. "And the Mediterranean, it's so far. You're only allowed to take two weeks off at a time."

"So we'll go in May," I said. "Next year is perfect. The Spring bank holiday is a week earlier so it doesn't clash with the accounting calendar for once. And Paul"—Paul was my boss—"Paul wants three weeks in July so he can go to Greece, and I said I'd cover. He'll owe me. He's not going to say no." I paused before lunging for the final and decisive shot. "We'll go in May because next year is our thirtieth anniversary. Our pearl wedding anniversary. Let's do something special. We'll do it paddling in the Med."

"Do you have a plan?" she asked, and I knew I'd landed it. 2009 would see us in the South of France... and beyond. I rubbed my hands together.

"Home to Kent. A night in that site we love, then an early start. Over to Calais on the boat before Calais to Dijon."

"Sounds a long way."

"It is. We'll have two nights in Dijon to recover."

"Okay."

"Then Dijon to Aix-en-Provence. Two more nights."

"Aix-en-Provence? The one in Provence?"

"Oh yes."

She'd been reading and enjoying a series of Carol Drinkwater books set on an olive farm in Provence. I sensed the scales tipping ever further in the right direction.

She smiled. "Go on."

"From Aix it's only ninety-odd miles to Cannes. We'll find a site near Cannes. Spend five nights."

"Only five?"

"Yes, because then we move on along the Riviera, past Monaco, to Sanremo. In Italy."

"Italy? Aren't we getting a little ambitious here?"

"No, because… From Sanremo we could go to Milan."

"Milan? I thought Milan was just a symbol? The next big adventure."

"This *is* the next big adventure," I said. "We should go because we always said we would."

"Why? What's there?"

She had a point. I didn't know. I racked my brains. Apart from clothes shops that nobody, especially us, could afford, I was coming up short on motive. I pointed to my head. "Milan has been stuck in here ever since Switzerland. You remember? We saw the road sign? Turn south, drive a little further and get to Milan. Well this time, *this* time, we can do it."

I could see doubt creeping into Sarah's eyes. I might have pushed too far.

"Seems a flimsy reason," she said. "Especially when we don't know anything about the place. Have you found a site near Milan?"

I hadn't found a site. There was the city, and outside the

city, as far as I could tell, was an industrial sprawl that filled northern Italy.

"We don't have to take the caravan all the way. There are trains from Sanremo." I didn't know this. I guessed there were. There's no reason why there wouldn't be.

"And trains in Italy are not expensive," I said. I didn't know this either, but again, I guessed it was true. "Imagine arriving in Milan, by train, from the Med."

We locked eyes. I tried to read her thoughts but failed. Sarah was right. We didn't have to do it. Milan had always stood for the next exciting destination that lay over a distant, hazy horizon. But if a journey all the way to the Italian Riviera was possible, why not hop on a train for a day and visit the world's capital of fashion and design?

Sarah leaned over and traced a finger along my hypothetical route. The map was of the South of France only, south of Geneva, with a teeny bit of Italy and Switzerland tacked on the side, so the gob-smacking scale of my proposed journey was obscured, not to mention the inconvenient three-hundred-mile crawl along the traffic jam from home to Dover.

Her finger looped up towards the Alps. "And going back? We could go back through the Alps," she said.

"Annecy, maybe?" I suggested. "We've always wanted to go to Annecy."

She nodded.

"Then Annecy to… here." My finger paused around Troyes on the thumbnail-sized map of Northern France on the back cover, but I didn't want to voice the name, Troyes, where we'd once been targets of an alleged gas attack.

Speaking it might break the delicate spell. "And then, from… somewhere round here to Calais. Easy."

"I'm not sure about 'easy'," said Sarah. "But… yes. I think we could do it."

"Really?"

"Really."

We had another day in Ripon before going home, but I was ready to go home then, that day. I wanted to get the European sites books out and turn the idea into a concrete plan. I wanted to get on the phone and book it.

We spent our final day somewhere, I can't remember where, I didn't have my mind on it. Next day we had a leisurely pack. I wanted to rush but at the same time didn't want to appear too keen to end the holiday. We arrived home at tea time.

We'd been away for two weeks and there was two weeks' of laundry to empty out of the 'van. We had to read through two weeks of mail, which was really just two weeks of free newspapers and adverts for double glazing, showers and block-paving driveways. By the time we were done it was late but that didn't stop me spending an hour with the European sites books. I already had the route, now I just needed the sites. By eleven PM I had the whole itinerary.

Sarah made the point that the offices would be closed at eleven PM, and also, it was only August. Why did I need to book so early? Couldn't it wait?

Of course it could wait, but great plans had turned to dust before because of procrastination. We'd lose impetus. We'd let it slip. We'd end up in Wales in the rain again.

"I'll ring them after work, tomorrow," I said.

We went to bed and I could hardly sleep with excitement. You'd think it was already the night before the big holiday. How was I going to contain myself for nine months?

I arrived at work and felt the beneficial effects of an excellent holiday leaking out through my pores, washing away all the high spirits and bonhomie in the old familiar way. By ten o'clock I was weighed down by an accounting month-end and two weeks' worth of emails and backlog.

My mobile phone rang. It was Sarah.

"You missed a call this morning. An American lady. She wants you to call back as soon as you can. Here's the number."

I scribbled it down.

"What did she say?"

"She said call her back."

"Do you think—?"

"I don't know, she wouldn't say. Call her. Then call me."

There was a little room under the stairs at work, called the post room, but it was the size of a phone box and useless for sorting post. It was the hiding place of choice for making personal calls. I dialled the number. I had to do it a few times because I needed the international code for America and it hadn't been included, so a trip back to my desk for a bit of surreptitious googling was needed first.

Back in the post room my heart was beating as an unusual foreign ring tone blurped away on my phone. Was this the call I'd been waiting for since May? Was it good news? Maybe they were just calling to tell me I'd lost. But would they bother to ring the losers? After three rings a very

American voice answered. I knew the voice. I'd spoken to her before.

I CALLED SARAH.

"You've been ages. I can't stand the suspense. What happened?"

"I had to find out the dialling code. It's hard, calling America. And I tried not to be away from my desk for too long. I've only just got back from holiday, you know?"

"Okay, okay, but what was the call about? Was it the writing competition?"

"Yeah, it was Joni." I said it as though she was an old friend. I tried to make my voice all casual and disinterested, the way we Brits do to manage pants-wetting excitement.

"Well? What did she say?"

"Okay, you know next year's holiday? The one we nearly booked, to the South of France and to Milan?"

"Yes?"

"Well, let's get back to thinking of Milan in the metaphorical sense again. You know, where it represents something big and exciting over the far horizon."

Silence. Then, "What do mean?"

"I mean, the horizon might be a little farther than we bargained for. Like California."

Sarah screamed. "*You won?*"

"Well, you know, I came second. But any of the top three places counts as a win. They'll be flying me out to Los Angeles for a week, next July or August. You'll come too, obviously. Thought we might go for three weeks. Visit your cousin. See California: San Francisco, Yosemite, Hollywood."

Sarah gave an incoherent gurgle.

"Pretty good, hey," I said, still nonchalant.

"You don't sound excited."

"I am, I am, it's just…"

"It's just what?"

"I'm not good with gushing emotion. And… we nearly booked Milan."

"Oh, come on. We could fly to Milan any time if you're that bothered."

"Fly? Ah, well. *There's* the other thing. Kind of big. Kind of scary."

"What other thing?"

"We'll have to go to California on a plane. We've never been on a plane."

Also by Mike Wood

Travelling in a Box (Book 1)

Flying in a Box (Book 3)

And if you fancy some sci-fi – writing as Mjke Wood:

Old Man in a Spacesuit

The Sphere of Influence Series:

Deep Space Accountant

The Lollipop of Influence

The Spherical Trust

Collected Short Stories:

Power for Two Minutes and Other Unrealities

Thanks for reading Two in a Box. I hope you enjoyed it as much as I enjoyed reliving those adventures. The story continues with *Flying in a Box*, in which I go on my first ever plane flight, get chased by a snake in Yosemite, collect an award at an Oscar-like ceremony in Hollywood, then come back down to Earth, fog bound, stranded and sleepless in Italy.

I do get to paddle in the Med though, after an epic thousand-mile tow across France. But do I reach Milan?

If you'd like me to drop an email right into your inbox the moment any future instalments roll off the presses, just pop over to my web site, Travellinginabox.com, and add your name to my list. And if you spot me on a campsite, hiding from the rain, come on over and say hi.

Best Wishes
   Mike

Printed in Great Britain
by Amazon